A DAUGHTER OF THE SIOUX

A TALE OF THE INDIAN FRONTIER

BY

GENERAL CHARLES KING

AUTHOR OF "THE COLONEL'S DAUGHTER," "FORT FRAYNE," "AN ARMY WIFE," ETC., ETC.

[ZHINGOORA BOOKS]

A DAUGHTER OF THE SIOUX

CONTENTS

A DAUGHTER OF THE SIOUX

A DAUGHTER OF THE SIOUX

A DAUGHTER OF THE SIOUX

A Rifled Desk,

A DAUGHTER OF THE SIOUX

CHAPTER XXIV

A Soldier Entangled,

L'ENVOI

A DAUGHTER OF THE SIOUX

ILLUSTRATIONS

A DAUGHTER OF THE SIOUX

CHAPTER I

FORESHADOWED EVENTS

The major commanding looked up from the morning report and surveyed the post adjutant with something of perturbation, if not annoyance, in his grim, gray eyes. For the fourth time that week had Lieutenant Field requested permission to be absent for several hours. The major knew just why the junior wished to go and where. The major knew just why he wished him not to go, but saw fit to name almost any other than the real reason when, with a certain awkward hesitancy he began:

"W—ell, is the post return ready?"

"It *will* be, sir, in abundant time," was the prompt reply.

"You know they sent it back for correction last month," hazarded the commander.

"And you know, sir, the error was not mine," was the instant rejoinder, so quick, sharp and positive as to carry it at a bound to the verge of disrespect, and the keen, blue eyes of the young soldier gazed, frank and fearless, into the heavily ambushed grays of the veteran in the chair. It made the latter wince and stir uneasily.

"If there's one thing I hate, Field, it is to have my papers sent back by some whipsnapper of a clerk, inviting attention to this or that error, and I expect my adjutant to see to it that they don't."

A DAUGHTER OF THE SIOUX

"Your adjutant does see to it, sir. I'm willing to bet a month's pay fewer errors have been found in the papers of Fort Frayne than any post in the Department of the Platte. General Williams told you as much when you were in Omaha."

The major fairly wriggled in his cane-bottomed whirligig. What young Field said was true, and the major knew it. He knew, moreover, there wasn't a more painstaking post adjutant from the Missouri to the mountains. He knew their monthly reports—"returns" as the regulations call them—were referred to by a model adjutant general as model papers. He knew it was due to young Field's care and attention, and he knew he thought all the world of that young gentleman. It was just because he thought so much of him he was beginning to feel that it was high time to put a stop to something that was going on. But, it was a delicate matter; a woman was the matter; and he hadn't the moral courage to go at it the straightforward way. He "whip sawed" again. Thrumming on the desk with his lean, bony fingers he began:—

"If I let my adjutant out so much, what's to prevent other youngsters asking similar indulgence?"

The answer came like the crack of a whip:—

"Nothing, sir; and far better would it be for everybody concerned if they spent more hours in the saddle and fewer at the store."

This was too much for the one listener in the room. With something like the sound of a suppressed sneeze, a tall, long-legged captain of cavalry started up from his chair, an outspread

A DAUGHTER OF THE SIOUX

newspaper still full-stretched between him and the desk of the commander, and, thus hidden as to his face, sidled sniggering off to the nearest window. Young Field had fearlessly, if not almost impudently, hit the nail on the head, and metaphorically rapped the thrumming fingers of his superior officer. Some commanders would have raged and sent the daring youngster right about in arrest. Major Webb knew just what Field referred to,—knew that the fascinations of pool, "pitch" and poker held just about half his commissioned force at all "off duty" hours of the day or night hanging about the officers' club room at the post trader's; knew, moreover, that while the adjutant never wasted a moment over cards or billiards, he, the post commander, had many a time taken a hand or a cue and wagered his dollars against those of his devoted associates. They all loved him. There wasn't "a mean streak in his whole system," said every soldier at Fort Frayne. He had a capital record as a volunteer—a colonel and, later, brigade commander in the great war. He had the brevet of brigadier general of volunteers, but repudiated any title beyond that of his actual rank in the regulars. He was that *rara avis*—a bachelor field officer, and a bird to be brought down if feminine witchery could do it. He was truthful, generous, high-minded, brave—a man who preferred to be of and with his subordinates rather than above them—to rule through affection and regard rather than the stern standard of command. He was gentle and courteous alike to officers and the rank and file, though he feared no man on the face of the globe. He was awkward, bungling and overwhelmingly, lavishly, kind and thoughtful in his dealings with the womenfolk of the garrison, for he stood in awe of the

A DAUGHTER OF THE SIOUX

entire sisterhood. He could ride like a centaur; he couldn't dance worth a cent. He could snuff a candle with his Colt at twenty paces and couldn't hit a croquet ball to save his soul. His deep-set gray eyes, under their tangled thatch of brown, gazed straight into the face of every man on the Platte, soldier, cowboy, Indian or halfbreed, but fell abashed if a laundress looked at him. Billy Ray, captain of the sorrel troop and the best light rider in Wyoming, was the only man he ever allowed to straddle a beautiful thoroughbred mare he had bought in Kentucky, but, bad hands or good, there wasn't a riding woman at Frayne who hadn't backed Lorna time and again, because to a woman the major simply couldn't say no.

And though his favorite comrades at the post were captains like Blake and Billy Ray, married men both whose wives he worshipped, the major's rugged heart went out especially to Beverly Field, his boy adjutant, a lad who came to them from West Point only three years before the autumn this story opens, a young fellow full of high health, pluck and principle—a tip top soldier, said everybody from the start, until, as Gregg and other growlers began to declaim, the major completely spoiled him. Here, three years only out of military leadingstrings, he was a young cock of the walk, "too dam' independent for a second lieutenant," said the officers' club element of the command, men like Gregg, Wilkins, Crane and a few of their following. "The keenest young trooper in the regiment," said Blake and Ray, who were among its keenest captains, and never a cloud had sailed across the serene sky of their friendship and esteem until this

A DAUGHTER OF THE SIOUX

glorious September of 188-, when Nanette Flower, a brilliant, beautiful brunette came a visitor to old Fort Frayne.

And it was on her account the major would, could he have seen the way, said no to the adjutant's request to be absent again. On her account and that of one other, for that request meant another long morning in saddle with Miss Flower, another long morning in which "the sweetest girl in the garrison," so said they all, would go about her daily duties with an aching heart. There was no woman at Fort Frayne who did not know that Esther Dade thought all the world of Beverly Field. There was only one man who apparently had no inkling of it—Beverly Field himself.

She was the only daughter of a veteran officer, a captain of infantry, who at the age of fifty, after having held a high command in the volunteers during the civil war, was still meekly doing duty as a company officer of regulars nearly two decades after. She had been carefully reared by a most loving and thoughtful mother, even in the crude old days of the army, when its fighting force was scattered in small detachments all over the wide frontier, and men, and women, too, lived on soldier rations, eked out with game, and dwelt in tents or ramshackle, one-storied huts, "built by the labor of troops." At twelve she had been placed at school in the far East, while her father enjoyed a two years' tour on recruiting service, and there, under the care of a noble woman who taught her girls to be women indeed—not vapid votaries of pleasure and fashion, Esther spent five useful years, coming back to her fond father's soldier roof a winsome picture of girlish health and grace and comeliness—a girl who

A DAUGHTER OF THE SIOUX

could ride, walk and run if need be, who could bake and cook, mend and sew, cut, fashion and make her own simple wardrobe; who knew algebra, geometry and "trig" quite as well as, and history, geography and grammar far better than, most of the young West Pointers; a girl who spoke her own tongue with accuracy and was not badly versed in French; a girl who performed fairly well on the piano and guitar, but who sang full-throated, rejoiceful, exulting like the lark—the soulful music that brought delight to her ageing father, half crippled by the wounds of the war days, and to the mother who so devotedly loved and carefully planned for her. Within a month from her graduation at Madame Piatt's she had become the darling of Fort Frayne, the pet of many a household, the treasure of her own. With other young gallants of the garrison, Beverly Field had been prompt to call, prompt to be her escort when dance or drive, ride or picnic was planned in her honor, especially the ride, for Mr. Adjutant Field loved the saddle, the open prairie or the bold, undulating bluffs. But Field was the busiest man at the post. Other youngsters, troop or company subalterns, had far more time at their disposal, and begged for rides and dances, strolls and sports which the post adjutant was generally far too busy to claim. It was Esther who brought lawn tennis to Frayne and found eager pupils of both sexes, but Field had been the first to meet and welcome her; had been for a brief time at the start her most constant cavalier. Then, as others began to feel the charm of her frank, cordial, joyous manner, and learned to read the beauty that beamed in her clear, truthful eyes and winsome, yet not beautiful face, they became assiduous in turn,—two of them almost

A DAUGHTER OF THE SIOUX

distressingly so,—and she could not wound them by refusals. Then came a fortnight in which her father sat as a member of a court-martial down at old Fort Laramie, where were the band, headquarters and four troops of the ——th, and Captain and Mrs. Freeman, who were there stationed, begged that Mrs. Dade and Esther should come and visit them during the session of the court. There would be all manner of army gaieties and a crowd of outside officers, and, as luck would have it, Mr. Field was ordered thither as a witness in two important cases. The captain and his good wife went by stage; Esther and Beverly rode every inch of the way in saddle, camping over night with their joyous little party at La Bontè. Then came a lovely week at Laramie, during which Mr. Field had little to do but devote himself to, and dance with, Esther, and when his final testimony was given and he returned to his station, and not until then, Esther Dade discovered that life had little interest or joy without him; but Field rode back unknowing, and met at Frayne, before Esther Dade's return, a girl who had come almost unheralded, making the journey over the Medicine Bow from Rock Springs on the Union Pacific in the comfortable carriage of old Bill Hay, the post trader, escorted by that redoubtable woman, Mrs. Bill Hay, and within the week of her arrival Nanette Flower was the toast of the bachelors' mess, the talk of every household at Fort Frayne.

And well she might be. Dark and lustrous were her eyes; black, luxuriant and lustrous was her hair; dark, rich and lustrous her radiant beauty. In contour her face was well nigh faultless. It might have been called beautiful indeed but for the lips, or something about the mouth, that in repose had not a soft or

Page 15

A DAUGHTER OF THE SIOUX

winsome line, but then it was never apparently in repose. Smiles, sunshine, animation, rippling laughter, flashing, even, white teeth—these were what one noted when in talk with Miss Flower. There was something actually radiant, almost dazzling, about her face. Her figure, though *petite*, was exquisite, and women marked with keen appreciation, if not envy, the style and finish of her varied and various gowns. Six trunks, said Bill Hay's boss teamster, had been trundled over the range from Rawlins, not to mention a box containing her little ladyship's beautiful English side-saddle, Melton bridle and other equine impedimenta. Did Miss Flower like to ride? She adored it, and Bill Hay had a bay half thoroughbred that could discount the major's mare 'cross country. All Frayne was out to see her start for her first ride with Beverly Field, and all Frayne reluctantly agreed that sweet Essie Dade could never sit a horse over ditch or hurdle with the superb grace and unconcern displayed by the daring, dashing girl who had so suddenly become the centre of garrison interest. For the first time in her life Mrs. Bill Hay knew what it was to hold the undivided attention of army society, for every woman at Fort Frayne was wild to know all about the beautiful newcomer, and only one could tell.

Hay, the trader, had prospered in his long years on the frontier, first as trader among the Sioux, later as sutler, and finally, when Congress abolished that title, substituting therefore the euphemism, without material clog upon the perquisites, as post trader at Fort Frayne. No one knew how much he was worth, for while apparently a most open-hearted, whole-souled fellow, Hay was reticence itself when his fortunes or his family were matters

A DAUGHTER OF THE SIOUX

of question or comment. He had long been married, and Mrs. Hay, when at the post, was a social sphinx,—kind-hearted, charitable, lavish to the soldiers' wives and children, and devotion itself to the families of the officers when sickness and trouble came, as come in the old days they too often did. It was she who took poor Ned Robinson's young widow and infant all the way to Cheyenne when the Sioux butchered the luckless little hunting party down by Laramie Peak. It was she who nursed Captain Forrest's wife and daughter through ten weeks of typhoid, and, with her own means, sent them to the seashore, while the husband and father was far up on the Yellowstone, cut off from all communication in the big campaign of '76. It was she who built the little chapel and decked and dressed it for Easter and Christmas, despite the fact that she herself had been baptized in the Roman Catholic faith. It was she who went at once to every woman in the garrison whose husband was ordered out on scout or campaign, proffering aid and comfort, despite the fact long whispered in the garrisons of the Platte country, that in the old, old days she had far more friends among the red men than the white. That could well be, because in those days white men were few and far between. Every one had heard the story that it was through her the news of the massacre at Fort Phil Kearny was made known to the post commander, for she could speak the dialects of both the Arapahoe and the Sioux, and had the sign language of the Plains veritably at her fingers' ends. There were not lacking those who declared that Indian blood ran in her veins—that her mother was an Ogalalla squaw and her father a French Canadian fur trapper, a story to which her raven black

A DAUGHTER OF THE SIOUX

hair and brows, her deep, dark eyes and somewhat swarthy complexion gave no little color. But, long years before, Bill Hay had taken her East, where he had relatives, and where she studied under excellent masters, returning to him summer after summer with more and more of refinement in manner, and so much of style and fashion in dress that her annual advent had come to be looked upon as quite the event of the season, even by women of the social position of Mrs. Ray and Mrs. Blake, the recognized leaders among the young matrons of the ———th Cavalry, and by gentle Mrs. Dade, to whom every one looked up in respect,— almost in reverence. Despite the mystery about her antecedents there was every reason why Mrs. Hay should be held in esteem and affection. Bill Hay himself was a diamond in the rough,— square, sturdy, uncompromising, generous and hospitable; his great pride and glory was his wife; his one great sorrow that their only child had died almost in infancy. His solecisms in syntax and society were many. He was given at times to profanity, and at others, when madame was away, to draw poker; but officers and men alike proclaimed him a man of mettle and never hesitated to go to him when in financial straits, sure of unusurious aid. But, even had this not been the case, the popularity of his betterhalf would have carried him through, for there was hardly a woman at Frayne to speak of her except in terms of genuine respect. Mrs. Hay was truth telling, sympathetic, a peacemaker, a resolute opponent of gossip and scandal of every kind, a woman who minded her own business and was only mildly insistent that others should do likewise. She declined all overtures leading to confidences as to her past, and

Page 18

A DAUGHTER OF THE SIOUX

demanded recognition only upon the standard of the present, which was unimpeachable.

All the same it came something like a shock to society at Frayne that, when she appeared at the post this beautiful autumn of 188-, nearly three months later than the usual time, she should be accompanied by this brilliant and beautiful girl of whom no one of their number had previously heard, and whom she smilingly, confidently presented as, "My niece, Miss Flower."

"The Major sought to block that morning's ride in vain."

A DAUGHTER OF THE SIOUX

There was a dance the night the Dades got home from Laramie. Nearly all day long had they driven in the open buckboard over the rough, winding road along the Platte, and Mrs. Dade was far too tired to think of going, but Esther was so eager that her father put aside his precious paper, tucked her under his arm and trudged cheerily away across the parade toward the bright lights of the hop room. They had a fairly good string orchestra at Frayne that year, and one of Strauss's most witching waltzes— "Sounds from the Vienna Woods"—had just been begun as father and daughter entered. A dozen people, men and women both, saw them and noted what followed. With bright, almost dilated, eyes, and a sweet, warm color mantling her smiling face, Esther stood gazing about the room, nodding blithely as she caught the glance of many a friend, yet obviously searching for still another. Then of a sudden they saw the bonny face light up with joy uncontrollable, for Mr. Field came bounding in at the side door, opening from the veranda of the adjutant's office. He saw her; smiled joyous greeting as he came swiftly toward her; then stopped short as a girl in black grenadine dropped the arm of her cavalier, the officer with whom she was promenading, and without a moment's hesitation, placed her left hand, fan-bearing, close to the shoulder knot on his stalwart right arm, her black-gloved right in his white-kidded left, and instantly they went gliding away together, he nodding half in whimsical apology, half in merriment, over the black spangled shoulder, and the roseate light died slowly from the sweet, smiling face—the smile itself seemed slowly freezing—as the still dilated eyes followed the graceful movements of the couple, slowly, harmoniously winding

A DAUGHTER OF THE SIOUX

and reversing about the waxen floor. Even at the Point she had never seen more beautiful dancing. Even when her stanchest friend, Mrs. Blake, pounced upon her with fond, anxious, welcoming words, and Mrs. Ray, seeing it all, broke from her partner's encircling arm, and sped to add her greeting, the child could hardly regain self-control, and one loving-hearted woman cried herself to sleep that night for the woe that had come into the soft and tender eyes which had first beamed with joy at sight of Beverly Field, then filled with sudden dread immeasurable.

But the major sought to block that morning ride in vain. The impetuous will of the younger soldier prevailed, as he might have known it would, and from the rear gallery of his quarters, with his strong fieldglass, Major Webb watched the pair fording the Platte far up beyond Pyramid Butte. "Going over to that damned Sioux village again," he swore between his set teeth. "That makes the third time she's headed him there this week," and with strange annoyance at heart he turned away to seek comfort in council with his stanch henchman, Captain Ray, when the orderly came bounding up the steps with a telegraphic despatch which the major opened, read, turned a shade grayer and whistled low.

"My compliments to Captains Blake and Ray," said he, to the silent young soldier, standing attention at the doorstep, "and say I should be glad to see them here at once."

That night the sentries had just called off half past one when there was some commotion at the guard-house. A courier had ridden in post haste from the outlying station of Fort Beecher, far up under the lee of the Big Horn range. The corporal of the guard took charge of his reeking horse, while the sergeant led the messenger to the commander's quarters. The major was already awake and half dressed. "Call the adjutant," was all he said, on reading the despatch, and the sergeant sped away. In less than five minutes he was back.

"I could get no answer to my knock or ring, sir, so I searched the house. The adjutant isn't there!"

CHAPTER II

ABSENT FROM DUTY

For a moment the major stood in silence; then, briefly saying, "Call Captain Ray," turned again to the dimly lighted hallway of his commodious quarters, (the women thought it such a shame there should be no "lady of the house" for the largest and finest of the long line known as "Officers' Row") while the sergeant of the guard scurried away to the soldier home of the senior cavalry captain on duty at the post. When the major again came forth his field glasses were in his hand and he had hurried down the steps and out into the broad sheen of the moonlight when he caught sight of the courier seated on the horseblock at the gate, wearily leaning his head upon his gauntleted hand. Webb stopped short:

"Come right in here, my lad," he cried, "I want to speak with you," and, followed slowly by the soldier, he entered his parlor, and whirled an easy chair in front of the open fireplace. "Sit right down there now, and I'll be with you in a minute," he added; bustled into the rear room and presently reappeared with a decanter and glass; poured out a stiff tot of Monongahela; "A little water?" he asked, as the trooper's eye brightened gratefully. A little water was added and off came the right hand gauntlet. "I drink the major's health and long life to him," said the soldier, gulping down the fluid without so much as a wink. Then, true to his training, set down the glass and stood strictly at attention.

"You've had nothing to eat since yesterday morning, I'll be bound," said Webb. "Now, I've got to see some of my officers at

A DAUGHTER OF THE SIOUX

once. You make yourself at home here. You'll find cold beef, bread, cheese, pickles, milk, if you care for it, and pie right there in the pantry. Take the lamp in with you and help yourself. If you want another nip, there's the decanter. You've made splendid time. Did you meet no Indians?"

"Not one, sir, but I saw smokes at sunset out toward Eagle Butte."

"Your name—I see you belong to Captain Truscott's troop."

"Kennedy, sir; and I thank the major."

"Then I'll leave you in charge until you've had your fill," said the commander. "Then go over to 'F' Troop's quarters and get a bed. Tell anybody who comes I've gone to the flagstaff." With that the major stalked from the room, followed by the Irishman's adoring eyes. A moment later he stood by the tall white staff at the edge of the northward bluff, at whose feet the river swept by in musical murmurings. There he quickly focussed his glass, and gazed away westward up the Platte to where but the evening before a score of Indian lodges dotted the other bank, perhaps two miles away. The September moon was at its full and, in that rare, cloudless atmosphere, flooding the valley with its soft, silvery light so that close at hand, within the limits of the garrison, every object could be almost as distinctly seen as in broad day-light, but, farther away, over the lowlands and the river bottom and the rolling prairie stretching to the northern horizon, the cottonwoods along the stream or in the distant swales made only black blotches against the vague, colorless surface, and the bold

A DAUGHTER OF THE SIOUX

bluffs beyond the reservation limits south of the flashing waters, the sharp, sawlike edge of the distant mountain range that barred the way to the west, even the cleancut outlines of Eagle Butte, the landmark of the northward prairie, visible for fifty miles by day, were now all veiled in some intangible filament that screened them from the soldier's searching gaze. Later in the season, on such a night, their crests would gleam with radiance almost intolerable, the glistening sheen of their spotless crown of snow. All over this broad expanse of upland prairie and wooded river bed and boldly undulating bluff line not so much as a spark of fire peeped through the wing of night to tell the presence of human wayfarer, white, halfbreed or Indian, even where the Sioux had swarmed, perhaps two hundred strong, at sunset of the day gone by.

Close at hand, northernmost of the brown line, was the double set of quarters occupied by Captains Blake and Ray, the latter, as senior, having chosen the half nearest the bluff because of the encircling veranda and the fine, far-extending view. A bright light gleamed now behind the blinds of the corner room of the second floor, telling that the captain was up and dressing in answer to the commander's summons, but all the rest of the dozen houses were black, save where at the middle of the row a faint glow came from the open doorway at the commanding officer's. Across the broad level of the parade were the long, low barracks of the troops, six in number, gable-ending east and west. Closing the quadrangle on the south were the headquarters buildings and the assembly room, the offices of the adjutant and quartermaster, the commissary and quartermaster's storehouses, etc. At the

A DAUGHTER OF THE SIOUX

southwest angle stood the guard-house, where oil lamps, backed by their reflectors of polished tin, sent brilliant beams of light athwart the roadway. Beyond these low buildings the black bulk of the Medicine Bow Mountains, only a dozen miles away, tumbled confusedly against the sparkling sky. All spoke of peace, security, repose, for even in the flats under the westward bluff, where lay the wide extended corrals, hay and wood yards and the stables, not one of the myriad dogs that hung about the post was lifting up his voice to bay the autumn moon. Even those easily-started night trumpeters, the big Missouri mules, sprawled about their roomy, sand-floored stables and drowsed in placid comfort, wearied with their musical efforts of the earlier hours of the night and gathering impetus for the sonorous braying with which they should presently salute the dawn.

Beyond the guard-house, at the edge of the plateau overlooking the westward flats, but invisible from the flagstaff bluff, stood the big wooden edifice known as the store, with its card and billiard room for the officers on the southern side, another for the enlisted men upon the northern, the bar and general merchandise establishment compressed between them. Southward, farther still, surrounded by crude greenhouses abounding in potted plants and beds of vine and vegetables, was the big and somewhat pretentious house of the post trader himself, his own stables and corral being half way down the slope and well away from those of the garrison. "Out of sight," muttered Webb, "but by no means out of mind," for it was safe to say the thoughts of more than half the men and women making up the social element of Fort Frayne had been centering

A DAUGHTER OF THE SIOUX

within the last few days beneath the roof that gave shelter to that brilliant, fascinating beauty Nanette Flower.

Ten days a denizen of the fort, it seemed as though she had been there as many weeks, so completely had she accepted the situation and possessed herself of the ins and outs of garrison life. The women had called, of course, and gone away filled with unwilling admiration, for the girl's gowns and graces were undeniable. The married men, as was the army way, had called with their wives on the occasion of the first visit. The bachelors, from Webb down to the junior subaltern, had called in little squads at first; afterwards, except the major, they sought to see Miss Flower when other fellows were not present. Even Hartley and Donovan, the two whose devotions to Esther Dade had been carried to the verge of oppression, and who were on terms of distant civility only when compelled to appear together in the presence of women or their other superiors, had been moved to more than one visit at the Hays', but Hartley speedily returned to his undesired siege at the quarters of Captain Dade, while Donovan joined forces with two other youngsters, Bruce and Putney, because it gave them comfort to bother Field; who, being the adjutant, and a very busy man, could visit only at certain hours of the day or evening. Now, it had become apparent to the boys that despite her general attitude of cordiality their attentions were not what Mrs. Hay so much desired as those of the major commanding. Twice had he been invited to dine within the week of Nanette's coming. Once he accepted. The second time he begged off on plea of a previous engagement, subsequently made, to go shooting with Blake. It was the bachelor heart and home of

Major Webb to which Mrs. Hay would have laid vicarious siege, small blame to her, for that indomitable cross-examiner, Mrs. Wilkins, wife and manager of the veteran ranker now serving as post quartermaster, had wormed out of Mrs. Hay the admission that Nanette had no fortune. She was the only daughter of a half brother, very dear to Mrs. Hay, whom she had lost, she said, long years before. To do her justice, it was quite apparent that Miss Flower was no party to the plan, for, though she beamed on Webb as she did on all, she frankly showed her preference for the younger officers who could dance as well as ride, and either dancing or riding was her glory. She danced like a sylph; she seemed to float about the room as though on air; she rode superbly, and shirked no leap that even Ray and Field took with lowered hands and close gripping knees. She was joyous, laughing, radiant with all the officers, and fairly glowed with cordiality for all the women. But it speedily developed that she would rather dance with Field than any of the others, probably because he was by far the best waltzer, and to ride with him, because, Ray excepted, there was none to excel him in the saddle. Ten days had she been at Frayne and within that time had become as thoroughly at ease and home as though it had been her abiding place since babyhood. It was plain to see that big Bill Hay almost worshipped this lovely *protegée* of the wife he more than worshipped. It was plain to see that Webb uneasily held aloof, as though fearful of singeing his shrivelling wings. It was plain to see that the hitherto indomitable Mrs. Wilkins was puzzled. It was not so plain to see that there were two women at the post on whom Miss Flower's charms made slight

A DAUGHTER OF THE SIOUX

impression—Mesdames Blake and Ray—two wise young matrons who were known to have few secrets from each other and no intimacies—or rather no confidences—with any other woman at Fort Frayne—Mrs. Dade possibly excepted.

But what they thought, their liege lords stood ready to swear to; and it was to them Webb turned in his perplexity when it became apparent that his young adjutant was ensnared. It was to Ray he promptly opened his heart, as that veteran of a dozen Indian campaigns, then drawing his fourth "fogy," came hastening out to join the commander.

"Here's confirmation of the telegram. Read that, Ray," said Webb, handing him the despatch from Fort Beecher. "Then come with me to Field's. He's missing."

"Missing!" cried Ray, in consternation, as he hurriedly opened the page. "In God's name what do you mean?"

"I mean he isn't in quarters and hasn't been in bed to-night. Now I need him—and it's two o'clock."

Even as he spoke the voice of the sentry at the guard-house rang out the watch call through the still and sparkling night. It was taken up by Number Two back of the storehouses, and his "All's well" was still echoing among the foothills, prolonged and powerful, when Number Three, down at the quartermaster's corral, began his soldier song; and so, alert, cheery, reassuring, the sentries sent their deep-voiced assurance on its unbroken round to the waking guardian at the southwest angle, and as his final

A DAUGHTER OF THE SIOUX

"A-a-a-ll's W-e-ell" went rolling away over bluff and stream and prairie, Ray lifted a grave and anxious face from the fateful paper.

"Lame Wolf out? That's bad in itself! He's old Red Cloud's nephew and a brute at best. Stabber's people there yet?" he suddenly asked, whirling on his heel and gazing westward.

"Can't make out even with my glasses. All dark as pitch among the cottonwoods, but Kennedy, who made the ride, says he saw smokes back of Eagle Butte just before sunset."

"Then you can bet they won't be there at dawn—the warriors at least. Of course the women, the kids and old men will stay if only for a blind. He had forty fighting men, and Wolf's got at least two hundred. What started the row?"

"The arrest of those two young bucks on charge of killing Finn, the sheep herder, on the Piney last week. I don't believe the Sioux began it. There's a bad lot among those damned rustlers," said Webb, snapping the glass into its well-worn case. "But no matter who starts, we have to finish it. Old Plodder is worried and wants help. Reckon I'll have to send you, Ray."

"Ready whenever you say, sir," was the prompt and soldierly reply. Even marriage had not taken the edge from Ray's keen zest for campaigning. "Shall I have out my sergeant and cooks at once? We'll need to take rations."

"Yes, but wait with me till I wire the chief at Laramie. Come to the office." So saying the post commander turned and strode away. The captain glanced at the upper window where the light

A DAUGHTER OF THE SIOUX

now dimly burned, but blind and window were open, and a woman's form appeared.

"It's all right, Maidie," called the captain, softly. "May have to start out on scout at daybreak. That's all. Home soon," and with a reassuring wave of the hand, turned again to his stanch friend and commander.

"I hate to send you—again," said Webb. "You were out in June, and the others have had only short scouts since—"

"Don't bother. What's a cavalryman for? Shall we?—I—can't believe it—some how," and Ray stopped, glanced inquiringly at the major, and then nodded toward the doorway of the third house on the row. The ground floor was occupied by Field as his quarters, the up-stair rooms by Putney and Ross.

"Come in," said the major, briefly, and, pushing through the gate they softly entered the dark hallway and struck a light in the front room. A wood fire was smouldering on the andirons in the wide brick chimney place. An open book, face downward, was on the centre table. Two embroidered slippers lay as though hurriedly kicked off, one under the sofa beyond the mantelpiece, the other half way across the worn carpet. Striking another match at the doorway, Ray passed on to the little inner room,—the bed chamber. On the bed, carelessly thrown, were the young officer's best and newest forage cap, undress uniform coat and trousers. He had used them during the evening when calling at the Hays'. On the floor were the enamelled leather buttoned boots he wore on such occasions. The bed was otherwise untouched. Other

A DAUGHTER OF THE SIOUX

boots and shoes in orderly row stood against the wall beside the plain, unpainted wardrobe. The spurred riding boots and the knee-tight breeches were gone. Turning back to the front room, Ray found the major, his face gray and disturbed, holding forth to him an open envelope. Ray took it and glanced at the superscription. "Lieutenant Beverly Field, Fort Frayne," and returned it without a word. Both knew the strange, angular, slashing hand-writing at a glance, for both had seen and remarked it before. It was Nanette Flower's.

Dropping the envelope on the table—he had found it on the floor—Webb led the way to the open air. There was then no time to compare views. There stood the sergeant.

"Sir," said he, with a snap of the gloved left hand at the brown tube nestling in the hollow of the shoulder, "Number Five reports that he has heard galloping hoofbeats up the bench twice in the last half hour, and thought he saw distant horsemen,— three;—couldn't say whether they were Indians or cowboys."

"Very good, sergeant," was the major's brief answer. "Send for the telegraph operator and my orderly."

The sergeant turned.

"One moment," called Ray,—"your pardon, Major—My first sergeant, too, and—sergeant, have any sentries reported horses taken out from the stables to-night?"

"Not one, sir," and, stanch and sturdy, the commander of the guard stood ready to vouch for his men.

A DAUGHTER OF THE SIOUX

"That's all!"

A quick salute, a face to the right about and the sergeant was gone. Webb turned and looked inquiringly at Ray.

"I asked, sir," was that officer's brief explanation, "because wherever Field has gone he wore riding dress."

A DAUGHTER OF THE SIOUX

CHAPTER III

A NIGHT ENCOUNTER

Comforted by abundant food, refreshed and stimulated by more than two or three enthusiastic toasts to the health of the major the men so loved, Trooper Kennedy, like a born dragoon and son of the ould sod, bethought him of the gallant bay that had borne him bravely and with hardly a halt all the long way from Beecher to Frayne. The field telegraph had indeed been stretched, but it afforded more fun for the Sioux than aid to the outlying posts on the Powder and Little Horn, for it was down ten days out of twelve. Plodder, lieutenant colonel of infantry commanding at Beecher, had been badly worried by the ugly demonstrations of the Indians for ten days past. He was forever seeing in mind's eye the hideous details of the massacre at Fort Phil Kearny, a few miles further on around the shoulder of the mountains, planned and carried out by Red Cloud with such dreadful success in '67. Plodder had strong men at his back, whom even hordes of painted Sioux could never stampede, but they were few in number, and there were those ever present helpless, dependent women and children. His call for aid was natural enough, and his choice of Kennedy, daring, dashing lad who had learned to ride in Galway, was the best that could be made. No peril could daunt the light-hearted fellow, already proud wearer of the medal of honor; but, duty done, it was Kennedy's creed that the soldier merited reward and relaxation. If he went to bed at "F" Troop's barracks there would be no more cakes and ale, no more of the major's good grub and rye. If he went down to look after the gallant steed he loved—saw to it that Kilmaine was rubbed down, bedded, given abundant hay and later water—sure then, with clear conscience, he could accept the major's "bid," and call again on his bedward way and toast the major to his Irish heart's and stomach's content. Full of pluck and fight and enthusiasm, and only quarter full, he would insist, of rye, was Kennedy as he strode whistling down the well-remembered road to the flats, for he, with Captain Truscott's famous troop, had served some months at Frayne before launching forth to Indian story land in the shadows of the Big Horn range. Kennedy, in fact, essayed to sing when once out of earshot of the guard-house, and singing, he strolled on past the fork of the winding road where he should have turned to his right, and in the fulness of his heart went striding southward down the slope, past the once familiar haunt the store, now dark and deserted, past the big house of the post trader, past the trader's roomy stables and corral, and so wended his moonlit way along the Rawlins trail, never noting until he had chanted over half a mile and most of the songs he knew, that Frayne was well behind him and the rise to the Medicine Bow in front. Then Kennedy began to laugh and call himself names, and then, as he turned about to retrace his steps by a short cut over the bottom, he was presently surprised, but in no wise disconcerted, to find himself face to face with a painted Sioux. There by the path side, cropping the dewy grass, was the trained pony. Here, lounging by the trail, the thick black braids of his hair interlaced with beads, the quill gorget heaving at his massive throat; the heavy blanket slung negligently, gracefully about his stalwart form; his

A DAUGHTER OF THE SIOUX

nether limbs and feet in embroidered buckskin, his long-lashed quirt in hand; here stood, almost confronting him, as fine a specimen of the warrior of the Plains as it had ever been Trooper Kennedy's lot to see, and see them he had—many a time and oft.

In that incomparable tale, "My Lord the Elephant," the great Mulvaney comes opportunely upon a bottle of whiskey and a goblet of water. "The first and second dhrink I didn't taste," said he, "bein' dhry, but the fourth and fifth took hould, an' I began to think scornful of elephants." At no time stood Kennedy in awe of a Sioux. At this time he held him only in contempt.

"How, John," said he, with an Irishman's easy insolence, "Lookin' for a chance to steal somethin'—is it?" And then Kennedy was both amazed and enraptured at the prompt reply in the fervent English of the far frontier.

"Go to hell, you pock-marked son-of-a-scut! Where'd *you* steal your whiskey?"

For five seconds Kennedy thought he was dreaming. Then, convinced that he was awake, an Irishman scorned and insulted, he dashed in to the attack. Both fists shot out from the brawny shoulders; both missed the agile dodger; then off went the blanket, and with two lean, red, sinewy arms the Sioux had "locked his foeman round," and the two were straining and swaying in a magnificent grapple. At arms' length Pat could easily have had the best of it, for the Indian never boxes; but, in a bear hug and a wrestle, all chances favored the Sioux. Cursing and straining, honors even on both for a while, Connaught and wild

A DAUGHTER OF THE SIOUX

Wyoming strove for the mastery. Whiskey is a wonderful starter but a mighty poor stayer of a fight. Kennedy loosed his grip from time to time to batter wildly with his clinched fists at such sections of Sioux anatomy as he could reach; but, at range so close, his blows lacked both swing and steam, and fell harmless on sinewy back and lean, muscular flanks. Then he tried a Galway hitch and trip, but his lithe antagonist knew a trick worth ten of that. Kennedy tried many a time next day to satisfactorily account for it, but never with success. He found himself speedily on the broad of his back, gasping for breath with which to keep up his vocal defiance, staring up into the glaring, vengeful black eyes of his furious and triumphant foeman. And then in one sudden, awful moment he realized that the Indian was reaching for his knife. Another instant it gleamed aloft in the moonlight, and the poor lad shut his eyes against the swift and deadly blow. Curses changed to one wordless prayer to heaven for pity and help. He never saw the glittering blade go spinning through the air. Vaguely, faintly he heard a stern young voice ordering "Hold there!" then another, a silvery voice, crying something in a strange tongue, and was conscious that an unseen power had loosed the fearful grip on his throat; next, that, obedient to that same power,—one he dare not question,—the Indian was struggling slowly to his feet, and then for a few seconds Kennedy soared away into cloudland, knowing naught of what was going on about him. When he came to again, he heard a confused murmur of talk about him, and grew dimly aware that his late antagonist was standing over him, panting still and slightly swaying, and that an officer, a young athlete, was

A DAUGHTER OF THE SIOUX

saying rebukeful words. Well he knew him, as what trooper of the ——th did not?—Lieutenant Beverly Field; but, seeing the reopened eyes it was the Indian again who sought to speak. With uplifted hand he turned from the rescuer to the rescued.

"You're saved this time, you cur of a Mick," were, expurgated of unprintable blasphemy, the exact words of the semi-savage lord of the frontier, "but by the God that made us both I'll get you before another moon, dash dash you, and when I do I'll cut out your blackguard heart and eat it." Then bounding on his pony, away he sped at mad gallop, westward.

For a moment no further word was spoken. The officer presently helped the soldier to his feet and stayed him, for the latter's legs seemed wobbly. Field let his salvage get its breath before asking questions. Yet he was puzzled, for the man's face was strange to him. "Who are you?" he asked, at length, "and what on earth are you doing out here this time of night?"

"Kennedy, sir. Captain Truscott's troop, at Fort Beecher. I got in with despatches an hour ago—"

"What!" cried Field. "Despatches! What did you do—"

"Gave 'em to the major, sir. Beg pardon; they was lookin' for the adjutant, sir, an' Sergeant Hogan said he wasn't home."

Even in the moonlight the Irishman saw the color fade from the young officer's face. The hand that stayed him dropped nerveless. With utter consternation in his big blue eyes, Field stood for a moment, stunned and silent. Then the need of instant action spurred him. "I must go—at once," he said. "You are all right now—You can get back? You've been drinking, haven't you?"

"The major's health, sir—just a sup or two."

"I've no time now to listen to how you came to be out here. I'll see you by and by." But still the young officer hesitated. One hand grasped the rein of his horse. He half turned to mount, then turned again. "Kennedy," he faltered, "you'd have been a dead man if we—if I—hadn't reached you at that moment."

"I know it, sir," burst in Pat, impetuously. "I'll never forget it—"

"Hush, Kennedy, you *must* forget—forget that you saw—spoke with me—forget that you saw or heard—any other soul on earth out here to-night. Can you promise?"

"I'll cut my tongue out before I ever spake the word that'll harm the lieutenant, or the—the—or any one he says, sir. But never will I forget! It ain't in me, sir."

"Let it go at that then. Here, shake hands, Kennedy. Now, good-night!" Another instant and Field was in saddle and speeding away toward the post where lights were now dancing about the quartermaster's corral, and firefly lamps were flitting down the slope toward the stables on the flats. Ray's men were already up and doing. Slowly, stiffly following, Pat Kennedy rubbed his aching head, with a hand that shook as never did his resolution. His bewildered brain was puzzling over a weighty problem. "The lieutenant's safe all right," he muttered, "but what's gone wid the squaw that was shoutin' Sioux at that murdherin' buck?"

A DAUGHTER OF THE SIOUX

Meantime all Fort Frayne had seemed to wake to life. No call had sounded on the trumpet. No voice had been raised, save the invariable call of the sentries, passing from post to post the half hours of the night; but the stir at the guard-house, the bustle over at the barracks, the swift footsteps of sergeants or orderlies on the plank walk or resounding wooden galleries, speedily roused first one sleeper, then another, and blinds began to fly open along the second floor fronts, and white-robed forms to appear at the windows, and inquiring voices, male and female, hailed the passerby with "What's the matter, sergeant?" and the answer was all sufficient to rouse the entire garrison.

"Captain Ray's troop ordered out, sir," or "ma'am," as the case might be. No need to add the well-worn cause of such night excursions—"Indians."

The office was brightly lighted, and there, sleepy-eyed and silent, were gathered many of the officers about their alert commander. Ray was down at his stables, passing judgment on the mounts. Only fifty were to go, the best half hundred in the sorrel troop, for it was to be a forced march. Neither horse nor man could be taken unless in prime condition, for a break down on part of either on the way meant delay to the entire command, or death by torture to the hapless trooper left behind. Small hope was there of a march made unobserved, for Stabber's band of Ogalallas had been for weeks encamped within plain view. Less hope was there of Stabber's holding aloof now that his brethren at the Big Horn had declared for war. He was a recalcitrant of the first magnitude, a sub-chief who had never missed the warpath when the Sioux were afield, or the consolation trip to Washington between times. Where Stabber went his young men followed unquestioning. It was a marvel that Kennedy had succeeded in getting through. It meant that the Indian runners, or the Indian smokes and signals, had not at once so covered the country with scouts that couriers could by no possibility slip between them. But now the signal fire was gleaming at Eagle Butte, and an answering blaze had flared from Stabber's camp. Invisible from Fort Frayne, they had both been seen by shrewd non-commissioned officers, sent scouting up the Platte by Major Webb within half an hour of the coming of the alarm.

"Ray will push ahead at once," said Webb, to his silent subordinates. "You see Colonel Plodder has only two troops up there, and he will need all his infantry to defend the post. I've wired to Laramie and to Department Headquarters, and further orders will come before noon. Let all the cavalry be ready. Then if we push out, Dade, we leave Fort Frayne to you. They'll hardly venture south of the Platte this time."

"Is—Mr. Field going with Captain Ray?" presently ventured young Ross, who knew Ray had but one subaltern for duty at the moment, and whose soul was burning with eagerness to accompany the first troop to take the field.

"No," said the major, shortly. "Captain Ray needs no more."

"I only asked because Field isn't here, and I thought—maybe—" stumbled Ross, ingloriously, but the mischief was done.

A DAUGHTER OF THE SIOUX

"Mr. Field is—busy," answered the major, still more shortly, then reddened to his bushy brows, for at the doorway, in riding dress, and with a face the color of parchment, stood the officer in question. It was a moment that threatened panic, but Webb met the crisis with marked aplomb.

"Oh, Field," he cried, "there's another matter. I want two good men to slip out at once and see how many of Stabber's people start or have started. It may be daybreak before they can tell. Sergeant Schreiber would be a tiptop man for one—and little Duffy. You 'tend to it."

And so, mercifully, he sent the lad away until the crowd should have dispersed. Only Blake and Ray were with him when, after awhile, Mr. Field returned and stood silently before them. Well he knew that the post commander could hardly overlook the absence of his adjutant at such a time.

"Have you anything to tell me, Field?" was the major's only query, his tone full of gentle yet grave reproach.

"I was restless. I could not sleep, sir. I went out—purposely."

"You know no horse can be taken from the stables at night except in presence of the sergeant or corporal of the guard."

"I took none, sir," was the answer, and now both faces were white. "I rode one of—Mr. Hay's."

For one moment there was no sound but the loud ticking of the big office clock. Then came the question.

A DAUGHTER OF THE SIOUX

"Who rode the others, Field? The sentries say they heard three."

There was another moment of silence. Ray stepped on tiptoe to the door as though he wanted not to hear. Blake looked blankly out of the window. Then the young soldier spoke.

"I—cannot tell you, sir."

For full ten seconds the post commander sat with grave, pallid face, looking straight into the eyes of his young staff officer. White as his senior, but with eyes as unflinching, Field returned the gaze. At last the major's voice was heard again, sad and constrained.

"Field, Captain Ray starts on a forced march at once for Fort Beecher. I—wish you to go with him."

CHAPTER IV

THE SIGN OF THE BAR SHOE

Many a time has it happened in the old days of the old army that the post adjutant has begged to be allowed to go with some detachment sent after Indians. Rarely has it happened, however, that, without any request from the detachment commander or of his own, has the post adjutant been ordered to go. No one could say of Beverly Field that he had not abundantly availed himself of every opportunity for active service in the past. During his first two years with the regiment he had spent more than half the time in saddle and afield, scouting the trails of war parties or marauding bands, or watching over a peaceable tribe when on the annual hunt. Twice he had been out with Ray, which meant a liberal education in plainscraft and frontier duty. Twice twenty times, probably, had he said he would welcome a chance to go again with Captain Ray, and now the chance had come, so had the spoken order, and, so far from receiving it with rejoicing, it was more than apparent that he heard it with something like dismay.

But Webb was not the man to either explain or defend an order, even to a junior for whom he cherished such regard. Field felt instinctively that it was not because of a wish expressed in the past he was so suddenly bidden to take the field. Ray's senior subaltern, as has been said, was absent, being on duty at West Point, but his junior was on hand, and Ray really did not need, and probably had not applied for, the services of Mr. Field. It was all the major's doing, and all, reasoned he, because the major deemed it best that for the time being his young adjutant should be sent away from the post. Impulse prompted Field to ask wherein he had offended or failed. Reflection taught him, however, that he would be wise to ask no questions. It might well be that Webb knew more of what had happened during the night than he, Beverly Field, would care to have mentioned.

"You can be ready, can you not?" asked the major.

"I am ready now, sir," was the brief, firm reply, but the tone told unerringly that the lad resented and in heart rebelled at the detail. "To whom shall I turn over the post fund, sir?"

"I do not care to have you transfer funds or—anything, Field. This is but a temporary affair, one that will take you away perhaps a fortnight."

"I prefer that it should be permanent, sir," was the young officer's sudden interruption, and, though his eyes were blazing, he spoke with effort, his face still white with mingled sense of indignity and indignation.

"Gently, Mr. Field," said Webb, with unruffled calm, even while uplifting a hand in quiet warning. "We will consider that, if need be, on your return. Meantime, if you desire, I will receipt to you for the post fund or any other public money."

"That is the trouble, sir. The best I can do is give you an order for it. Post treasurers, as a rule, have not had to turn over their funds at four o'clock in the morning," which statement was true enough, however injudicious it might be to bruit it. Mild-

A DAUGHTER OF THE SIOUX

mannered commanding officers sometimes amaze their subordinates by most unlooked for and unwelcome eruptiveness of speech when they feel that an unwarrantable liberty has been taken. Webb did not take fire. He turned icy.

"The quartermaster's safe can be opened at any moment, Mr. Field," said he, the blue gray eyes glittering, dangerously. "I presume your funds are there."

"It was because the quartermaster would *not* open it at any moment that I took them out and placed them elsewhere," hotly answered Field, and not until then did Webb remember that there had been quite a fiery talk, followed by hyperborean estrangement, between his two staff officers, and now, as the only government safe at the post was in the office of the quartermaster, and the only other one was Bill Hay's big "Phoenix" at the store, it dawned upon the major that it was there Mr. Field had stowed his packages of currency—a violation of orders pure and simple—and that was why he could not produce the money on the spot. Webb reflected. If he let Ray start at dawn and held Field back until the trader was astir, it might be eight o'clock before the youngster could set forth. By that time Ray would be perhaps a dozen miles to the northward, and with keen-eyed Indian scouts noting the march of the troop and keeping vigilant watch for possible stragglers, it might be sending the lad to certain death, for Plodder had said in so many words the Sioux about him had declared for war, had butchered three ranchmen on the Dry Fork, had fired on and driven in his herd guards and wood choppers, and, what started with Lane

A DAUGHTER OF THE SIOUX

Wolf's big band, would spread to Stabber's little one in less than no time, and what spread to Stabber's would soon reach a host of the Sioux. Moreover, there was another reason. It would give Field opportunity for further conference with—inmates of the trader's household, and the major had his own grave reasons for seeking to prevent that.

"Your written order will be sufficient, Mr. Field," said he. "Send me memorandum of the amounts and I will receipt at once, so that you can go without further thought of them. And now," with a glance at the clock, "you have hardly half an hour in which to get ready."

Raising his hand in mechanical salute, Field faced about; cast one look at Blake, standing uncomfortably at the window, and then strode angering away to his quarters, smarting under a sense of unmerited rebuke yet realizing that, as matters looked, no one was more to blame than himself.

Just as the first faint flush of coming day was mantling the pallid eastern sky, and while the stars still sparkled aloft and the big, bright moon was sinking to the snow-tipped peaks far away to the occident, in shadowy column a troop of fifty horse filed slowly from The Sorrels' big corral and headed straight for the Platte. Swift and unfordable in front of Frayne in the earlier summer, the river now went murmuring sleepily over its stony bed, and Ray led boldly down the bank and plunged girth deep into the foaming waters. Five minutes more and every man had lined up safely on the northward bank. In low tone the order was given, starting as Ray ever did, in solid column of fours. In dead

A DAUGHTER OF THE SIOUX

silence the little command moved slowly away, followed by the eyes of half the garrison on the bluff. Many of these were women and children, who gazed through a mist of tears. Ray turned in saddle as the last of his men went by; looked long at the dim light in the upper window of his home, where, clasping her children to her heart, his devoted wife knelt watching them, her fond lips moving in ceaseless prayer. Dimly she could see the tried leader, her soldier husband, sitting in saddle at the bank. Bravely she answered the flutter of his handkerchief in farewell. Then all was swallowed up in the shadows of the distant prairie, and from the nursery adjoining her room there rose a querulous wail that told that her baby daughter was waking, indifferent to the need that sent the soldier father to the aid of distant comrades, threatened by a merciless foe, and conscious only of her infantile demands and expectations. Not yet ten years wed, that brave, devoted wife and mother had known but two summers that had not torn her husband from her side on just such quest and duty, for these were the days of the building up of the West, resisted to the bitter end by the red wards of the nation.

The sun was just peering over the rough, jagged outline of the eastward buttes, when a quick yet muffled step was heard on the major's veranda and a picturesque figure stood waiting at the door. Scout, of course, a stranger would have said at a glance, for from head to foot the man was clad in beaded buckskin, without sign of soldier garb of any kind. Soldier, too, would have been the expert testimony the instant the door opened and the commanding officer appeared. Erect as a Norway pine the strange figure stood to attention, heels and knees together,

A DAUGHTER OF THE SIOUX

shoulders squared, head and eyes straight to the front, the left hand, fingers extended, after the precise teachings of the ante-bellum days, the right hand raised and held at the salute. Strange figure indeed, yet soldierly to the last degree, despite the oddity of the entire make-up. The fur-trimmed cap of embroidered buckskin sat jauntily on black and glossy curls that hung about the brawny neck and shoulders. The buckskin coat, heavily fringed as to the short cape and the shorter skirt, was thickly covered with Indian embroidery of bead and porcupine quill; so, too, were the fringed trousers and leggings; so, too, the moccasins, soled with thick, yet pliant hide. Keen black eyes shone from beneath heavy black brows, just sprinkled, as were the thick moustache and imperial, with gray. The lean jowls were closely shaved. The nose was straight and fine, the chin square and resolute. The face and hands were tanned by sun and wind well nigh as dark as many a Sioux, but in that strange garb there stood revealed one of the famous sergeants of a famous regiment, the veteran of a quarter century of service with the standard, wounded time and again, bearing the scars of Stuart's sabre and of Southern lead, of Indian arrow and bullet both; proud possessor of the medal of honor that many a senior sought in vain; proud as the Lucifer from whom he took his Christian name, brave, cool, resolute and ever reliable—Schreiber, First Sergeant of old "K" Troop for many a year, faced his post commander with brief and characteristic report:—

"Sir, Chief Stabber, with over thirty warriors, left camp about three o'clock, heading for Eagle Butte."

A DAUGHTER OF THE SIOUX

"Well done, sergeant! I knew I could count on you," answered Webb, in hearty commendation. "Now, one thing more. Go to 'F' Troop's quarters and see how Kennedy is faring. He came in with despatches from Fort Beecher, and later drank more, I fancy, than was good for him, for which I assume all responsibility. Keep him out of mischief this morning."

"I will, sir," said the sergeant, and saluting turned away while Webb went back to set a dismantled pantry in partial order, against the appearance of his long-suffering house-keeper, whose comments he dreaded as he did those of no inspector general in the army. For fifteen years, and whithersoever Webb was ordered, his bachelor *ménage* had been presided over by Mistress Margaret McGann, wife of a former trooper, who had served as Webb's "striker" for so many a year in the earlier days that, when discharged for disability, due to wounds, rheumatism and advancing years, and pensioned, as only Uncle Sam rewards his veterans, McGann had begged the major to retain him and his buxom better half at their respective duties, and Webb had meekly, weakly yielded, to the end that in the fulness of time Dame Margaret had achieved an ascendancy over the distinguished cavalry officer little short of that she had exercised over honest Michael since the very day she consented to become Mistress McGann. A sound sleeper was she, however, and not until morning police call was she wont to leave her bed. Then, her brief toilet completed, she would descend to the kitchen and set the major's coffee on the fire, started by her dutiful spouse an hour earlier. Then she proceeded to lay the table, and put the rooms in order against the major's coming, and woe betide him if

A DAUGHTER OF THE SIOUX

cigar stubs littered the bachelor sittingroom or unrinsed glasses and half empty decanters told of even moderate symposium over night. Returning that eventful morning from his office at first call for reveillé, after seeing the last of Ray's gallant troop as it moved away across the dim vista of the northward prairie, Webb had been concerned to find his decanter of Monongahela half empty on the pantry table and the *débris* of a hurried feast on every side. Kennedy, who had begun in moderation, must have felt the need of further creature comfort after his bout with the stalwart Sioux, and had availed himself to the limit of his capacity of the major's invitation. Webb's first thought was to partially remove the traces of that single-handed spree; then, refilling the decanter from the big five-gallon demijohn, kept under lock and key in the cupboard—for Michael, too, had at long intervals weaknesses of his own—he was thinking how best to protect Kennedy from the consequences of his, Webb's, rash invitation when Schreiber's knock was heard.

Ten minutes more and the sergeant was back again.

"Sir, I have to report that Trooper Kennedy has not been seen about the quarters," said he.

"Then try the stables, sergeant," answered the veteran campaigner, and thither would Schreiber next have gone, even had he not been sent. And, sure enough, there was Kennedy, with rueful face and a maudlin romaunt about a moonlit meeting with a swarm of painted Sioux, over which the stable guard were making merry and stirring the trooper's soul to wrath ungovernable.

A DAUGHTER OF THE SIOUX

"I can prove ut," he howled, to the accompaniment of clinching fists and bellicose lunges at the laughing tormentors nearest him. "I can whip the hide off'n the scut that says I didn't. Ask Lootn't Field, bejabers! He saw it. Ask—Oh, Mother of God! what's this I'm sayin'?"—And there, with stern, rebuking gaze, stood the man they knew and feared, every soul of them, as they did no commissioned soldier in the ——th, Sergeant Schreiber, the redoubtable, and Schreiber had heard the insane and damaging boast.

"Come with me, Kennedy," was all he said, and Kennedy snatched his battered felt headgear down over his eyes and tacked woefully after his swift-striding master, without ever another word.

But it was to his own room Schreiber took the unhappy Irishman, not to the quarters of Company "F." He had heard words that, coupled with others that fell through the darkness on his keenly listening ears some two hours earlier, had given him cause for painful thought. "Lie down here, Kennedy. Pull off your boots," said he, "and if you open your fool head to any living soul until I give you leave, py Gott—I'll gill you!" It was Schreiber's way, like Marryatt's famous Boatswain, to begin his admonitions in exact English, and then, as wrath overcame him, to lapse into dialect.

It was but a few minutes after seven when Major Webb, having previously despatched a messenger to the post trader's to say he had need to see Mr. Hay as soon as possible, mounted his horse and, followed by Sergeant Schreiber and an orderly, rode quietly

A DAUGHTER OF THE SIOUX

past the guard-house, touching his hat to the shouted "Turn out the guard—commanding officer" of the sentry on Number One. Mr. Hay was dressing hurriedly, said the servant, so Webb bade Schreiber and the orderly ride slowly down to the flats and await him at the forks of the road. It was but five minutes before Hay appeared, pulling on his coat as he shot from the door, but even before he came the major had been carefully, cautiously scanning the blinds of the second story, even while feigning deep interest in the doings of a little squad of garrison prisoners—the inevitable inmates of the guard-house in the days before we had our safeguard in shape of the soldier's club—the post exchange—and now again in the days that follow its ill-judged extinction. The paymaster had been at Frayne but five days earlier. The prison room was full of aching heads, and Hay's coffers' of hard-earned, ill-spent dollars. Webb sighed at sight of the crowded ranks of this whimsically named "Company Q," but in no wise relaxed his vigilance, for the slats of the blind of the corner window had partially opened. He had had a glimpse of feminine fingers, and purposely he called Hay well out into the road, then bent down over him:

"All your horses in and all right, this morning, Hay?"

"None have been out," said Hay, stoutly, "unless they've gone within the hour. I never let them have the keys, you know, over night. Pete brought them to me at eight last evening and got 'em at six this morning, the usual time."

"Where does he get them—without waking you?" asked Webb.

A DAUGHTER OF THE SIOUX

"They hang behind the door in my sleeping room. Pete gets them when he takes my boots to black at six o'clock."

"Come over to the stables," said the commanding officer, and, wondering, Hay followed.

They found the two hostlers busily at work grooming. In his box stall, bright as a button, was "Harney," Hay's famous runner, his coat smooth as satin. Hay went rapidly from stall to stall. Of the six saddlers owned by him not one gave the faintest sign of having been used over night, but Webb, riding through the gangway, noted that "Crapaud," the French halfbreed grooming in the third stall, never lifted his head. Whatever evidence of night riding that might earlier have existed had been deftly groomed away. The trader had seen suspicion in the soldier's eye, and so stood forth, triumphant:—

"No, Major Webb," said he, in loud, confident, oracular tone, "no horse of mine ever gets out without my knowing it, and never at night unless you or I so order it."

"No?" queried the major, placidly. "Then how do you account for—this?"

Among the fresh hoof prints in the yielding sand, with which the police party had been filling the ruts of the outer roadway, was one never made by government horse or mule. In half a dozen places within a dozen rods, plain as a pikestaff, was the print of a bar shoe, worn on the off fore foot of just one quadruped at the post—Hay's swift running "General Harney."

CHAPTER V

A GRAVE DISCOVERY

Only an hour was the major away from his post. He came back in time for guard mounting and the reports of the officers-of-the-day. He had reason to be on the parade at the "assembly of the details," not so much to watch the work of the post adjutant *pro tempore*, as the effect of the sudden and unlooked for change on certain of the customary spectators. He had swiftly ridden to the camp of the recreant Stabber and purposely demanded speech with that influential chieftain. There had been the usual attempt on part of the old men left in charge to hoodwink and to temporize, but when sharply told that Stabber, with his warriors, had been seen riding away toward Eagle Butte at three in the morning, the sages calmly confessed judgment, but declared they had no other purpose than a hunt for a drove of elk reported seen about the famous Indian race course in the lower hills of the Big Horn. Circling the camp, however, Webb had quickly counted the pony tracks across the still dewy bunchgrass of the bench, and found Schreiber's estimate substantially correct. Then, stopping at the lodge of Stabbers's uncle, old "Spotted Horse," where that superannuated but still sagacious chief was squatted on his blanket and ostentatiously puffing a long Indian pipe, Webb demanded to know what young men remained in the village. Over a hundred strong, old men, squaws and children, they thronged about him, silent, big-eyed and attentive, Schreiber interpreting as best he could, resorting to the well-known sign

A DAUGHTER OF THE SIOUX

language when the crafty Sioux professed ignorance of the meaning of his words:—

"No young men. All gone," was the positive declaration of the venerable head of the bailiwick, when compelled at last to answer. But Schreiber had studied the pony herd and knew better. Moreover, not more than six of their ponies had been led along with the war party that set forth in the early hours of the moonlit morning. Others, both men and mounts, unavoidably left behind, would surely be sent forward at the first possible opportunity, and, much as Webb might wish to turn back to capture the party, well as he might know that other bands were in revolt and Stabber gone to help them, he was powerless under his orders to interfere until by some openly hostile act these laggards of the little band invited his reprisal. The rule of the road, as prescribed by the civil authorities, to which the soldier had sworn obedience, being practically, "Don't defend until you are hit. Don't shoot until you are shot."

Webb came cantering back assured that these frowsy, malodorous lodges concealed, perhaps, half a score of fighting men who were a menace to the neighborhood and who could be counted on to make it more than interesting for any couriers that might have to be sent between the fort and the forces at the front. Calling Schreiber to his side, as, with long easy stride their trained mounts went loping swiftly homeward, he gave instructions the veteran heard with kindling eyes. Then, parting from him at the corrals, the commander rode on and dismounted at his quarters

A DAUGHTER OF THE SIOUX

just as the trumpeters were forming on the broad, grassy level of the parade.

Even without a band young Field had managed to make his guard mount a pretty and attractive ceremony. Frayne was a big post and needed a daily guard of twenty-four men, with the usual quota of non-commissioned officers. Cowboys, herders, miners, prospectors, rustlers (those pirates of the plains) and occasional bands of Indians, Sioux or Arapahoe, were forever hovering about its borders in search of supplies, solid or fluid, and rarely averse to the conversion of public property to personal use. Like many a good citizen of well-ordered municipalities within the confines of civilization, they held that what belonged to the government belonged to them, and the fact that some officer would have to pay for whatsoever they stole, from a horse to a hammer, cut no figure in their deliberations. Frayne had long been a favorite place for fitting out depleted stock, animal, vegetable or mineral, and there had been times when Webb found as many as forty men almost too small a guard, and so gave it to be understood that sentries whose carbines were unlawfully discharged at night, without the formality of preliminary challenge or other intimation of business intentions, would be held blameless, provided they had something to show for their shot. A remarkable feature of the winter's depredation had been that Hay's corral was never molested, although unguarded by the garrison and quite as much exposed as the most remote of the government shops, shanties or stables.

A DAUGHTER OF THE SIOUX

Field mounted his guard, except in cold or stormy weather, in full uniform, and the daily "march past" in review brought many of the garrison ladies, most of the children and all of the dogs to the scene. Some of the households breakfasted just before,— some just after—guard mounting, but, as a rule, no one sat at table when almost everybody else was gathered along the westward edge of the broad parade. It was there the plans for the social day were discussed and determined. Rides, drives, hunts or picnics away from the post; dances, dinners, croquet or tennis within the garrison limits. It was the hour when all the girls were out, looking fair and fresh as daisies, and while the mothers sedately gossiped along the row of broad verandas, their daughters blithely chatted in little groups, or, as might often be, paced slowly with downcast eyes and mantling cheeks at the side of some young gallant who had no thought for other duty than that of the thrilling moment. And here they were, well nigh a dozen of them, of all ages from twelve to twenty, as the major sent his mount to the stables and made quick survey of the scene, and a moment's glance was sufficient to show that among them all there was stir and excitement beyond that which would be caused by so common an incident as the sending forth of a troop on scout.

It was the fact that Field had gone and that young Ross was acting in his place that set them all to speculating on the cause. One of their number, promenading with Lieutenant Hartley, glanced up at Major Webb as they passed him by, with such a world of mingled question and reproach in her soft blue eyes that his heart for the moment smote him. He had never seen Esther

A DAUGHTER OF THE SIOUX

Dade looking so languid or so wan, yet more *of* her and *for* her had he been thinking during the week gone by than of any other girl in or out of the army. To-day, however, there was another he eagerly sought to see, and, with something akin to keen disappointment, noted that she was not among the strollers along the board walk or the chatting groups about the steps and gateways. Not once during her brief visit had she as yet missed guard mounting. Now her absence was significant. In the very eyes of the little party hastening toward him—three young girls and a brace of subalterns—he read question and cross-question, and was thankful to see Hay, the trader, trudging up the walk to join him. So seldom did the old frontiersman enter the quadrangle that people remarked upon his coming;—remarked still more when Webb hurried down to meet him.

"You're right about the horses, major," said Hay, mopping a moist and troubled face with a big bandana. "My racer and my best single footer, Dan, were out last night. Dan's saddle cloth was wet and so was Harney's. Some one outside has got false keys,—I'll put new padlocks on at once,—but for the life of me I can't think who would play me such a trick. To *steal* the horses,—run 'em off to Rawlins or up the Sweetwater or off to the Hills—I could understand that! but to borrow them for an hour or two,—why, it beats me hollow!" And Hay in deep perplexity leaned against the low fence and almost imploringly gazed into the major's face. They all leaned on Webb.

"Any idea who they were?" asked the commander.

A DAUGHTER OF THE SIOUX

"Not the skin of a shadow, 'cept that one man rode shorter stirrups'n I do. They forgot to set 'em back. They had my California saddle on Dan and that light Whitman of mine on Harney."

"Sure it was two men?" queried Webb, looking straight into the trader's eyes.

"What else could it be?" demanded Hay, in no little excitement.

"Well, I thought possibly Miss Flower might have been moved to take a moonlight ride. No reason why she shouldn't, you know, and not wishing to disturb you——"

"Then she would have used her own side-saddle. What's she doing with a man's? Besides, she'd have told me!"

"Oh! You've seen her then this morning? I thought perhaps she wasn't up," hazarded Webb.

"Up? Why, hang it, she was up at daybreak—up hours ago, my wife says. Haven't you seen her? She's over here somewhere?"

No, Webb had not seen her, and together the two started in search, first to the flagstaff, and there at the point of bluff beyond the Rays',—there she stood, gazing up the Platte toward the Indian village through a pair of signal glasses that weighed heavily in her daintily gloved hands. Captain Tracy, a bachelor assistant surgeon, stood faithfully by her side, listening to her lively chatter, with ears that absorbed and eyes that worshipped.

A DAUGHTER OF THE SIOUX

"Come away," said Webb. "I have an order on you for Field's currency in your safe. When are you going to try to get your cash to bank?" And Webb keenly eyed his man as he asked the question.

"To-morrow or next day sure,—even if I have to go part way with the stage myself. When do you want this money?" said Hay, tapping the envelope Webb had given him.

"Well, now, if agreeable to you. I prefer to keep such funds at the quartermaster's. Oh—Good morning, Mrs. Ray!" he cheerily called, lifting his cap, at sight of a young matron at an upper window. "Can you see them still?" he added, for the elder of the two boys was peering through a long telescope, perched on its brass tripod upon a little shelf projecting from the sill. Many a time had the "Rays' spyglass" been the last to discern some departing troop as it crossed the low divide ten miles away to the north. Many a time had the first announcement of "courier coming" reached headquarters through Master Sandy, the first born of their olive branches. There were unshed tears in the gentle voice that answered. There was wordless anxiety in the sweet, pallid face that smiled so bravely through its sorrow. "The troop passed out of sight quarter of an hour ago, major," said Mrs. Ray. "But Sandy could see the flankers on their left until within the last five minutes."

"*Way* out on their left, major!" interposed that young gentleman, big with importance. "If old Stabber tries any of his tricks with *that* troop he'll—he'll get his belly full!" and Master Sandy plainly intimated both in tone and manner, not to mention the

Page 62

A DAUGHTER OF THE SIOUX

vernacular of the soldier, that Stabber might take liberties with any other troop or company at the post, but would best beware of Daddy's. And yet, not three months agone he had stoutly taken up the cudgels for the Frayne garrison, as a whole, against the field, the wordy battle with the son and heir of the colonel commanding at Laramie culminating in a combat only terminated by the joint efforts of the stable sergeant and sentry, for both youngsters were game as their sires. What Sandy Ray was now praying to see was an attack by Stabber's band upon the isolated troop, but Stabber, it may be said, knew a trick worth ten of that. There was no sense in pitching into the sorrel troop on even terms when by waiting another day, perhaps, and the answer of Lame Wolf to the appeal of his speedy messenger, he might outnumber and overwhelm them with five to one.

"We should be hearing from Omaha and Laramie by ten o'clock, Mrs. Ray," said the major, reassuringly, "and I will send you word at once. And, of course, Corporal Ray," he continued, and now with martial formality addressing the lad at the telescope, "I can rely upon you to report at once in case you see anything suspicious toward the Big Horn."

"Yes, sir," answered the boy, straightening up to attention. Then, scrupulously exchanging salutes, the old soldier and the young parted company, and the major returned to receive the reports of the old and new officers of the day. These gentlemen were still with him, Captain Chew, of the Infantry, and the senior first lieutenant for duty with the ----th, when Hay came hurrying up the board walk from the direction of the store. For reasons of his

A DAUGHTER OF THE SIOUX

own, Webb had sent his orderly to the guard-house to say to the officers in question that he would await them at his quarters instead of the little building known as the adjutant's office, in which were the offices of the commander, the record room in which were placed the desks of the sergeant-major and his three clerks, and the sleeping rooms of the special duty soldiers. It had happened more than once in the past that garrison stories of matters not supposed to be known outside the office had been traced back to that desk room, and now Webb's questions of his old officer of the day, and his instructions to the new were not things he cared to have bruited about the post. He was listening intently to the captain's report of the sentries' observations during the night gone by when Hay reached the gate and stopped, not wishing to intrude at such a moment.

"Come in, Mr. Hay," said the commander, cordially. "This all will interest you," and, thus bidden, the trader joined the soldiers three on the veranda, and some of the young people of the garrison, setting up their croquet arches on the parade, looked curiously toward the group, and wondered what should keep the old officer-of-the-day so long. Sauntering down the walk, smiling radiantly upon the occupants of the various verandas that she passed, then beaming between times into the face of her smitten escort, her black eyes and white teeth flashing in the rare sunshine, Nanette Flower was gradually nearing the major's quarters. She was barely twenty yards away when, in obedience to some word of the major, Mr. Hay held forth two white packages that, even at the distance, could be recognized, so far as the outer

Page 64

A DAUGHTER OF THE SIOUX

covering was concerned, as official envelopes. She was too far away, perhaps, to hear what was said.

"It seems," began Webb, to his officers, as he mechanically opened the first packet, "that Field took fire at Wilkins's growls about the bother of keeping his funds, so the youngster stowed his money with Hay. He insisted on turning over everything before he left, so I receipted to him. Let's see," he continued, glancing at the memorandum in his hand. "Three hundred and seventy-two dollars and eighty-five cents post fund, and four hundred belonging to various enlisted men. I may as well count it in your presence."

By this time the long, lean fingers had ripped open the package marked four hundred, and were extracting the contents,—a sheet of official paper with figures and memoranda, and then a flat package, apparently, of currency. Topmost was a five dollar treasury note; bottom-most another of the same denomination. Between them, deftly cut, trimmed and sized, were blank slips of paper to the number of perhaps thirty and the value of not one cent. With paling faces the officers watched the trembling fingers slash open the second, its flap, as was that of the first envelope, securely gummed,—not sealed. A nickel or two and a few dimes slid out before the packet came. It was of like consistency with the first—and of about the same value. Webb lifted up his eyes and looked straight into the amazed,—almost livid, face of the trader.

"My God! Major Webb," cried Hay, aghast and bewildered. "Don't look at me like that! No man on earth has ever accused me of a crime. This means that not only my stable but my safe has been robbed,—and there is a traitor within my gates."

Dr. Tracy, absorbed in contemplation of Miss Flower's radiant face, and in the effort to make his own words eloquent, had no ears for those of others. He never heeded the trader's excited outburst. He only saw her suddenly flinch, suddenly pale, then sway. His ready arm was round her in a twinkling. In a twinkling she twisted free from the undesired clasp.

"Just—my foot turned!—a pebble!" she gasped.

But when, all assiduity, Tracy would have seated her on the horseblock and examined the delicate ankle, she refused straightway, and with almost savage emphasis, and with rigid lips from which all loveliness had fled, bade him lead on home, where, despite protest and appeal, personal and professional, she dismissed him curtly.

A DAUGHTER OF THE SIOUX

CHAPTER VI

FIRST SIGHT OF THE FOE

Ray's gallant half hundred, as has been said, took the route for the north at break of day. Before them spread the open prairie, apparently level and unbroken for full five miles to the front and either flank, the distant slopes and ridges bounding the level expanse growing more distinct with every moment, and presently lighting up in exulting radiance in response to the rosy blushes of the eastward sky. Scorning the dusty stage road, the troop commander pointed to a distant height just visible against the northward horizon, bade the leading guide march straight on that; then gave the order "Right by Twos," that he might the more readily note the gait and condition of every horse and the bearing and equipment of his rider. There was still time to weed out weaklings of either class should any such there be. Riding slowly along the left flank, one after another, he carefully scanned every man and mount in his little detachment, then, at quicker pace, passed around to the eastward side of the column, and as critically, carefully studied them from that point of view. A light of quiet satisfaction shone in his fine, dark eyes as he finished, for, next to his wife and children, that troop was Ray's supreme delight. The preliminary look-over by lantern light had been all sufficient. This later inspection on the move revealed not a steed amiss, not an item of equipment either misplaced or lacking. "Steady as planets," barring the irrepressible tendency of some young, high-spirited horse to dance a bit until quieted by the monotony of the succeeding miles, at quick, light-hoofed walk, the sorrels tripped easily along in precise, yet companionable couples. "One yard from head to croup," said the drill book of the day, and, but for that, the riders might have dropped their reins upon the pommel as practically unnecessary. But, for the first hour or so, at least, the tendency toward the rear of column was ever to crowd upon the file leaders, a proceeding resented, not infrequently, in less disciplined commands than Ray's, by well-delivered kicks, or at least such signs of equine disapprobation as switching tail or set-back ears. But Ray's troop horses moved like so many machines, so constant and systematic had been their drill; and Ray's men rode in the perfection of uniform, so far as armament and equipment were concerned. Each greatcoat, precisely rolled, was strapped with its encircling poncho at the pommel. Each blanket, as snugly packed, with the sidelines festooned upon the top, was strapped at the cantle. Lariat and picket pin, coiled and secured, hung from the near side of the pommel. The canteen, suspended from its snap hook, hung at the off side. Saddle-bags, with extra horse shoes, nails, socks, underwear, brushes and comb, extra packages of carbine and revolver cartridges and minor impedimenta, equally distributed as to weight, swung from the cantle and underneath the blanket roll. From the broad, black leather carbine sling, over each trooper's left shoulder, the hard-shooting brown barrelled little Springfield hung suspended, its muzzle thrust, as was the fashion of the day, into the crude socket imposed so long upon our frontier fighters by officials who had never seen the West, save, as did a certain writer of renown, from a car window, thereby limiting their horizon. Ray despised that socket as he did

A DAUGHTER OF THE SIOUX

the Shoemaker bit, but believed, with President Grant, that the best means to end obnoxious laws was their rigorous enforcement. Each man's revolver, a trusty brown Colt, hung in its holster at the right hip. Each man was girt with ammunition belt of webbing, the device of an old-time Yankee cavalryman that has been copied round the world, the dull-hued copper cartridges bristling from every loop. Each man wore, as was prescribed, the heavy, cumbrous cavalry boot of the day and generation, but had stowed in his saddle-bags light moccasins and leggings with which to replace them when, farther afield, their clear-headed commander should give the word. Each man, too, wore the gauntlets of Indian-tanned buckskin, a special pattern that Ray had been permitted to use experimentally. Each man was clad in dark blue flannel shirt and blouse, the latter soon probably to be stored with the big, weighty boots in Truscott's saddle room at Beecher, with, probably too, many of the light blue riding breeches, saddle-pieced with canvas—the uniform at the start destined, in the case of veteran troopers, at least, to be shed in favor of brown duck hunting trousers, or even, among certain extremists, fringed, beaded and embroidered buckskin, than which the present chronicler knows no more uncomfortable garb when soaked by pelting rains or immersion in some icy mountain stream. Even the brown campaign hats, uniformly "creased," as the fifty left the ford, would soon be knocked out of all semblance to the prescribed shape, and made at once comfortable and serviceable. Add to these items the well-filled haversack and battered tin quart cup, (for on a forced march of two or three days Captain Ray would have no pack mules,) and

A DAUGHTER OF THE SIOUX

the personal equipment of his men was complete. As for the mounts, each sorrel tripped easily along under the sextuple folds of the saddle blanket, and the black-skinned McClellan saddle tree, with its broad horsehair cincha and hooded wooden stirrups, minus the useless skirts and sweat leathers. Neither breast strap, crupper nor martingale hampered the free movements of the sturdy, stocky little weight carriers. The black, single-reined curb bridle, fastened as to the throat latch by a light buckle, was slipped on over the headstall of the so-called watering bridle, whose toggled and detachable snaffle bit was generally "toted" from start to finish of a field scout in the saddle bags,—a twist of the flexible lariat, Indian fashion, between the complaisant jaws of his pet, being the troop's ready substitute. Add to this that, full, free and unmutilated, in glossy waves the beautiful manes and tails tossed in the upland breeze (for the heresies of Anglomania never took root in the American cavalry) and you have Ray's famous troop as it looked, fresh started from old Fort Frayne this glorious autumn morning of 188-, and with a nod of approbation, and "It couldn't be better, sergeant," to his devoted right hand man, the veteran senior non-commissioned officer of the troop, Ray rang out the command "At ease," and placed himself beside the silent young lieutenant at the head of column.

A DAUGHTER OF THE SIOUX

A DAUGHTER OF THE SIOUX

Ray's Troop.

As has been said, Ray's senior subaltern was on detached service. His junior, Mr. Clayton, had joined but the year before, and this threw Mr. Field in command of the leading platoon and to the side of the leading guide. Now, as the senior officer took the head of column and Mr. Clayton fell back to the rear, the silence of the first mile of march was broken and, though sitting erect in saddle and forbidden to lounge or "slouch," the troop began its morning interchange of chaff and comment. Every mother's son of them rejoiced to be once more afield with a chance of stirring work ahead.

"It's time to throw out our advance, Field," said Ray, in kindly, cordial tone, as he scanned the low divide still some miles ahead and reined in beside the stern-faced young soldier. "Send Sergeant Scott forward with three men and the same number on each flank—corporals in charge."

He had more than liked Webb's adjutant. He had been his stanchest friend and supporter among the troop and company commanders, and was eager to befriend him now. He had expressed no wish to have him sent on the hurried move, but well he knew the post commander's reasons and approved his course. Still, now that Field was being removed, for the time at least, from the possibility of an entangling alliance that might prove disastrous, in every way in his power Ray meant to show the mortified, indeed sorely angered, officer that his personal regard for him had suffered no change whatever. If he could succeed in winning Field's confidence it might well be that he could bring

A DAUGHTER OF THE SIOUX

him to see that there were good and sufficient grounds for the post commander's action—that for Field's own good, in fact, it was a most desirable move. The soul of loyalty and square dealing himself, Ray had never for a moment dreamed that anything other than a foolish escapade had occurred—a ride by moonlight, perhaps, demanded of her devotee by a thoughtless, thoroughbred coquette, whose influence over the young fellow was beginning to mar his usefulness, if not indeed his future prospects. Just what to think of Nanette Flower Ray really did not know. Marion, his beloved better half, was his unquestioned authority in all such matters, and it was an uncommon tenet of that young matron never to condemn until she had cause. Instinctively she shrank from what she had seen of Miss Flower, even though her woman's eye rejoiced in the elegance of Miss Flower's abundant toilets; and, conscious of her intuitive aversion, she would utter no word that might later prove unjust. Oddly enough, that instinctive aversion was shared by her closest friend and neighbor, Mrs. Blake; but, as yet, the extent of their condemnation had found vent only in the half whimsical, half petulant expression on part of the younger lady—Blake's beautiful wife, "I wish her name weren't—so near like mine," for "Nan" had been her pet name almost from babyhood. Vaguely conscious were they both, these lords of creation, Messrs. Blake and Ray, that the ladies of their love did not approve of Miss Flower, but Ray had ridden forth without ever asking or knowing why, and so, unknowing, was ill prepared to grapple with the problem set before him. It is easier to stem a torrent with a shingle than convince a lover that his idol is a shrew.

A DAUGHTER OF THE SIOUX

Without a word of reply, Field reined out of column, glanced along the double file of his platoon, nodded a signal "Fall out" to Sergeant Scott, and the men nearest him at the front, merely said "Advance guard," and then proceeded to choose his corporals and men for flankers. No need to tell Scott what to do! He had been leading scouts in Arizona long ere Field had even dreamed of West Point. In five minutes, riding at easy lope, carbines advanced, three little parties of four troopers each were spreading far out to the front and flank, guarding the little column against the possibility of sudden assault from hidden foe. Here upon the level prairie one would think such precaution needless, but every acre of the surface was seamed and gullied by twisting little water courses, dry as a chip at the moment, and some of them so deep as to afford cover even for the biggest pony of the wild warriors of the plains. Then, to the front, the barrier ridges, streaked with deep winding ravines, were now billowing against the northward sky, and once among those tangled land waves no chances could be taken now that it was known that the Sioux had declared for war, and that Stabber's band was out to join their red brethren in the oft recurring outbreak. Until their lands were criss-crossed by the railways and their mountain haunts re-echoed to the scream of the iron horse, next to nothing would start an Indian war: it took so long to reach the scene with troops in sufficient numbers to command their respect.

And at this moment the situation was grave in the extreme. There had been bad blood and frequent collision between the cattlemen, herders, "hustlers,"—especially hustlers,—and the hunting parties of the Sioux and the Northern Cheyenne, who

A DAUGHTER OF THE SIOUX

clung to the Big Horn Range and the superb surrounding country with almost passionate love and with jealous tenacity. There had been aggression on both sides, then bloodshed, then attempts on part of frontier sheriffs to arrest accused or suspected red men, and equally determined and banded effort to prevent arrest of accused and identified whites. By due process of law, as administered in the days whereof we write, the Indian was pretty sure to get the worst of every difference, and therefore, preferred, not unnaturally, his own time-honored methods of settlement. In accordance therewith, had they scalped the sheriff's posse that had shot two of their young braves who had availed themselves of a purposely given chance to escape, and then in their undiscriminating zeal, the Sioux had opened fire from ambush on Plodder's hunting parties and the choppers at the wood camp, who defended themselves as best they could, to the end that more men, red and white, were killed. The Indians rallied in force and closed in about Fort Beecher, driving the survivors to shelter within its guarded lines, and then, when Plodder needed every man of his force to keep the foe at respectful distance, so that his bullets could not reach the quarters occupied by the women and children at the post, there reached him by night a runner from the stage station far over to the southeast, on a dry fork of the Powder, saying that the north and south bound stages had taken refuge there, with only ten men, all told, to stand off some fifty warriors, and therefore imploring assistance. Not daring to send a troop, Plodder called for volunteers to bear despatches to Major Webb, at Frayne, and Pat Kennedy, with half a dozen brave lads, had promptly stepped forward. Kennedy had managed to slip through the encircling Sioux by night, and to reach Fort Frayne after a daring and almost desperate ride. Then Ray was ordered forth, first to raise the siege at the stage station, then, either to hold that important relay ranch or go on to reinforce Plodder as his judgment and the situation might dictate.

He knew enough of the stout adobe walls of the corral on the Dry Fork, and of the grit of the few defenders, to feel reasonably sure that, with ammunition, provisions and water in plenty, they could easily hold out a week if need be against the Sioux, so long as they fought on the defensive and the Indians were not strongly reinforced. He reasoned that Stabber and his people were probably gone to strengthen the attack, and that having an hour's start at least, and riding faster, they would get there somewhat ahead of him. But one of his own old sergeants, a veteran of twenty years in the cavalry, was now stationmaster on the Dry Fork, and all the Sioux from the Platte to Paradise couldn't stampede old Jim Kelly. Many a forced march had Ray made in the past, and well he knew that the surest way to bring his horses into action, strong and sound at the finish, was to move "slow and steady" at the start, to move at the walk until the horses were calm and quiet, was his rule. Then on this bright September day would come the alternating trot and lope, with brief halts to reset saddles; then, later still, the call upon his willing men and mounts for sustained effort, and by sunset he and they could count on riding in, triumphant, to the rescue, even though Stabber himself should seek to bar the way.

A DAUGHTER OF THE SIOUX

And that Stabber meant to watch the road, if not to block it, became evident before the head of column began the gradual ascent of Moccasin Ridge, from whose sharp crest the little band could take their last look, for the time, at least, at the distant walls of Frayne. Somewhere toward seven-thirty Corporal Connors' foremost man, far out on the left flank, riding suddenly over a low divide, caught sight of a bonneted warrior bending flat over his excited pony and lashing that nimble, fleet-footed creature to mad gallop in the effort to reach the cover of the projecting point of bluff across the shallow ravine that cut in toward the foothills. Stone, the trooper, lifted his campaign hat on high once, and then lowered his arm to the horizontal, hat in hand, pointing in the direction the darting savage was seen, and thus, without a syllable having been spoken at the front, word was passed in to Ray that one Indian had been sighted far out to the northwest.

"They may try to hold us among the breaks of the Mini Pusa," said he, to his still unreconciled second in command. Field had been civil, respectful, but utterly uncommunicative in his replies to the captain's repeated cordialities. Any attempt to even remotely refer to the causes that led to his being ordered out with the detachment had been met with chilling silence. Now, however, the foe had been seen and could be counted on to resist if his rallied force much exceeded that of the troop, or to annoy it by long-range fire if too weak to risk other encounter. The command halted one moment at the crest to take one long, lingering look at the now far-distant post beyond the Platte; then, swinging again into saddle, moved briskly down into the long, wide hollow between them and the next divide, well nigh three

A DAUGHTER OF THE SIOUX

miles across, and as they reached the low ground and traversed its little draining gully, a muttered exclamation "Look there!" from the lips of the first sergeant, called their attention again to the far left front. Stone, the trooper who had reported the first Indian, had turned his horse over to the second man, as had the corporal on that flank, and together they were crouching up along the eastward face of a billowing hillock, while, straight to the front Sergeant Scott, obedient to a signal from his left hand man, was speeding diagonally along the rise to the north, for all three advance troopers had halted and two were cautiously dismounting. Ray watched one moment, with kindling eyes, then turned to his young chief of platoons:

"Take your men, Field, and be ready to support. There's something behind that second ridge!"

CHAPTER VII

BLOOD WILL TELL

As Webb had predicted, even before nine o'clock, came prompt, spirited response from Laramie, where the colonel had ordered the four troops to prepare for instant march, and had bidden the infantry to be ready for any duty the general might order. From Omaha,—department headquarters,—almost on the heels of the Laramie wire came cheery word from their gallant chief: "Coming to join you noon train to-day. Cheyenne 1:30 to-morrow. Your action in sending Ray's troop approved. Hold others in readiness to move at a moment's notice. Wire further news North Platte, Sidney or Cheyenne to meet me."

So the note of preparation was joyous throughout the barracks on the eastward side and mournful among the married quarters elsewhere. But even through the blinding tears with which so many loving women wrought, packing the field and mess kits of soldier husbands whose duties kept them with their men at barracks or stables, there were some, at least, who were quick to see that matters of unusual moment called certain of the major's stanchest henchmen to the office, and that grave and earnest consultation was being held, from which men came with sombre faces and close-sealed lips. First to note these indications was the indomitable helpmate of old Wilkins, the post quartermaster. She had no dread on his account, for rheumatism and routine duties, as the official in charge of Uncle Sam's huge stack of stores and supplies, exempted her liege from duty in the field; and, even while lending a helping hand where some young wife

A DAUGHTER OF THE SIOUX

and mother seemed dazed and broken by the sudden call to arms, she kept eyes and ears alert as ever, and was speedily confiding to first one household, then another, her conviction that there was a big sensation bundled up in the bosom of the post commander and his cronies, and she knew, she said, it was something about Field. Everybody, of course, was aware by eight o'clock that Field had gone with Ray, and while no officer presumed to ask if it was because Ray, or Field, had applied for the detail, no woman would have been restrained therefrom by any fear of Webb. Well he realized this fact and, dodging the first that sought to waylay him on the walk, he had later intrenched himself, as it were, in his office, where Dade, Blake and the old post surgeon had sat with him in solemn conclave while Bill Hay brought his clerk, bar-keeper, store-keeper, Pete, the general utility man, and even "Crapaud," the halfbreed, to swear in succession they had no idea who could have tampered with either the safe or the stables. Closely had they been cross-examined; and, going away in turn, they told of the nature of the cross-examination; yet to no one of their number had been made known what had occurred to cause such close questioning. Hay had been forbidden to speak of it, even to his household. The officers-of-the-day were sworn to secrecy. Neither Wilkins nor the acting adjutant was closeted with the council, and neither, therefore, could do more than guess at the facts. Yet that somebody knew, in part at least, the trend of suspicion, was at once apparent to Webb and his councilors when, about nine o'clock, he took Blake and Dade to see those significant "bar shoe" hoof prints. Every one of them had disappeared.

A DAUGHTER OF THE SIOUX

"By Jove!" said Webb, "I know *now* I should have set a sentry with orders to let no man walk or ride about here. See! He's used his foot to smear this—and this—and here again!"

There in a dozen places were signs old Indian trailers read as they would read an open book. Places where, pivoting on the heel, a heavy foot had crushed right and left into the yielding soil of the roadway, making concentric, circular grooves and ridges of sandy earth, where, earlier in the morning Dan's and Harney's dainty hoof prints were the only new impressions. For nearly fifty yards had this obliterating process been carried on, and in a dozen spots, until the road dipped over the rounding edge and, hard and firm now, went winding down to the flats. Here Webb, with Dade and Hay, returned, while Blake meandered on, musing over what he had been told. "It's a government heel, not a cowboy's," had Hay said, hopefully, of the print of that pivoting lump of leather.

"That gives no clue to the wearer," answered Blake. "Our men often sell their new boots, or give their old ones, to these hangers-on about the post. So far as I'm concerned, the care with which the print has been erased is proof to me that the major saw just what he said. Somebody about Hay's place was mighty anxious to cover his tracks."

But a dozen "somebodies" besides the stablemen hung there at all hours of the day, infesting the broad veranda, the barroom and stores, striving to barter the skin of coyote, skunk or beaver, or, when they had nothing to sell, pleading for an unearned drink. Half a dozen of these furtive, beetle-browed, swarthy sons of the

A DAUGHTER OF THE SIOUX

prairie lounged there now, as the elder officers and the trader returned, while Blake went on his way, exploring. With downcast eyes he followed the road to and across a sandy watercourse in the low ground, and there, in two or three places found the fresh imprint of that same bar shoe, just as described by Webb. Then with long, swift strides he came stalking up the hill again, passing the watchful eyes about the corral without a stop, and only checking speed as he neared the homestead of the Hays, where, once again, he became engrossed in studying the road and the hard pathways at the side. Something that he saw, or fancied that he saw, perhaps a dozen yards from the trader's gate, induced him to stop, scrutinize, turn, and, with searching eyes, to cross diagonally the road in the direction of the stables, then again to retrace his steps and return to the eastward side. Just as he concluded his search, and once more went briskly on his way, a blithe voice hailed him from an upper window, and the radiant face and gleaming white teeth of Nanette Flower appeared between the opening blinds. One might have said he expected both the sight and question.

"Lost anything, Captain Blake?"

"Nothing but—a little time, Miss Flower," was the prompt reply as, without a pause, the tall captain, raising his forage-cap, pushed swiftly on. "But I've found something," muttered he to himself, between his set teeth, and within five minutes more was again closeted with the post commander.

"You saw it?" asked Webb.

A DAUGHTER OF THE SIOUX

"Yes. Three or four places—down in the arroyo. More than that—Where's Hay?" he broke off suddenly, for voices were sounding in the adjoining room.

"Here, with Dade and the doctor."

"Then—" But Blake got no further. Breathless and eager, little Sandy Ray came bounding through the hallway into the presence of the officers. He could hardly gasp his news:

"Major, you told me to keep watch and let you know. There's a courier coming—hard! Mother saw him—too, through the—spyglass. She says they—see him, too at Stabber's—and she's afraid——"

"Right!" cried Webb. "Quick, Blake; rush out half a dozen men to meet him. Those devils may indeed cut him off. Thank you, my little man," he added, bending down and patting the dark curly head, as Blake went bounding away. "Thank you, Sandy. I'll come at once to the bluff. We'll save him. Never you fear."

In less than no time, one might say, all Fort Frayne seemed hurrying to the northward bluff. The sight of tall Captain Blake bounding like a greyhound toward his troop barracks, and shouting for his first sergeant,—of Major Webb almost running across the parade toward the flagstaff,—of Sandy rushing back to his post at the telescope,—of the adjutant and officer of the day tearing away toward the stables, where many of the men were now at work, were signs that told unerringly of something stirring, probably across the Platte. As luck would have it, in anticipation of orders to move, the troop horses had not been

A DAUGHTER OF THE SIOUX

sent out to graze, and were still in the sunshiny corrals, and long before the news was fully voiced through officers' row, Blake and six of his men were in saddle and darting away for the ford, carbines advanced the instant they struck the opposite bank.

From the bluff Webb had shouted his instructions. "We could see him a moment ago," for half a dozen field glasses were already brought to bear, "six miles out,—far east of the road. Feel well out to your left to head off any of Stabber's people. Three of them have been seen galloping out already."

"Aye, aye, sir," came the answering shout, as Blake whirled and tore away after his men. There had been a time in his distant past when the navy, not the army, was his ambition, and he still retained some of the ways of the sea. Just as Webb feared, some few of Stabber's young warriors had been left behind, and their eagle-eyed lookout had sighted the far-distant courier almost as soon as Sandy's famous telescope. Now they were hastening to head him off.

But he seemed to have totally vanished. Level as appeared the northward prairie from the commanding height on which stood the throng of eager watchers, it was in reality a low, rolling surface like some lazily heaving sea that had become suddenly solidified. Long, broad, shallow dips or basins lay between broad, wide, far-extending, yet slight, upheavals. Through the shallows turned and twisted dozens of dry arroyos, all gradually trending toward the Platte,—the drainage system of the frontier. Five miles out began the ascent to the taller divides and ridges that gradually, and with many an intervening dip, rose to the

A DAUGHTER OF THE SIOUX

watershed between the Platte and the score of tiny tributaries that united to form the South Cheyenne. It was over Moccasin, or Ten Mile, Ridge, as it was often called, and close to the now abandoned stage road, Ray's daring little command had disappeared from view toward eight o'clock. It was at least two, possibly three, miles east of the stage-road that the solitary courier had first been sighted, and when later seen by the major and certain others of the swift gathering spectators, he was heading for Frayne, though still far east of the highroad.

And now Mrs. Ray, on the north piazza, with Webb by her side and Nannie Blake, Mrs. Dade and Esther in close attendance, was briefly telling the major what she had seen up stream. One glance through Sandy's glass had told her the little fellow had not watched in vain.

Then, with the ready binocular, she had turned to the Indian encampment up the Platte, and almost instantly saw signs of commotion,—squaws and children running about, ponies running away and Indian boys pursuing. Then, one after another, three Indians,—warriors, presumably,—had lashed away northward and she had sent Sandy on the run to tell the major, even while keeping watch on this threatening three until they shot behind a long, low ridge that stretched southward from the foothills. Beyond doubt they were off in hopes of bagging that solitary horseman, speeding with warning of some kind for the shelter of Fort Frayne.

By this time there must have been nearly two hundred men, women and children lining the crest of the bluff, and speaking in

A DAUGHTER OF THE SIOUX

low, tense voices when they spoke at all, and straining their eyes for the next sight of the coming courier or the swift dash of the intercepting Sioux. Well out now, and riding at the gallop, Blake and his half dozen, widely separating so as to cover much of the ground, were still in view, and Dade and his officers breathed more freely. "See what a distance those beggars of Stabber's will have to ride," said the veteran captain to the little group about him. "They dare not cross that ridge short of three miles out. It's my belief they'll see Blake and never cross at all."

Then up rose a sudden shout. "There he is!" "There he comes!" "See!" "See!" and fifty hands pointed eagerly northeastward where a little black dot had suddenly popped into view out of some friendly, winding watercourse, four miles still away, at least count, and far to the right and front of Blake's easternmost trooper. Every glass was instantly brought to bear upon the swiftly coming rider, Sandy's shrill young voice ringing out from the upper window. "It isn't one of papa's men. His horse is a gray!" Who then could it be? and what could it mean, this coming of a strange courier from a direction so far to the east of the travelled road? Another moment and up rose another shout. "Look!"—"There they are!" "Sioux for certain!" And from behind a little knob or knoll on the meridian ridge three other black dots had swept into view and were shooting eastward down the gradual slope. Another moment and they were swallowed up behind still another low divide, but in that moment they had seen and been seen by the westernmost of Blake's men, and now, one after another as the signals swept from the left, the seven swerved. Their line of direction had been west of north. Now,

A DAUGHTER OF THE SIOUX

riding like mad, they veered to the northeast, and a grand race was on between the hidden three and the would-be rescuers;—all heading for that part of the low-rolling prairie where the lone courier might next be expected to come into view;—friends and foes alike, unconscious of the fact that, following one of those crooked arroyos with its stiff and precipitous banks, he had been turned from his true course full three quarters of a mile, and now, with a longer run, but a clear field ahead, was steering straight for Frayne.

Thus the interest of the on-lookers at the bluff became divided. Women with straining eyes gazed at the lonely courier, and then fearfully scanned the ridge line between him and the northward sky; praying with white lips for his safety; dreading with sinking hearts that at any moment those savage riders should come darting over the divide and swooping down upon their helpless prey. Men, with eyes that snapped and fists that clinched, or fingers that seemed twitching with mad desire to clasp pistol butt or sabre hilt, or loud barking carbine, ran in sheer nervous frenzy up and down the bluffs, staring only at Blake's far-distant riders, swinging their hats and waving them on, praying only for another sight of the Sioux in front of the envied seven, and craving with all their soldier hearts to share in the fight almost sure to follow. On the Rays' piazza, with pallid face and quivering lips, Esther Dade clung to her mother's side. Mrs. Ray had encircled with her arm the slender waist of Nannie Blake, whose eyes never for an instant quit their gaze after the swift-speeding dots across the distant prairie. All her world was there in one tall, vehement horseman. Other troopers, mounting at the

A DAUGHTER OF THE SIOUX

stables, had spurred away under Captain Gregg, and were splashing through the ford. Other denizens of Fort Frayne, hearing of the excitement, came hurrying to the bluff, hangers-on from the trader's store and corral, the shopman himself, even the bar-keeper in his white jacket and apron; two or three panting, low-muttering halfbreeds, their eyes aflame, their teeth gleaming in their excitement; then Hay himself, and with him,—her dark face almost livid, her hair disordered and lips rigid and almost purple, with deep lines at the corners of her mouth,—Nanette Flower. Who that saw could ever forget her as she forced her way through the crowd and stood at the very brink, saying never a word, but swiftly focussing her ready glasses? Hardly had she reached the spot when wild, sudden, exultant, a cheer burst fiercely from the lips of the throng. "Look!" "Look!" "By God, they've got 'em!" yelled man after man, in mad excitement. Three black dots had suddenly swept into view, well to the right of Blake's men, and came whirling down grade straight for the lone courier on the gray. Theirs had been the short side, ours the long diagonal of the race. Theirs was the race, perhaps, but not the prize, for he had turned up far from the expected point. Still they had him, if only,—if only those infernal troopers failed to see them. There was their hope! Plainly in view of the high bluff at the fort, they were yet hidden by a wave of the prairie from sight of the interceptors, still heading for the ridge the warriors had just left behind. Only for a second or two, however. A yell of fierce rejoicing went up from the crowd on the bluff as the easternmost of Blake's black specks was seen suddenly to check, then to launch out again, no longer to the north, but straight to

A DAUGHTER OF THE SIOUX

his right, followed almost immediately by every one of the seven. Then, too, swerved the would-be slayers, in long, graceful circles, away from the wrath to come. And, while the unconscious courier still rode, steadily loping toward the desired refuge, away for the breaks and ravines of the Sleeping Bear lashed the thwarted Sioux,—away in hopeless stern chase spurred the pursuers, and while women sobbed and laughed and screamed, and men danced and shouted and swore with delight, one dark face, livid, fearsome, turned back from the bluff, and Dr. Tracy, hastening to the side of his enchantress, caught, in amaze, these words, almost hissed between set and grinding teeth.

"Seven to three—Shame!"

CHAPTER VIII

MORE STRANGE DISCOVERIES

But Frayne was far from done with excitement for the day. For a while all eyes seemed centred on the chase, now scattered miles toward the east, and, save for two of the number left behind, blown, spent and hopelessly out of the race, soon lost to view among the distant swales and ravines. Then everyone turned to welcome the coming harbinger, to congratulate him on his escape, to demand the reason for his daring essay. Gregg and his men were first to reach him, and while one of them was seen through the levelled glasses to dismount and give the courier his fresh horse, thereby showing that the gray was well nigh exhausted, the whole party turned slowly toward the post. Then one of their number suddenly darted forth from the group and came spurring at top speed straight for the ford.

"That means news of importance," said Webb, at the instant. "And Gregg and all of his squad are coming in,—not following Blake. That means he and they are more needed elsewhere. Come on, Mr. Ross. We'll go down and meet that fellow. Orderly, have my horse sent to the ford." So, followed by three or four of the younger officers,—the married men being restrained, as a rule, by protesting voices, close at hand,—the commanding officer went slipping and sliding down a narrow, winding pathway, a mere goat track, many of the soldiers following at respectful distance, while all the rest of the gathered throng remained at the crest, eagerly, almost breathlessly awaiting the result. They saw the trooper come speeding in across the flats

A DAUGHTER OF THE SIOUX

from the northeast; saw as he reached the "bench" that he was spurring hard; heard, even at the distance, the swift batter of hoofs upon the resounding sod; could almost hear the fierce panting of the racing steed; saw horse and rider come plunging down the bank and into the stream, and shoving breast deep through the foaming waters; then issue, dripping, on the hither shore, where, turning loose his horse, the soldier leaped from saddle and saluted his commander. But only those about the major heard the stirring message:

"Captain Gregg's compliments, sir. It's Rudge from the Dry Fork. Sergeant Kelly feared that Kennedy hadn't got through, for most of Lame Wolf's people pulled away from the Fork yesterday morning, coming this way, and the sergeant thought it was to unite with Stabber to surround any small command that might be sent ahead from here. Rudge was ordered to make a wide sweep to the east, so as to get around them, and that's what took him so long. He left not two hours after Kennedy."

A DAUGHTER OF THE SIOUX

"The soldier leaped from his saddle."

A DAUGHTER OF THE SIOUX

In spite of his years of frontier service and training in self control, Webb felt, and others saw, that his face was paling. Ray, with only fifty men at his back, was now out of sight—out of reach—of the post, and probably face to face with, if not already surrounded by, the combined forces of the Sioux. Not a second did he hesitate. Among the swarm that had followed him was a young trumpeter of "K" Troop, reckless of the fact that he should be at barracks, packing his kit. As luck would have it, there at his back hung the brazen clarion, held by its yellow braid and cord. "Boots and Saddles, Kerry, Quick!" ordered the major, and as the ringing notes re-echoed from bluff and building wall and came laughing back from the distant crags at the south, the little throng at the bank and the crowd at the point of the bluff had scattered like startled coveys,—the men full run for the barracks and stables, never stopping to "reason why."

Nearly half an hour later, gray-haired Captain Dade stood at the point of bluff near the flagstaff, Esther, pale and tearful, by his side, waving adieu and Godspeed to Webb, who had halted in saddle on reaching the opposite bank and was watching his little column through the ford,—three stanch troops, each about sixty strong, reinforced by half a dozen of Ray's men left behind in the forward rush at dawn, but scorning disqualification of any kind now that danger menaced their beloved captain and their comrades of the sorrel troop. In all the regiment no man was loved by the rank and file as was Billy Ray. Brilliant soldiers, gifted officers, sterling men were many of his comrades, but ever since he first joined the ——th on the heels of the civil war, more than any one of its commissioned list, Ray had been

A DAUGHTER OF THE SIOUX

identified with every stirring scout and campaign, fight or incident in the regimental history. Truscott, Blake, Hunter and Gregg among the junior captains had all had their tours of detached duty—instructing at West Point, recruiting in the big Eastern cities, serving as aide-de-camp to some general officer, but of Ray it could be said he had hardly been east of the Missouri from the day he joined until his wedding day, and only rarely and briefly since that time. More than any officer had he been prominent in scout after scout—Arizona, Mexico, Texas, the Indian Territory, Kansas, Colorado, Nebraska, Wyoming, the Dakotas, Montana, even parts of Idaho and Utah he knew as he used to know the roads and runways of the blue grass region of his native state. From the British line to the Gulfs of Mexico and California he had studied the West. The regiment was his home, his intense pride, and its men had been his comrades and brothers. The veterans trusted and swore by, the younger troopers looked up to and well nigh worshipped him, and now, as the story that the Sioux had probably surrounded the sorrel troop went like wild fire through the garrison, even the sick in hospital begged to be allowed to go, and one poor lad, frantic through fever and enforced confinement, broke from the hold of the half-hearted attendant; tore over to "K" Troop barracks, demanding his "kit" of Sergeant Schreiber, and, finding the quarters deserted, the men all gone to stables, dared to burst into that magnate's own room in search of his arms and clothing, and thereby roused a heavily sleeping soldier, who damned him savagely until, through wild raving, he gathered that some grave danger menaced Captain Ray. Even his befuddled senses could

A DAUGHTER OF THE SIOUX

fathom that! And while guards and nurses bore the patient, shrieking and struggling, back to hospital, Kennedy soused his hot head in the cooling waters of their frontier lavatory and was off like a shot to the stables.

It was long before he found his horse, for the guard had taken Kilmaine to "F" Troop's stables, and Kennedy had been housed by "K." It was longer still before he could persuade the guard that he "had a right," as he put it, to ride after the major. Not until Captain Dade had been consulted would they let him go. Not, indeed, until in person Kennedy had pleaded his cause with that cool-headed commander. Dade noted the flushed and swollen face, but reasoned that nothing would more speedily shake the whiskey from his system than a long gallop in that glorious air and sunshine. "Major Webb is following the trail of Captain Ray," said he. "You follow the major's. You can't miss him, and there are no more Indians now to interpose. You should catch him by noon—then give him this."

"This" was a copy of a late despatch just in from Laramie, saying that the revolt had reached the Sioux at the agencies and reservations on the White Earth, and would demand the attention of every man at the post. No reinforcement, therefore, could be looked for from that quarter until the general came. It was no surprise to Dade. It could be none to Webb, for old Red Cloud had ever been an enemy, even when bribed and petted and fed and coddled in his village on the Wakpa Schicha. His nephew led the bolt afield. No wonder the old war chief backed

A DAUGHTER OF THE SIOUX

him with abundant food, ammunition and eager warriors sent "from home."

But it was after eleven when Kennedy drove his still wearied horse through the Platte and, far to the north, saw the dun dust cloud that told where Webb's little column was trotting hard to the support of the sorrels. His head was aching and he missed the morning draught of soldier coffee. He had eaten nothing since his cold lunch at the major's, and would have been wise had he gone to Mistress McGann and begged a cup of the fragrant Java with which she had stimulated her docile master ere he rode forth, but the one idea uppermost in Kennedy's muddled brain was that the sorrels were trapped by the Sioux and every trooper was needed to save them. At three in the morning he felt equal to fighting the whole Sioux nation, with all its dozen tribes and dialects. At 3:30 he had been whipped to a stand by just one of their number, and, "Mother av Moses," one that spoke English as well, or as ill, as any man in the ——th.

Sore in soul and body was Kennedy, and sore and stiff was his gallant bay, Kilmaine, when these comrades of over three years' service shook the spray of the Platte from their legs and started doggedly northward on the trail. Northward they went for full three miles, Kilmaine sulky and protesting. The dust cloud was only partially visible now, hidden by the ridge a few miles ahead, when, over that very ridge, probably four miles away to the right front, Kennedy saw coming at speed a single rider, and reined to the northeast to meet him. Blake and his men had gone far in that direction. Two of their number, with horses too slow for a

A DAUGHTER OF THE SIOUX

chase after nimble ponies, had, as we have seen, drifted back, and joined, unprepared though they were for the field, the rear of Webb's column. But now came another, not aiming for Webb, but heading for Frayne. It meant news from the chase that might be important. It would take him but little from the direct line to the north, why not meet him and hear? Kennedy reined to the right, riding slowly now and seeking the higher level from which he could command the better view.

At last they neared each other, the little Irish veteran, sore-headed and in evil mood, and a big, wild-eyed, scare-faced trooper new to the frontier, spurring homeward with panic in every feature, but rejoicing at sight of a comrade soldier.

"Git back; git back!" he began to shout, as soon as he got within hailing distance. "There's a million Indians just over the ridge. They've got the captain——"

"What captain?" yelled Kennedy, all ablaze at the instant. "Spake up, ye shiverin' loon!"

"Blake! He got way ahead of us——"

"Then it's to him you should be runnin', not home, ye cur! Turn about now! Turn about or I'll——" And in a fury Pat had seized the other's rein, and, spurring savagely at Kilmaine,—both horses instantly waking, as though responsive to the wrath and fervor of their little master,—he fairly whirled the big trooper around and, despite fearsome protests, bore him onward toward the ridge, swift questioning as they rode. How came they to send a raw rookie on such a quest? Why, the rookie gasped in explanation

A DAUGHTER OF THE SIOUX

that he was on stable guard, and the captain took the first six men in sight. How happened it that the captain got so far ahead of him? There was no keepin' up with the captain. He was on his big, raw-boned race horse, chasin' three Indians that was firin' and had hit Meisner, but there was still three of the troop to follow him, and the captain ordered "come ahead," until all of a sudden, as they filed round a little knoll, the three Indians they'd been chasin' turned about and let 'em have it, and down went another horse, and Corporal Feeney was killed sure, and he, the poor young rookie, saw Indians in every direction, "comin' straight at 'em," and what else could he do but gallop for home—and help? All this, told with much gasping on his part, and heard with much blasphemy by Kennedy, brought the strangely assorted pair at swift gallop over the springy turf back along the line of that panicky, yet most natural retreat. Twice would the big fellow have broken away and again spurred for home, but the little game cock held him savagely to his work and so, together, at last they neared the curtaining ridge. "Now, damn you!" howled Kennedy, "whip out your carbine and play you're a man till we see what's in front! an' if ye play false, the first shot from this barker," with a slap at the butt of his Springfield, "goes through your heart."

And this was what they saw as, together, they rounded the hillock and came in view of the low ground beyond.

Half way down the long, gradual slope, in a shallow little dip, possibly an old buffalo wallow, two or three horses were sprawled, and a tiny tongue of flame and blue smoke spitting from over the broad, brown backs told that someone, at least, was on the alert and defensive. Out on the prairie, three hundred yards beyond, a spotted Indian pony, heels up, was rolling on the turf, evidently sorely wounded. Behind this rolling parapet crouched a feathered warrior, and farther still away, sweeping and circling on their mettlesome steeds, three more savage braves were darting at speed. Already they had sighted the coming reinforcements, and while two seemed frantically signalling toward the northwest, the third whirled his horse and sped madly away in that direction.

"Millions, be damned!" yelled Kennedy. "There's only three. Come on, ye scut!" And down they went, full tilt at the Sioux, yet heading to cover and reach the beleaguered party in the hollow. Someone of the besieged waved a hat on high. Two more carbines barked their defiance at the feathered foe, and then came a pretty exhibit of savage daring and devotion. Disdainful of the coming troopers and of the swift fire now blazing at them from the pit, the two mounted warriors lashed their ponies to mad gallop and bore down straight for their imperilled brother, crouching behind the stricken "pinto." Never swerving, never halting, hardly checking speed, but bending low over and behind their chargers' necks, the two young braves swept onward and with wild whoop of triumph, challenge and hatred, gathered up and slung behind the rider of the heavier pony the agile and bedizened form on the turf; then circled away, defiant, taunting, gleeful, yes and even more:—With raging eyes, Kennedy sprang from saddle and, kneeling, drove shot after shot at the scurrying pair. Two of the three troopers at the hollow followed suit. Even

A DAUGHTER OF THE SIOUX

the big, blubbering lad so lately crazed with fear unslung his weapon and fired thrice into empty space, and a shout of wrath and renewed challenge to "come back and fight it out" rang out after the Sioux, for to the amaze of the lately besieged, to the impotent fury of the Irishman, in unmistakable, yet mostly unquotable, English, the crippled warrior was yelling mingled threat and imprecation.

"Who was it, Kennedy?—and where did you ever see him before?" a moment later, demanded Captain Blake, almost before he could grasp the Irishman's hands and shower his thanks, and even while stanching the flow of blood from a furrow along his sun-burnt cheek. "What's that he said about eating your heart?"

And Kennedy, his head cleared now through the rapture of battle, minded him of his promise to Field, and lied like a hero. "Sure, how should I know him, sorr? They're all of the same spit."

"But, he called you by name. I heard him plainly. So did Meisner, here," protested Blake. "Hello, what have you there, corporal?" he added, as young Feeney, the "surely killed," came running back, bearing in his hand a gaily ornamented pouch of buckskin, with long fringes and heavy crusting of brilliant beads.

"Picked it up by that pony yonder, sir," answered the corporal, with a salute. "Beg pardon, sir, but will the captain take my horse? His is hit too bad to carry him."

Two, indeed, of Blake's horses were crippled, and it was high time to be going. Mechanically he took the pouch and tied it to

A DAUGHTER OF THE SIOUX

his waist belt. "Thank God no *man* is hurt!" he said. "But—now back to Frayne! Watch those ridges and be ready if a feather shows, and spread out a little—Don't ride in a bunch."

But there was bigger game miles to the west, demanding all the attention of the gathered Sioux. There were none to spare to send so far, and though three warriors,—one of them raging and clamoring for further attempt despite his wounds,—hovered about the retiring party, Blake and his fellows within another hour were in sight of the sheltering walls of Frayne; and, after a last, long-range swapping of shots, with Blake and Meisner footing it most of the way, led their crippled mounts in safety toward that Rubicon of the West—the swift flowing Platte. They were still three miles out when Blake found leisure to examine the contents of that beaded pouch, and the first thing drawn from its depths was about the last a Christian would think to find in the wallet of a Sioux—a dainty little billet, scented with wood violet,—an envelope of delicate texture, containing a missive on paper to match, and the envelope was addressed in a strange, angular, characteristic hand that Blake recognized at once, to a man of whom, by that name at least, he had never heard before:

"Mr. Ralph Moreau,

En Ville."

A DAUGHTER OF THE SIOUX

CHAPTER IX

BAD NEWS FROM THE FRONT

It might well be imagined that a man returning from such a morning's work as had been Blake's could be excused from duty the rest of the day. He and his little party had had a spirited running fight of several hours with an evasive and most exasperating trio of warriors, better mounted for swift work than were the troopers. He had managed eventually to bring down one of the Indians who lingered a little too long within short range of the carbines, but it was the pony, not the rider, that they killed. Meanwhile other Indians had appeared on distant divides, and one feathered brave had galloped down to meet his comrades, and fire a few shots at the pursuing pale faces. But at no time, until near their supports and far from the fort, had the Sioux halted for a hand to hand fight, and Blake's long experience on the frontier had stood him in good stead. He saw they were playing for one of two results;—either to lure him and his fellows in the heat of pursuit far round to the northwest, where were the united hundreds of Lame Wolf and Stabber stalking that bigger game, or else to tempt Blake himself so far ahead of his fellows as to enable them to suddenly whirl about, cut him off, and, three on one, finish him then and there; then speed away in frenzied delight, possessors of a long-coveted scalp.

They well knew Blake,—almost as well as they did Ray. Many a year he had fought them through the summer and fed them through the winter. They, their squaws and pappooses, had fattened on his bounty when the snows were deep and deer were

Page102

A DAUGHTER OF THE SIOUX

gone, and their abundant rations had been feasted or gambled away. Many of their number liked him well, but now they were at the war game again, and, business is business with the aborigines. Blake was a "big chief," and he who could wear at his belt the scalp of so prominent a pale face leader would be envied among his people. "Long Legs," as they called him, however, was no fool. Brave and zealous as he was, Blake was not rash. He well knew that unless he and his few men kept together they would simply play into the hands of the Indians. It would have been easy for him, with his big racer, to outstrip his little party and close with the Sioux. Only one of the troopers had a horse that could keep pace with Pyramus, but nothing he could gain by such a proceeding would warrant the desperate risk. Matchless as we have reason to believe our men, we cannot so believe our mounts. Unmatched would better describe them. Meisner's horse might have run with the captain's, until crippled by the bullets of the Sioux, but Bent's and Flannigan's were heavy and slow, and so it resulted that the pursuit, though determined, was not so dangerous to the enemy but that they were able to keenly enjoy it, until the swift coming of Kennedy and his captive comrade turned the odds against them, for then two of Blake's horses had given out through wounds and weakness, and they had the pursuers indeed "in a hole."

That relief came none too soon. Blake and his fellows had been brought to a stand; but now the Sioux sped away out of range; the crippled party limped slowly back to the shelter of Frayne, reaching the post long hours after their spirited start, only to find the women and children, at least, in an agony of dread and

A DAUGHTER OF THE SIOUX

excitement, and even Dade and his devoted men looking grave and disturbed. Unless all indications failed, Ray and his people must have been having the fight of their lives. Two couriers had galloped back from Moccasin Ridge to say that Major Webb's scouts could faintly hear the sound of rapid firing far ahead, and that, through the glass, at least a dozen dead horses or ponies could be seen scattered over the long slope to the Elk Tooth range, miles further on. Webb had pushed forward to Ray's support, and Blake, calling for fresh horses for himself and two of his men, bade the latter get food and field kits and be ready to follow him. Then he hastened to join his devoted young wife, waiting with Mrs. Ray upon the piazza. Dade, who had met him at the ford, had still much to tell and even more to hear; but at sight of those two pale, anxious faces, lifted his cap and called out cheerily, "I hand him over to you, Mrs. Blake, and will see him later," then turned and went to his own doorway, and took Esther's slender form in his strong arms and kissed the white brow and strove to think of something reassuring to say, and never thought to ask Blake what he had in that fine Indian tobacco pouch swinging there at his belt, for which neglect the tall captain was more than grateful. It was a woman's letter, as we know, and that, he argued, should be dealt with only in a woman's way.

Sorely puzzled as Blake had been by the discovery, he had been able on the long homeward march,—walking until in sight of Frayne and safety, then galloping ahead on the corporal's horse,—to think it out, as he said, in several ways. Miss Flower had frequently ridden up the valley and visited the Indian village across the Platte. Miss Flower might easily have dropped that note, and some squaw, picking it up, had surrendered it to the first red man who demanded it, such being the domestic discipline of the savage. The Indian kept it, as he would any other treasure trove for which he had no use, in hopes of reward for its return, said Blake. It was queer, of course, that the Indian in whose pouch it was found should have been so fluent a speaker of English, yet many a Sioux knew enough of our tongue to swear volubly and talk ten words of vengeance to come. There were several ways, as Blake reasoned, by which that letter might have got into the hands of the enemy. But at any rate, with everything said, it was a woman's letter. He had no right to read it. He would first confide in his wife, and, if she said so, in Mrs. Ray. Then what they decided should decide him.

But now came a new problem. Despite the long morning of peril and chase and excitement, there was still much more ahead. His men were in saddle; his troop was afield; the foe was in force on the road to the north; the battle, mayhap, was on at the very moment, and Frayne and home was no place for him when duty called at the distant front. Only, there was Nan, silent, tremulous, to be sure, and with such a world of piteous dread and pleading in her beautiful eyes. It was hard to have to tell her he must go again and at once, hard to have to bid her help him in his hurried preparations, when she longed to throw herself in his arms and be comforted. He tried to smile as he entered the gate, and thereby cracked the brittle, sun-dried court plaster with which a sergeant had patched his cheek at the stables. The would-be glad-some grin started the blood again, and it trickled

A DAUGHTER OF THE SIOUX

down and splashed on his breast where poor Nan longed to pillow her bonny head, and the sight of it, despite her years of frontier training, made her sick and faint. He caught her in his left arm, laughing gayly, and drew her to the other side. "Got the mate to that scoop of Billy's," he cried, holding forth his other hand to Mrs. Ray. "'Tisn't so deep, perhaps, but 'twill serve, 'twill do, and I'll crow over him to-night. Come in with us, Mrs. Ray. I—I've something to show you."

"One minute," said that wise young matron. "Let me tell the children where to find me. Sandy and Billy are on post at the telescope. They wouldn't leave it even for luncheon." With that she vanished, and husband and wife were alone.

"You must go, Gerald," she sobbed—"I know it, but—isn't there *some* way?—Won't Captain Dade send more men with you?"

"If he did, Nan, they'd only hamper me with horses that drag behind. Be brave, little woman. Webb has swept the way clear by this time! Come, I need your help."

And the door closed on the soldier and his young wife. They never saw that Nanette Flower, in saddle, was riding swiftly up the row, and, for the first time since her coming to Frayne, without an escort. Dade reappeared upon his front gallery in time to greet her, but Esther, after one quick glance, had darted again within. Dade saw unerringly that Miss Flower was in no placid frame of mind. Her cheeks were pale; her mouth had that livid

A DAUGHTER OF THE SIOUX

look that robbed her face of all beauty; but her eyes were full and flashing with excitement.

"What news, captain?" she hailed, and the joyous, silvery ring had gone from her voice. "They tell me Captain Blake is back—two horses crippled, two men hit, including himself."

"His own share is a scratch he wouldn't think of mentioning outside the family, Miss Flower," answered Dade, with grim civility. He had his reasons for disapproving of the young woman; yet they were not such as warranted him in showing her the least discourtesy. He walked to his gate and met her at the curb beyond and stood stroking the arching neck of her spirited horse—"Harney" again.

"Did they—were there any Indians—killed?" she asked, with anxiety scarcely veiled.

"Oh, they downed one of them," answered the captain, eying her closely the while and speaking with much precision, "a fellow who cursed them freely in fluent English." Yes, she was surely turning paler.—"A bold, bad customer, from all accounts. Blake thought he must be of Lame Wolf's fellows, because he—seemed to know Kennedy so well and to hate him. Kennedy has only just come down from Fort Beecher, where Wolf's people have been at mischief."

"But what became of him? What did they do with him?" interrupted the girl, her lips quivering in spite of herself.

A DAUGHTER OF THE SIOUX

"Oh,—left him, I suppose," answered the veteran, with deliberate design. "What else could they do? There was no time for ceremony. His fellow savages, you know, can attend to that."

For a moment she sat there rigid, her black eyes staring straight into the imperturbable face of the old soldier. No one had ever accused Dade of cruelty or unkindness to man or woman, especially to woman; yet here he stood before this suffering girl and, with obvious intent, pictured to her mind's eye a warrior stricken and left unburied or uncared for on the field. Whatever his reasons, he stabbed and meant to stab, and for just one moment she seemed almost to droop and reel in saddle; then, with splendid rally, straightened up again, her eyes flashing, her lip curling in scorn, and with one brief, emphatic phrase ended the interview and, whirling Harney about, smote him sharply with her whip, and darted away:—

"True!" said she. "Civilized warfare!"

"If that girl isn't more than half savage," said Dade, to himself, as Harney tore away out of the garrison on the road to the ford, "I am more than half Sioux. Oh, for news of Ray!"

Ray indeed! It was now nearly four o'clock. Telegrams had been coming and going over the Laramie wire. "The Chief," as they called their general, with only one of his staff in attendance, had reached Cheyenne on time, and, quitting the train, declining dinner at the hotel and having but a word or two with the "Platform Club,"—the little bevy of officers from Fort Russell whose custom it was to see the westbound train through almost

A DAUGHTER OF THE SIOUX

every day—had started straightway for Laramie behind the swiftest team owned by the quartermaster's department, while another, in relay, awaited him at the Chugwater nearly fifty miles out. Driving steadily through the starlit night, he should reach the old frontier fort by dawn at the latest, and what news would Dade have to send him there? Not a word had he uttered to either the officers who respectfully greeted, or reporters who eagerly importuned, him as to the situation at Frayne; but men who had served with him in Arizona and on the Yellowstone many a year before, knew well that grave tidings had reached him. Dade had, in fact, supplemented Webb's parting despatch with another saying that Blake's little party, returning, had just been sighted through the telescope nine miles out, with two men afoot. But not until the general reached Lodge Pole Creek did the message meet him, saying that Webb's advance guard could hear the distant attack on Ray. Not until he reached the Chugwater in the early night could he hope to hear the result.

It was nightfall when the awful suspense of the garrison at Frayne was even measurably lifted. Blake, with three troopers at his back, had then been gone an hour, and was lost in the gloaming before Dr. Tracy's orderly, with a face that plainly told the nervous tension of his two hours' ride, left his reeking, heaving horse at the stables and climbed the steep path to the flagstaff, the shortest way to the quarters of the commanding officer. Despite the gathering darkness, he had been seen by a dozen eager watchers and was deluged with questions by trembling, tearful women and by grave, anxious men.

A DAUGHTER OF THE SIOUX

"There's been a fight; that's all I know," he said. "I was with the pack mules and the ambulances and didn't get to see it. All I saw was dead ponies way out beyond Ten Mile Ridge. Where's the major?—I mean the captain?" No! the orderly didn't know who was killed or wounded, or that anybody was killed and wounded. All he knew was that Dr. Tracy came galloping back and ordered the ambulances to scoot for the front and him to spur every bit of the way back to Frayne with the note for Captain Dade.

All this was told as he eagerly pushed his way along the board walk; soldiers' wives hanging on his words and almost on him; officers' wives and daughters calling from the galleries or running to the gates, and Dade heard the hubbub almost as quickly as did Esther, who hurried to the door. By the light of the hall lamp the commander read the pencilled superscription of the gummed envelope and the word "Immediate" at the corner. The same light fell on a dozen anxious, pleading faces beyond the steps. His hand shook in spite of himself, and he knew he could not open and read it in their presence. "One moment," he said, his heart going out to them in sympathy as well as dread. "You shall hear in one moment," and turned aside into the little army parlor.

But he could not turn from his wife and child. They followed and stood studying his pale face as he read the fateful words that told so little, yet so much:—

Reached Ray just in time. Sharp affair. Dr. Waller will have to come at once, as Tracy goes on with us to rescue stage people at Dry Fork. Better send infantry escort and all hospital attendants that can be possibly spared; also chaplain. Sergeants Burroughs

A DAUGHTER OF THE SIOUX

and Wing, Corporal Foot and Troopers Denny, Flood, Kerrigan and Preusser killed. Many wounded—Lieutenant Field seriously.

Webb.

A DAUGHTER OF THE SIOUX

CHAPTER X

"I'LL NEVER GO BACK"

A sharp affair indeed was that of this September day!—a fight long talked of on the frontier if soon forgotten in "the States." Obedient to his orders to push to the relief of the imperilled party on the Dry Fork, Ray had made good time to Moccasin Ridge, even though saving horses and men for the test of the later hours. Well he knew his march would be watched by some of Stabber's band, but little did he dream at starting that Indian strategy would take the unusual form of dropping what promised to be a sure thing, leaving the people at the stage station to the guardianship of less than a dozen braves, and launching out with a big band to aid a little one in attack on one lone detachment that might not come at all. But Lame Wolf reasoned that the people penned at the stage station were in no condition to attempt escape. They were safe whenever he chose to return to them, and Lame Wolf knew this of Stabber—that he had long been a hanger-on about the military reservations, that he had made a study of the methods of the white chiefs, that he was able to almost accurately predict what their course would be in such event as this, and that Stabber had recently received accessions whose boast it was that they had information at first hand of the white chief's plans and intentions. Stabber had sent swift runners to Lame Wolf urging him to bring his warriors to aid him in surrounding the first troops sent forth from Frayne. Stabber had noted, year after year, that it was the almost invariable policy of our leaders to order a small force at the start, and then, when that was crushed, to follow it with the big one that should have been sent in the first place. Kennedy's successful coming was known to Stabber quite as soon as it was to Webb. It may well be that Stabber let him through, feeling confident what the result would be, and then, despite a certain jealousy, not confined entirely to savage rival leaders, Lame Wolf had confidence in Stabber's judgment. Ray had expected long range flank fire, and possibly occasional resistance in front; but, assured of Stabber's paucity in numbers and believing Lame Wolf too busy to send Stabber substantial aid, he thought a sharp lesson or two would clear his front of such Indians as sought to check him, and so rode serenely forward, rejoicing in his mission and in his game and devoted little command.

"Something beyond that second ridge," he had said to Field, in sending him forward with the bulk of the platoon, and Field, who had been silent and brooding, woke at the summons and, all animation at the scent of danger, spurred swiftly ahead to join the advance and see for himself what manner of hindrance awaited them, leaving the baker's dozen of his platoon to trot steadily on under lead of its sergeant, while Ray, with his trumpeter, followed mid way between his advance and Clayton's platoon, intact, moving quietly at the walk and held in reserve.

Ordinarily Ray would himself have ridden to the far front and personally investigated the conditions, but he was anxious that Field should understand he held the full confidence of his temporary commander. He wished Field to realize that now he had opportunity for honorable distinction, and a chance to show

A DAUGHTER OF THE SIOUX

what was in him and, having sent him forward, Ray meant to rely on his reports and be ready to back, if possible, his dispositions. Nothing so quickly demolishes prejudice in garrison as prowess in the field. Not infrequently has an officer gone forth under a cloud and returned under a crown. It is so much easier to be a hero in a single fight than a model soldier through an entire season—at least it was so in the old days.

But the moment Mr. Field dismounted and, leaving his horse with the others along the slope, had gone crouching to the crest, he levelled his glasses for one look, then turned excitedly and began rapid signals to his followers. Presently a young trooper came charging down, making straight for Ray. "The lieutenant's compliments," said he, "but there's a dozen Sioux in sight, and he wishes to know shall he charge."

A dozen Sioux in sight! That was unusual. Ordinarily the Indian keeps in hiding, lurking behind sheltering crests and ridges in the open country, or the trees and underbrush where such cover is possible. A dozen in sight?

"How far ahead, Murray?" asked the captain, as he shook free his rein and started forward at the gallop. "Did you see them yourself?"

"Yes, sir. Most of 'em were bunched by the roadside, jabbing with their lances at something or other. Two or three were closer in. They must ha' been watching us, for they only quit the ridge just before we came up. Then they skedaddled." The vernacular of the civil war days, long since forgotten except about the few

Veteran Soldiers' Homes in the East, was still in use at times in regiments like the ——th, which had served the four years through with the Army of the Potomac. Old sergeants give the tone to younger soldiers in all the customs of the service. The captain and the two men now with him had caught up with Field's swift trotting support by this time, and the eyes of the men kindled instantly at sight of their leader speeding easily by, cool, confident and as thoroughly at home as though it were the most ordinary skirmish drill. Those who have never tried it, do not quite realize what it means to ride in closed ranks and compact column, silent and unswerving, straight forward over open fields toward some equally silent crest, that gives no sign of hostile occupancy, and yet may suddenly blaze with vengeful fires and spit its hissing lead into the faces of the advancing force. Even here where the ridge was already gained by two or three of the advance, proving, therefore, that the enemy could not be in possession, men saw by the excitement manifest in the signals of the lieutenant, and indeed of Sergeant Scott, who had spent fifteen years in the ranks, that Indians must be close at hand. The crest was barely five hundred yards in front of the section, and they were still "bunched," a splendid mark if the foe saw fit by sudden dash to regain the ridge and pour in rapid fire from their magazine rifles. Every ward of the nation, as a rule, had his Winchester or Henry,—about a six to one advantage to the red men over the sworn soldier of the government in a short range fight. The lieutenant was a brave lad and all that, and could be relied on to "do his share in a shindy," as the sergeant put it, but when it came to handling the troop to the best advantage, giving

A DAUGHTER OF THE SIOUX

them full swing when they met the foe on even terms and a fair field, but holding them clear of possible ambuscade, then "Captain Billy is the boss in the business," was the estimate of his men, and every heart beat higher at sight of him. He would know just what to do for them, and knowing, would do it.

Even as he went loping by Ray had half turned, with something like a smile in his dark eyes and a nod of his curly head to the sergeant commanding, and a gesture of the gauntleted hand,—a horizontal sweep to right and left, twice repeated,—had given the veteran his cue, and with another moment Winsor had the dozen in line at open, yet narrow, intervals, with carbines advanced and ready for business. They saw their captain ride swiftly up the gentle slope until close to the crest, then off he sprang, tossed his reins to the trumpeter and went hurrying afoot to join the lieutenant. They saw him kneeling as though to level his glasses and look fixedly forward; saw Field run back to his horse and mount in a twinkling; saw him whirl about as though coming to place himself at their head, yet rein in at once—his charger's fore feet ploughing the turf at some word from their leader. Field was eager to charge, but Ray had seen for himself and for his men, and Ray said, no. Another moment and all at the front were again in saddle—Field back with the advance, Ray coolly seated astride his pet sorrel,—scouting a second ridge, far to the north, with his glasses, and sending, as before, Scott and his three troopers straight on to the front, and signalling to the flankers to continue the move. Ten seconds' study of the position in the long, wide, shallow depression before him had fathomed the scheme of the savage. The little knot of Indians, jabbering,

A DAUGHTER OF THE SIOUX

yelping, prodding and circling about some unseen object on the turf, feigning ignorance of the soldiers' coming, was at the old-time trick to get the foremost troopers to charge and chase, to draw them on in all the dash and excitement of the moment, far ahead—three miles, perhaps—of the main body, and so enable all the lurking band behind that second curtain, the farther ridge, to come swooping down to surround, overwhelm and butcher the luckless few, then be off to safe distance long before the mass of the troop could possibly reach the scene.

"No you don't, Stabber!" laughed Ray, as Field, not a little chagrined, and the dozen at his back, came trotting within hearing distance. "That dodge was bald-headed when I was a baby. Look, Field," he continued. "They were jabbing at nothing there on the prairie. That was a fake captive they were stabbing to death. See them all scooting away now. They'll rally beyond that next ridge, and we'll do a little fooling of our own."

And so, with occasional peep at feathered warriors on the far left flank, and frequent hoverings of small parties on the distant front, Ray's nervy half hundred pushed steadily on. Two experiments had satisfied the Sioux that the captain himself was in command and they had long since recognized the sorrels. They knew of old Ray was not to be caught by time-worn tricks. They had failed to pick off the advance, or the officers, as the troop approached the second ridge. Lame Wolf's big band was coming fast, but only a dozen of his warriors, sent lashing forward, had as yet reached Stabber. The latter was too weak in numbers to think of fighting on even terms, and as Ray seemed

A DAUGHTER OF THE SIOUX

determined to come ahead, why not let him? Word was sent to Wolf not to risk showing south of the Elk Tooth spur. There in the breaks and ravines would be a famous place to lie in ambush, leaving to Stabber the duty of drawing the soldiers into the net. So there in the breaks they waited while Ray's long skirmish line easily manœuvred the red sharp-shooters out of their lair on the middle divide. Then, reforming column, the little command bore straight away for the Elk.

But all these diversions took time. Twenty miles to the north of Frayne stretched the bold divide between the Elk Fork, dry as a dead tooth much of the year, and the sandy bottom of the Box Elder. Here and there along the ridge were sudden, moundlike upheavals that gave it a picturesque, castellated effect, for, unlike the general run of the country, the Elk Tooth seemed to have a backbone of rock that shot forth southeastward from the southern limit of the beautiful Big Horn range; and, in two or three places, during some prehistoric convulsion of nature, it had crushed itself out of shape and forced upward a mass of gleaming rock that even in the course of centuries had not been overgrown with grass. "Elk teeth" the Indians had called these odd projections, and one of them, the middle one of the three most prominent, was a landmark seen for many a mile except to the south and west. Eagle Butte was the only point south of the Big Horn and in the valley of the Platte from which it could be seen, and famous were these two points in the old days of the frontier for the beacon fires that burned or the mirror signals that flashed on their summits when the war parties of the Sioux were afield.

A DAUGHTER OF THE SIOUX

It was the sight of puffs of smoke sailing skyward from the crest of the middle tooth that caught Ray's attention the moment he reached the second ridge. A moment more had been devoted to recalling some of his eager men who, from the extreme right of the swinging skirmish line, had broken away in pursuit of certain intentional laggards. Then a dozen of the Indians, finding themselves no longer followed, gathered at comparatively safe distance across the prairie, and, while in eager consultation, found time for taunting, challenging and occasionally firing at the distant and angering troopers, whom Sergeant Scott had sharply ordered back, and Ray, after calm survey of these fellows through his glass, had then levelled it at the trio of buttes along the distant ridge and turned to Field, sitting silent and disappointed by his side.

"There, Field," said the captain. "Take this glass and look at those signal smokes—Stabber has more men now at his call than he had when he started, and more yet are coming. They were just praying you would charge with a handful of men. They would have let you through, then closed around and cut you off. Do you see, boy?"

Field touched his hat brim. "You know them best, sir," was the brief answer. "What I wanted was a chance at those fellows hanging about our front and calling us names."

"You'll get it, I'm thinking, before we're an hour older. They know whither we're bound and mean to delay us all they can. Ah, Clayton," he added, as the junior lieutenant rode up to join them, while his platoon dismounted to reset saddles behind the

A DAUGHTER OF THE SIOUX

screen of the skirmish line. "Men look full of fight, don't they? There, if anywhere, is where we'll get it. I've just been showing Field those signal smokes. Mount and follow when we're half way down to that clump of cottonwoods yonder. We must reach those people at the stage station to-night, and I may have to give these beggars a lesson first. Watch for my signal and come ahead lively if I turn toward you and swing my hat. All ready, Field. Shove ahead."

And this was the last conference between the three officers that eventful morning. As once again the advance guard pushed cautiously forward toward the banks of the arroyo in the bottom, Ray turned to Field. "Skirmish work suits you better than office duty, Field. You look far livelier than you did yesterday. Don't you begin to see that the major was right in sending you out with us?" And the dark eyes of the trained and experienced soldier shone kindly into the face of the younger man.

"I'm glad to be with you, Captain Ray," was the prompt answer. "It isn't—my being sent, but the *way* I was sent, or the—cause for which I was sent that stings me. I thought then, and I think now, that if you had been post commander it wouldn't have been done. I don't know yet what charge has been laid at my door——"

"There was no time to talk of reasons, Field," interposed Ray, though his keen eyes were fixed on the distant ridge ahead, beyond which the last of the Indians had now disappeared. The outermost troopers, with Sergeant Scott, were within a few hundred yards of the little clump of cottonwoods that marked

A DAUGHTER OF THE SIOUX

the site of a water hole. To the right and left of it curved and twisted the dry water course between its low, jagged, precipitous banks. Behind the advance, full four hundred yards, rode the skirmish line from the first platoon, a dozen strong. Far out to the east and west the flankers moved steadily northward, keenly watching the slopes beyond them and scanning the crooked line of the arroyo ahead. Not a sign at the moment could be seen of the painted foe, yet every man in the troop well knew they swarmed by dozens behind the buttes and ridges ahead. Ray and Field, riding easily along in rear of the line, with only the trumpeter within earshot, relaxed in no measure the vigilance demanded by the situation, yet each was deeply concerned in the subject of the talk.

"There was no time. We had to start at once," continued Ray. "Wait until you are back at the old desk, Field, and you'll find the major is, and was, your stanch friend in this matter—"

"I'll never go back to it, captain!" broke in Field, impetuously. "If ordered to resume duty as adjutant, come what may, I shall refuse."

But before Ray could interpose again there came sudden and stirring interruption. From a point far down the "swale," from behind the low bank of the stream bed, three rifle shots rang out on the crisp morning air. The horse of the leading flanker, away out to the right, reared and plunged violently, the rider seeming vainly to strive to check him. Almost instantly three mounted warriors were seen tearing madly away northeastward out of the gully, their feathers streaming in the wind. Field spurred away to

A DAUGHTER OF THE SIOUX

join his men. Ray whirled about in saddle, and swung his broad-brimmed scouting hat high above his head, in signal to Clayton; then shouted to Field. "Forward to the cottonwoods. Gallop!" he cried. "We need them first of all!"

CHAPTER XI

A FIGHT WITH A FURY

The noonday sun was staring hotly down, an hour later, on a stirring picture of frontier warfare, with that clump of cottonwoods as the central feature. Well for Ray's half hundred, that brilliant autumn morning, that their leader had had so many a year of Indian campaigning! He now seemed to know by instinct every scheme of his savage foe and to act accordingly. Ever since the command had come in sight of the Elk Tooth the conviction had been growing on Ray that Stabber must have received many accessions and was counting on the speedy coming of others. The signal smokes across the wide valley; the frequent essays to tempt his advance guard to charge and chase; the boldness with which the Indians showed on front and flank; the daring pertinacity with which they clung to the stream bed for the sake of a few shots at the foremost troopers, relying, evidently, on the array of their comrades beyond the ridge to overwhelm any force that gave close pursuit; the fact that other Indians opened on the advance guard and the left flankers, and that a dozen, at least, tore away out of the sandy arroyo the moment they saw the line start at the gallop;—all these had tended to convince the captain that, now at last, when he was miles from home and succor, the Sioux stood ready in abundant force to give him desperate battle.

To dart on in chase of the three warriors would simply result in the scattering of his own people and their being individually cut off and stricken down by circling swarms of their red foes. To gather his men and attempt to force the passage of the Elk Tooth ridge meant certain destruction of the whole command. The Sioux would be only to glad to scurry away from their front and let them through, and then in big circle whirl all about him, pouring in a concentric fire that would be sure to hit some, at least, exposed as they would be on the open prairie, while their return shots, radiating wildly at the swift-darting warriors, would be almost as sure to miss. He would soon be weighted down with wounded, refusing to leave them to be butchered; unable, therefore, to move in any direction, and so compelled to keep up a shelterless, hopeless fight until, one by one, he and his gallant fellows fell, pierced by Indian lead, and sacrificed to the scalping knife as were Custer's three hundred a decade before.

No, Ray knew too much of frontier strategy to be so caught. There stood the little grove of dingy green, a prairie fortress, if one knew how to use it. There in the sand of the stream bed, by digging, were they sure to find water for the wounded, if wounded there had to be. There by the aid of a few hastily thrown intrenchments he could have a little plains fort and be ready to repel even an attack in force. Horses could be herded in the depths of the sandy shallows. Men could be distributed in big circle through the trees and along the bank; and, with abundant rations in their haversacks and water to be had for the digging, they could hold out like heroes until relief should come from the south.

Obviously, therefore, the cottonwood grove was the place, and thither at thundering charge Field led the foremost line, while

A DAUGHTER OF THE SIOUX

Ray waved on the second, all hands cheering with glee at sight of the Sioux darting wildly away up the northward slope. Ten men in line, far extended, were sent right forward half way across the flats, ordered to drive the Indians from the bottom and cripple as many as possible; but, if menaced by superior numbers, to fall back at the gallop, keeping well away from the front of the grove, so that the fire of its garrison might not be "masked." The ten had darted after the scurrying warriors, full half way to the beginning of the slope, and then, just as Ray had predicted, down came a cloud of brilliant foemen, seeking to swallow the little ten alive. Instantly their sergeant leader whirled them about and, pointing the way, led them in wide circle, horses well in hand, back to the dry wash, then down into its sandy depths. Here every trooper sprang from saddle, and with the rein looped on the left arm, and from the shelter of the straight, stiff banks, opened sharp fire on their pursuers, just as Clayton's platoon, dismounting at the grove, sprang to the nearest cover and joined in the fierce clamor of carbines. Racing down the slope at top speed as were the Sioux, they could not all at once check the way of their nimble mounts, and the ardor of the chase had carried them far down to the flats before the fierce crackle began. Then it was thrilling to watch them, veering, circling, sweeping to right or left, ever at furious gallop, throwing their lithe, painted bodies behind their chargers' necks, clinging with one leg and arm, barely showing so much as an eyelid, yet yelping and screeching like so many coyotes, not one of their number coming within four hundred yards of the slender fighting line in the stream bed; some of them, indeed, disdaining to stoop, riding defiantly along

A DAUGHTER OF THE SIOUX

the front, firing wildly as they rode, yet surely and gradually guiding their ponies back to the higher ground, back out of harm's way; and, in five minutes from the time they had flashed into view, coming charging over the mile away ridge, not a red warrior was left on the low ground,—only three or four luckless ponies, kicking in their last struggles or stiffening on the turf, while their riders, wounded or unhurt, had been picked up and spirited away with the marvellous skill only known to these warriors of the plains.

Then Ray and his men had time to breathe and shout laughing comment and congratulation. Not one, as yet, was hit or hurt. They were secure for the time in a strong position, and had signally whipped off the first assault of the Sioux.

Loudly, excitedly, angrily these latter were now conferring again far up the slope to the north. At least an hundred in one concourse, they were having hot discussion over the untoward result of the dash. Others, obedient to orders from the chief, were circling far out to east and west and crossing the valley above and below the position of the defence. Others, still, were galloping back to the ridge, where, against the sky line, strong bodies of warriors could be plainly seen, moving excitedly to and fro. Two little groups slowly making their way to the crest gave no little comfort to the boys in blue. Some, at least, of the charging force had been made to feel the bite of the cavalry weapon, and were being borne to the rear.

But no time was to be wasted. Already from far up the stream bed two or three Indians were hazarding long-range shots at the

A DAUGHTER OF THE SIOUX

grove, and Ray ordered all horses into a bend of the "wash," where the side lines were whipped from the blanket straps and the excited sorrels securely hoppled. Then, here, there and in a score of places along the bank and again at the edge of the cottonwoods, men had been assigned their stations and bidden to find cover for themselves without delay. Many burrowed in the soft and yielding soil, throwing the earth forward in front of them. Others utilized fallen trees or branches. Some two or three piled saddles and blanket rolls into a low barricade, and all, while crouching about their work, watched the feathered warriors as they steadily completed their big circle far out on the prairie. Bullets came whistling now fast and frequently, nipping off leaves and twigs and causing many a fellow to duck instinctively and to look about him, ashamed of his dodge, yet sure of the fact that time had been in the days of the most hardened veteran of the troop when he, too, knew what it was to shrink from the whistle of hostile lead. It would be but a moment or two, they all understood, before the foe would decide on the next move; then every man would be needed.

Meantime, having stationed Field on the north front, with orders to note every movement of the Sioux, and having assigned Clayton to the minor duty of watching the south front and the flanks, Ray was moving cheerily among his men, speeding from cover to cover, suggesting here, helping there, alert, even joyous in manner. "We couldn't have a better roost, lads," he said. "We can stand off double their number easy. We can hold out a week if need be, but you bet the major will be reaching out after us before we're two days older. Don't waste your shots. Coax them

A DAUGHTER OF THE SIOUX

close in. Don't fire at a galloping Indian beyond three hundred yards. It's waste of powder and lead."

Cheerily, joyously they answered him, these his comrades, his soldier children, men who had fought with him, many of their number, in a dozen fields, and men who would stand by him, their dark-eyed little captain, to the last. Even the youngest trooper of the fifty seemed inspired by the easy, laughing confidence of the lighter hearts among their number, or the grim, matter of fact pugnacity of the older campaigners. It was significant, too, that the Indians seemed so divided in mind as to the next move. There was loud wrangling and much disputation going on in that savage council to the north. Stabber's braves and Lame Wolf's followers seemed bitterly at odds, for old hands in the fast-growing rifle pits pointed out on one side as many as half a dozen of the former's warriors whom they recognized and knew by sight, while Ray, studying the shifting concourse through his glasses, could easily see Stabber himself raging among them in violent altercation with a tall, superbly built and bedizened young brave, a sub-chief, apparently, who for his part, seemed giving Stabber as good as he got. Lame Wolf was not in sight at all. He might still be far from the scene, and this tall warrior be acting as his representative. But whoever or whatever he was he had hearty following. More than three-fourths of the wrangling warriors in the group seemed backing him. Ray, after a few words to Sergeant Winsor, crawled over beside his silent and absorbed young second in command, and, bringing his glasses to bear, gazed across a low parapet of sand long and fixedly at the turbulent throng a thousand yards away.

A DAUGHTER OF THE SIOUX

"It's easy to make out Stabber," he presently spoke. "One can almost hear that foghorn voice of his. But who the mischief is that red villain opposing him? I've seen every one of their chiefs in the last five years. All are men of forty or more. This fellow can't be a big chief. He looks long years younger than most of 'em, old Lame Wolf, for instance, yet he's cheeking Stabber as if he owned the whole outfit." Another long stare, then again— "Who the mischief can he be?"

No answer at his side, and Ray, with the lenses still at his eyes, took no note for the moment that Field remained so silent. Out at the front the excitement increased. Out through the veil of surging warriors, the loud-voiced, impetuous brave twice burst his way, and seemed at one and the same time, in his superb poise and gesturings, to be urging the entire body to join him in instant assault on the troops, and hurling taunt and anathema on the besieged. Whoever he was, he was in a veritable fury. As many as half of the Indians seemed utterly carried away by his fiery words, and with much shouting and gesticulation and brandishing of gun and lance, were yelling approbation of his views and urging Stabber's people to join them. More furious language followed and much dashing about of excited ponies.

"Have you ever seen that fellow before?" demanded Ray, of brown-eyed Sergeant Winsor, who had spent a lifetime on the plains, but Winsor was plainly puzzled.

"I can't say for the life of me, sir," was the answer. "I don't know him at all—and yet—"

A DAUGHTER OF THE SIOUX

"Whoever he is, by Jove," said Ray, "he's a bigger man this day than Stabber, for he's winning the fight. Now, if he only leads the dash as he does the debate, we can pick him off. Who are our best shots on this front?" and eagerly he scanned the few faces near him. "Webber's tiptop and good for anything under five hundred yards when he isn't excited, and Stoltz, he's a keen, cool one. No! not you, Hogan," laughed the commander, as a freckled faced veteran popped his head up over a nearby parapet of sand, and grinned his desire to be included.

"I've never seen the time you could hit what you aimed at. Slip out of that hole and find Webber and tell him to come here—and you take his burrow." Whereupon Hogan, grinning rueful acquiescence in his commander's criticism, slid backwards into the stream bed and, followed by the chaff of the three or four comrades near enough to catch the words, went crouching from post to post in search of the desired marksman.

"You used to be pretty sure with the carbine in the Tonto Basin when we were after Apaches, sergeant," continued Ray, again peering through the glasses. "I'm mistaken in this fellow if he doesn't ride well within range, and we must make an example of him. I want four first class shots to single him out."

"The lieutenant can beat the best I ever did, sir," said Winsor, with a lift of the hand toward the hat brim, as though in apology, for Field, silent throughout the brief conference, had half risen on his hands and knees and was edging over to the left, apparently seeking to reach the shelter of a little hummock close to the bank.

A DAUGHTER OF THE SIOUX

"Why, surely, Field," was the quick reply, as Ray turned toward his junior. "That will make it complete."

"With one magnificent red arm uplifted."

But a frantic burst of yells and war whoops out at the front put sudden stop to the words. The throng of warriors that had pressed so close about Stabber and the opposing orator seemed all in an instant to split asunder, and with trailing war bonnet and followed by only two or three of his braves, the former lashed his way westward and swept angrily out of the ruck and went circling away toward the crest, while, with loud acclamation, brandishing shield and lance and rifle in superb barbaric tableau, the warriors lined up in front of the victorious young leader who, sitting high in his stirrups, with one magnificent red arm uplifted, began shouting in the sonorous tongue of the Sioux

A DAUGHTER OF THE SIOUX

some urgent instructions. Down from the distant crest came other braves as though to meet and ask Stabber explanation of his strange quitting the field. Down came a dozen others, young braves mad for battle, eager to join the ranks of this new leader, and Ray, who had turned on Field once more, fixed his glasses on that stalwart, nearly stark naked, brilliantly painted form, foremost of the Indian array and now at last in full and unimpeded view.

"By the gods of war!" he cried. "I never saw that scoundrel before, but if it isn't that renegade Red Fox—Why, here, Field! Take my glass and look. You were with the commissioners' escort last year at the Black Hills council. You must have seen him and heard him speak. Isn't this Red Fox himself?"

And to Ray's surprise the young officer's eyes were averted, his face pale and troubled, and the answer was a mere mumble—"I didn't meet Fox—there, captain."

He never seemed to see the glass held out to him until Ray almost thrust it into his hand and then persisted with his inquiry.

"Look at him anyhow. You may have seen him somewhere. Isn't that Red Fox?"

And now Ray was gazing straight at Field's half hidden face. Field, the soul of frankness hitherto, the lad who was never known to flinch from the eyes of any man, but to answer such challenge with his own,—brave, fearless, sometimes even defiant. Now he kept the big binocular fixed on the distant hostile array, but his face was white, his hand unsteady and his answer, when it

A DAUGHTER OF THE SIOUX

came, was in a voice that Ray heard in mingled pain and wonderment. Could it be that the lad was unnerved by the sight? In any event, he seemed utterly unlike himself.

"I—cannot say, sir. It was dark—or night at all events,—the only time I ever heard him."

CHAPTER XII

THE ORDEAL BY FIRE

That action had been resolved upon, and prompt action, was now apparent. Stabber, fighting chief though he had been in the past, had had his reason for opposing the plans of this new and vehement leader; but public sentiment, stirred by vehement oratory, had overruled him, and he had bolted the field convention in a fury. Lame Wolf, a younger chief than Stabber, had yet more power among the Ogalallas, being Red Cloud's favorite nephew, and among the Indians at least, his acknowledged representative. Whenever called to account, however, for that nephew's deeds, the wary old statesman promptly disavowed them. It was in search of Lame Wolf, reasoned Ray, that Stabber had sped away, possibly hoping to induce him to call off his followers. It was probably the deeper strategy of Stabber to oppose no obstacle to Ray's advance until the little troop was beyond the Elk Tooth ridge, where, on utterly shelterless ground, the Indian would have every advantage. He knew Ray of old; knew well that, left to himself, the captain would push on in the effort to rescue the stage people and he and his command might practically be at the mercy of the Sioux, if only the Sioux would listen and be patient. Stabber knew that to attack the troopers now entrenching at the cottonwoods meant a desperate fight in which the Indians, even if ultimately triumphant, must lose many a valued brave, and that is not the thoroughbred Indian's view of good generalship. Stabber was old, wily and wise. The new chief, whoever he might be, seemed

A DAUGHTER OF THE SIOUX

possessed of a mad lust for instant battle, coupled with a possible fear that, unless the golden moment were seized, Ray might be reinforced and could then defy them all. Indeed there were veteran campaigners among the troopers who noted how often the tall red chief pointed in sweeping gesture back to Moccasin Ridge—troopers who even at the distance caught and interpreted a few of his words. "That's it, sir," said Winsor, confidently to Ray. "He says 'more soldiers coming,' and—I believe he knows."

At all events he had so convinced his fellows and, even before Stabber reached the middle tooth—where sat a little knot of mounted Indians, signalling apparently to others still some distance to the north,—with a chorus of exultant yells, the long, gaudy, glittering line of braves suddenly scattered and, lashing away to right and left, dozens of them darted at top speed to join those already disposed about that big circle, while others still, the main body, probably seventy strong, after some barbaric show of circus evolutions about their leader, once more reined up for some final injunctions from his lips. Then, with a magnificent gesture of the hand, he waved them on and, accompanied by only two young riders, rode swiftly away to a little swell of the prairie just out of range of the carbines, and there took his station to supervise the attack.

"Damn him!" growled old Winsor. "He's no charger like Crazy Horse. He's a Sitting Bull breed of general—like some we had in Virginia," he added, between his set teeth, but Ray heard and grinned in silent appreciation. "Set your sights and give 'em their first volley as they reach that scorched line," he called to the men

Page 135

A DAUGHTER OF THE SIOUX

along the northward front, and pointed to a stretch of prairie where the dry grass had lately been burned away. "Five hundred yards will do it. Then aim low when they rush closer in."

"Look at the middle tooth, captain," came the sudden hail from his left. "Mirror flashes! See!" It was Field who spoke, and life and vim had returned to his voice and color to his face. He was pointing eagerly toward the highest of the knobs, where, all on a sudden, dazzling little beams of light shot forth toward the Indians in the lowlands, tipping the war bonnet and lance of many a brave with dancing fire. Whatever their purport, the signals seemed ignored by the Sioux, for presently two riders came sweeping down the long slope, straight for the point where sat Red Fox, as, for want of other name, we must for the present call him—who, for his part, shading his eyes with his hand, sat gazing toward the westward side of his warrior circle, evidently awaiting some demonstration there before giving signal for action elsewhere. Obedient to his first instructions, the main body had spread out in long, irregular skirmish rank, their mettlesome ponies capering and dancing in their eagerness. Chanting in chorus some shrill, weird song, the line was now slowly, steadily advancing, still too far away to warrant the wasting of a shot, yet unmistakably seeking to close as much as possible before bursting in with the final charge.

A DAUGHTER OF THE SIOUX

"Some few of their number borne away by their comrades."

A DAUGHTER OF THE SIOUX

And still the red leader sat at gaze, oblivious for the moment of everything around him, ignoring the coming of orders possibly from Lame Wolf himself. Suddenly the silver armlets once more gleamed on high. Then, clapping the palm of his right hand to his mouth, Red Fox gave voice to a ringing war whoop, fierce, savage and exultant, and, almost at the instant, like the boom and rumble that follows some vivid lightning flash, the prairie woke and trembled to the thunder of near a thousand hoofs. From every point of the compass—from every side, yelling like fiends of some orthodox hell, down they came—the wild warriors of the frontier in furious rush upon the silent and almost peaceful covert of this little band of brothers in the dusty garb of blue. One, two, three hundred yards they came, centering on the leafy clump of cottonwoods, riding at tearing gallop, erect, defiant, daring at the start, and giving full voice to their wild war cry. Then bending forward, then crouching low, then flattening out like hunted squirrel, for as the foremost in the dash came thundering on within good carbine range, all on a sudden the watch dogs of the little plains fort began to bark. Tiny jets of flame and smoke shot from the level of the prairie, from over dingy mounds of sand, from behind the trunks of stunted trees, from low parapet of log or leather. Then the entire grove seemed veiling itself in a drifting film of blue, the whole charging circle to crown itself with a dun cloud of dust that swept eastward over the prairie, driven by the stiff, unhampered breeze. The welkin rang with savage yell, with answering cheer, with the sputter and crackle of rifle and revolver, the loud bellow of Springfield, and then, still yelping, the feathered riders veered and circled, ever at

A DAUGHTER OF THE SIOUX

magnificent speed, each man for himself, apparently, yet all guided and controlled by some unseen, yet acknowledged, power; and, in five minutes, save where some hapless pony lay quivering and kicking on the turf, the low ground close at hand was swept clean of horse or man. The wild attack had been made in vain. The Sioux were scampering back, convinced, but not discomfited. Some few of their number, borne away stunned and bleeding by comrade hands from underneath their stricken chargers,—some three or four, perhaps, who had dared too much,—were now closing their eyes on the last fight of their savage lives.

To Ray and to many of his men it was all an old story. Stabber would never have counselled or permitted attack on seasoned troopers, fighting behind even improvised shelter. Something, perhaps, had occurred to blind his younger rival to the peril of such assault, and now, as three or four little parties were seen slowly drifting away toward the ridge, burdened by some helpless form, other couriers came thundering down at Red Fox, and wild excitement prevailed among the Elk Teeth. More signals were flashing. More Indians came popping into view, their feathered bonnets streaming in the rising wind, and about the prairie wave, where the savage general had established field headquarters, a furious conference was going on. Stabber had again interposed, and with grim but hopeful eyes, Ray and his fellows watched and noted. Every lull in the fight was so much gain for them.

"Twelve fifty-two," said the dark-eyed commander, swinging his watch into the pocket of his hunting shirt, and sliding backward

A DAUGHTER OF THE SIOUX

into the stream bed. "All serene so far. Watch things on this front, Field, while I make the rounds and see how we came out."

"All serene so far" it was! Not a man hurt. Two of the sorrels had been hit by flying bullets and much amazed and stung thereat, but neither was crippled. Bidding their guards to dig for water that might soon be needed, Ray once more made his way to the northward side and rejoined Field and Winsor.

In an almost cloudless sky of steely blue the sun had just passed the meridian and was streaming hotly down on the stirring picture. Northward the ridge line and the long, gradual slope seemed alive with swarms of Indian warriors, many of them darting about in wild commotion. About the little eminence where Stabber and the Fox had again locked horns in violent altercation, as many as a hundred braves had gathered. About the middle knob, from whose summit mirror flashes shot from time to time, was still another concourse, listening, apparently, to the admonitions of a leader but recently arrived, a chieftain mounted on an American horse, almost black, and Ray studied the pair long and curiously through his glasses. "Lame Wolf, probably," said he, but the distance was too great to enable him to be certain. What puzzled him more than anything was the apparent division of authority, the unusual display of discord among the Sioux. These were all, doubtless, of the Ogalalla tribe, Red Cloud's own people, yet here were they wrangling like ward "heelers" and wasting precious time. Whatever his antecedents this new comer had been a powerful sower of strife and sedition, for, instead of following implicitly the counsels of one leader, the Indians were divided now between three.

True to its practice, the prairie wind was sweeping stronger and stronger with every moment, as the sun-warmed strata over the wide, billowing surface sought higher levels, and the denser, cooler current from the west came rushing down. And now all sounds of the debate were whisked away toward the breaks of the South Shyenne,[*] and it was no longer possible for old Sioux campaigners to catch a word of the discussion. The leaves of the cottonwoods whistled in the rising gale, and every time a pony crossed the stream bed and clambered the steep banks out to the west, little clouds of dun-colored dust came sailing toward the grove, scattered and spent, however, far from the lair of the defence.

[* Oddly enough, that method of spelling the river's name became official.]

But, while the discussion seemed endless among the Indians on the northward side, never for a moment was the vigilance of the circle relaxed. South, east and west the slopes and lowlands were dotted with restless horsemen, and from young Clayton came the word that through his glass he could make out three or four warriors far away toward the Moccasin Ridge. "That's good," said Ray. "It means they, too, are looking for a column coming out from Frayne. But where on earth did all these rascals come from? There must be four hundred now in sight."

A DAUGHTER OF THE SIOUX

Well might he ask and marvel! Stabber's little village had never more than fifty warriors. Lame Wolf's band was counted at less than two hundred and forty fighting men, and these, so said the agents of the omniscient Bureau, were all the Ogalallas away from the shelter of the reservation when the trouble started. No more should be allowed to go, was the confident promise, yet a fortnight nearly had elapsed since the frontier fun began. News of battle sweeps with marvellous speed through Indian haunted lands, and here were warriors by the score, come to strengthen the hands of kindred in the field, and, more were coming. The mirror signals plainly told them that. Yet it was now well nigh one o'clock and not another hostile move was made. Fox then was being held by stronger hands. It meant that Lame Wolf had listened to reason,—and Stabber, and would permit no fresh attack until his numbers should be so increased that resistance would practically be vain. It meant even more—that the Indian leader in chief command felt sure no force was yet within helping distance of the corralled troopers. He could, therefore, take his time.

But this was a theory Ray would not whisper to his men. He knew Webb. He knew Webb would soon read the signs from the north and be coming to his relief, and Ray was right. Even as he reasoned there came a message from across the grove. Lieutenant Clayton said the Indians he had seen away to the south were racing back. "Thank God!" was the murmured answer no man heard. "Now, lads, be ready!" was the ringing word that roused the little troop, like bugle call "To Arms." And even as eager faces lifted over the low parapets to scan the distant foe, fresh signals

A DAUGHTER OF THE SIOUX

came flashing down from the northward ridge, fresh bands of warriors came darting to join the martial throng about the still wrangling chieftains, and then, all on a sudden, with mighty yelling and shrill commotion, that savage council burst asunder, and, riding at speed, a dozen braves went lashing away to the westward side, while with fierce brandishing of arms and shields and much curveting and prancing of excited ponies, the wild battle lines were formed again. The Sioux were coming for the second trial.

"Meet them as before! Make every shot tell!" were the orders passed from man to man and heard and noted amidst the whistling of the wind and the sounds of scurry and commotion at the front. Then, silent and crouching low, the soldiers shoved the brown barrels of their carbines forth again and waited. And then the grim silence of the little fortress was broken, as, with startling, sudden force there went up a shout from the westward side:—

"My God, boys, they're setting fire to the prairie!"

Ray sprang to his feet and gazed. Away out to the west and southwest, whence came the strong breeze blowing from the Sweetwater Hills, half a dozen dark, agile forms, bending low, were scudding afoot over the sward, and everywhere they moved there sprang up in their tracks little sheets of lambent flame, little clouds of bluish, blinding smoke, and almost in less time than it takes to tell it, a low wall of fire, started in a dozen places, reaching far across the low ground, fencing the valley from stream bed to the southward slopes, crowned by its swift-sailing

A DAUGHTER OF THE SIOUX

crest of hot, stifling fume, came lapping and seething and sweeping across the level, licking up the dry buffalo grass like so much tow, mounting higher and fiercer with every second, and bearing down upon the little grove and its almost helpless defenders in fearful force, in resistless fury—a charge no bullet could stop, an enemy no human valor could hope to daunt or down.

"Quick, men!" yelled Ray. "Out with you, you on the west front! Stay you here, you others! Watch the Sioux! They'll be on us in an instant!" And away he sped from the shelter of the bank, out from the thick of the cottonwoods, out to the open prairie, straight toward the coming torrent of flame still, thank God, full seven hundred yards away, but leaping toward them with awful strides. Out with him rushed Field, and out from Clayton's front sped half a dozen old hands, every man fumbling for his match box; out until they had reached a line with their captain, already sprawled upon the turf, and there, full an hundred yards from the grove, they spread in rude skirmish line and, reckless of the mad chorus of yells that came sweeping down the wind, reckless of the clamor of the coming charge, reckless of the whistling lead that almost instantly began nipping and biting the turf about them, here, there and everywhere, they, too, had started little fires; they, too had run their line of flame across the windward front; they, too, had launched a wall of flame sailing toward the grove, and then, back through blinding smoke they ran for their saddle blankets, just as the sharp sputter of shots burst forth on the northward side, and the Sioux, with magnificent dash, came thundering within range.

A DAUGHTER OF THE SIOUX

Then followed a thrilling battle for life—two red enemies now enrolled against the blue. "Fight fire with fire" is the old rule of the prairie. Ray had promptly met the on-coming sweep of the torrent by starting a smaller blaze that should at least clear the surface close at hand, and, by eating off the fuel, stop, possibly, the progress of the greater flame.

But the minor blaze had also to be stopped lest it come snapping and devouring within the grove. It is no easy matter to check a prairie fire against a prairie gale when every human aid is summoned. It is desperate work to try to check one when to the fires of nature are added the furious blaze of hostile arms, every rifle sighted by savage, vengeful foe. "Check it, lads, ten yards out!" shouted Ray, to his gallant fellows, now lost in the smoke, while he again rushed across the front to meet the charging Sioux. With his brave young face all grime, Field was already at work, guiding, urging, aiding his little band. "Both hands! Both hands!" he cried, as, wielding his folded blanket, he smote the fringe of flame. "Stamp it out! Great God! Wing, are you hit?"

For answer the sergeant by his side went plunging down, face foremost, and little Trooper Denny, rushing to aid his young officer in the effort to raise the stricken man, as suddenly loosed his hold and, together again, these two sworn comrades of many a campaign lay side by side, as they had lain in camp and bivouac all over the wide frontier, and poor Denny could only gasp a loyal word of warning to his officer. "Get back, sir; for God's sake, get back!" ere the life blood came gushing from his mouth. Bending low, Field grabbed the faithful fellow in his strong arms

A DAUGHTER OF THE SIOUX

and, calling to the nearmost men to look to Wing, bore his helpless burden back through stifling smoke clouds; laid him on the turf at the foot of a cottonwood, then ran again to the perilous work of fighting the flame, stumbling midway over another prostrate form. "Both hands! Both hands!" he yelled as again his blanket whirled in air; and so, by dint of desperate work, the inner line of flame at last was stayed, but every man of the gallant little squad of fire fighters had paid the penalty of his devotion and felt the sting of hissing lead—Field the last of all. Westward now, well nigh an hundred yards in width, a broad, black, smoking patch stretched across the pathway of the swift-coming wall of smoke and flame, a safeguard to the beleaguered command worth all the soldier sacrifice it cost. In grand and furious sweep, the scourge of the prairie sent its destroying line across the wide level to the south of the sheltering grove, but in the blood and sweat of heroic men the threatening flames of the windward side had sputtered out. The little garrison was safe from one, at least, of its dread and merciless foes, though five of its best and bravest lay dead or dying, and others still sore stricken, in the midst of the smoking grove.

"Field, old boy," said Ray, with brimming eyes, as he knelt and clasped the hand of the bleeding lad, while the Sioux fell back in wrath and dismay from the low-aimed, vengeful fire of the fighting line. "This means the Medal of Honor for you, if word of mine can fetch it!"

A DAUGHTER OF THE SIOUX

CHAPTER XIII

WOUNDED—BODY AND SOUL

To say the Sioux were furious at the failure of their second attempt would be putting it far too mildly. The fierce charge from the northward side, made under cover of the blinding smoke sent drifting by the gale across the level flats, had been pushed so close to the grove that two red braves and half a dozen ponies had met their death within sixty paces of the rifle pits. There lay the bodies now, and the Indians dare not attempt to reach them. The dread, wind-driven flame of the prairie fire, planned by the Sioux to burn out the defence, to serve as their ally, had been turned to their grave detriment.

Ray and his devoted men had stopped the sweep of so much of the conflagration as threatened their little stronghold, but, ranging unhampered elsewhere, the seething wall rolled on toward the east, spreading gradually toward its flanks, and so, not only consuming vast acres of bunch grass, but checking the attack that should have been made from the entire southern half of the Indian circle. Later, leaping the sandy stream bed a little to the west of the cottonwoods, it spread in wild career over a huge tract along the left bank, and now, reuniting with the southern wing some distance down the valley, was roaring away to the bluffs of the Mini Pusa, leaving death and desolation in its track. Miles to the east the war parties from the reservation, riding to join Lame Wolf, sighted the black curtain of smoke, swift sailing over the prairie, and changed their course accordingly. Not so many miles away to the south Webb's skirmishers, driving before them three

A DAUGHTER OF THE SIOUX

or four Sioux scouts from the northward slope of the Moccasin Ridge, set spurs to their horses and took the gallop, the main body following on.

With their eyelids blistered by heat and smoke, Ray's silent, determined little band could see nothing of the coming force, yet knew relief was nigh; for, close at hand, both east and west, large bodies of the enemy could be seen swift riding away to the north.

They had hoped, as "Fox" had planned and promised, to burn out and overwhelm the little troop at the grove before the column from Frayne could possibly reach the spot. They had even anticipated the probable effort of the command to check the flames, and had told off some fifty braves to open concentric fire on any party that should rush into the open with that object in view. They had thought to send in such a storm of lead, even from long range, that it should daunt and drive back those who had dared the attempt. They had stormed indeed, but could neither daunt nor drive back. Ray's men had braved death itself in the desperate essay, and, even in dying, had won the day.

But their losses had been cruel. Three killed outright; three dying and eight more or less severely wounded had reduced their fighting strength to nearly thirty. The guards of the sorrels, herded in the stream bed, had all they could do to control the poor, frightened creatures, many of them hit, several of them felled, by the plunging fire from the far hillsides. Even though driven back, the Sioux never meant to give up the battle. On every side, leaving their ponies at safe distance, by dozens the warriors crawled forward, snake-like, to the edge of the burned

A DAUGHTER OF THE SIOUX

and blackened surface, and from there poured in a rapid and most harassing fire, compelling the defence to lie flat or burrow further, and wounding many horses. The half hour that followed the repulse of their grand assault had been sorely trying to the troop, for the wounded needed aid, more men were hit, and there was no chance whatever to hit back. Moving from point to point, Ray carried cheer and courage on every side, yet was so constantly exposed as to cause his men fresh anxiety. Even as he was bending over Field a bullet had nipped the right shoulderstrap, and later another had torn through the crown of his campaign hat. In all the years of their frontier fighting they had never known a hotter fire; but Ray's voice rang out through the drifting vapor with the same old cheer and confidence. "They can't charge again till the ground cools off," he cried. "By that time they'll have their hands full. See how they're scudding away at the southward even now. Just keep covered and you're all right." And, barring a growl or two from favored old hands who sought to make the captain take his own medicine and himself keep covered, the answer was full of cheer.

And so they waited through the hot smoke and sunshine of the autumn afternoon, and, even while comforting the wounded with assurance of coming relief, kept vigilant watch on every hostile move, and at last, toward three o'clock, the sharp fire about them slackened away, the smouldering roots of the bunch grass had burned themselves out. The smoke drifted away from the prairie, and, as the landscape cleared to the south and west, a cheer of delight went up from the cottonwoods, for the slopes three miles away were dotted here and there and everywhere with

A DAUGHTER OF THE SIOUX

circling, scurrying war ponies—they and their wild riders steadily falling back before a long rank of disciplined horsemen, the extended skirmish line of Webb's squadron, backed by supports at regular intervals, and all heading straight on for the broad lowlands of the Elk.

"Send six of your men over to the south front, sergeant," were Ray's orders to Winsor, as he hurried over to join Clayton again. "They may try one final charge from that side, and give us a chance to empty a few more saddles." Creeping and crouching through the timber the chosen men obeyed, and were assigned to stations under Clayton's eye. The precaution was wise indeed, for, just as the captain foresaw, a rally in force began far out over the southward slopes, the Indians gathering in great numbers about some chieftain midway between the coming force and the still beleaguered defenders of the grove. Then, brandishing lance and shield and rifle, as before, they began spreading out across the prairie, heading now for the cottonwoods, while others still faced and fired on the far blue skirmish line. The fierce wind, sweeping across the direction of the attack, deadened all sound of hoof or war chant, but there was no mistaking the signs, no doubt of the intent, when, in a little moment more, the earth began to tremble beneath the dancing pony feet, telling, almost with the swiftness of sight, that the grand advance had again begun. But other eyes were watching too. Other soldiers, keen campaigners as these at the Elk, were there afield, and almost at the moment the wild barbaric horde burst yelling into their eager gallop, and before the dust cloud hid the distant slopes beyond, the exultant shout went up from the captain's lips, as he threw

A DAUGHTER OF THE SIOUX

down his glass and grabbed his carbine. "It's all right, men! The major's coming at their heels. Now let 'em have it!"

In former days there had been scenes of wild rejoicing, sometimes of deep emotion, when relief came to some Indian-besieged detachment of the old regiment. Once, far to the south in the wild, romantic park country of Colorado, a strong detachment had been corralled for days by an overwhelming force of Utes. Their commander,—a dozen of their best men,—all the horses killed and many troopers sorely wounded. They had been rescued at last by their skilled and gallant colonel, after a long and most scientific march by both night and day. Another time, still farther in their past, and yet within a dozen years, away down the broad valley of the very stream of which this little Elk was a tributary, the Cheyennes had hemmed in and sorely hammered two depleted troops that owed their ultimate rescue to the daring of the very officer who so coolly, confidently headed the defence this day—to a night ride through the Indian lines that nearly cost him his brave young life, but that brought Captain Truscott with a fresh and powerful troop sweeping in to their succor with the dawn. Then there had been men who strained other men to their hearts and who shed tears like women, for gallant comrades had bitten the dust in the desperate fighting of the day before, and hope itself had almost gone—with the ammunition of the beleaguered command.

Now, with heavier losses than had befallen Wayne in '76, Ray's command beheld with almost tranquil hearts the coming of the fierce array in final charge. Behind them, not two miles, to be

Page 151

A DAUGHTER OF THE SIOUX

sure, rode in swift, well-ordered pursuit the long line of comrade troopers. But there had been intervening years of campaign experiences that dulled to a degree the earlier enthusiasms of the soldier, and taught at least the assumption of professional composure that was the secret wonder of the suckling trooper, and that became his chief ambition to acquire. It is one thing to charge home at a hard-fighting command when friends and comrades back the effort and cheer the charging line. It is another to charge home conscious that other chargers are coming at one's heels. Magnificent as a spectacle, therefore, this closing dash of Lame Wolf's warriors was but a meek reminder of their earlier attack. Long before they came within four hundred yards of the leafy stronghold,—the moment, indeed, the brown Springfields began their spiteful bark,—to right and left the warriors veered, far out on either flank. Screeching and yelling as was their savage way, they tore madly by, flattened out against their ponies' necks and, those who could use their arms at all, pumping wild shots that whistled harmless over the heads of the defenders and bit the blackened prairie many a rod beyond. Only jeers rewarded the stirring spectacle,—jeers and a few low-aimed, sputtering volleys that brought other luckless ponies to their knees and sprawled a few red riders. But in less than five minutes from the warning cry that hailed their coming, Lame Wolf and his hosts were lining Elk Tooth ridge and watching with burning hate and vengeful eyes the swift, steady advance of Webb's long blue fighting line, and the utter unconcern of the defence. Even before the relieving squadron was within carbine range certain of Ray's men had scrambled out upon the northward bank and, pushing forward

A DAUGHTER OF THE SIOUX

upon the prairie, were possessing themselves of the arms and ornaments of the two dead warriors whom the Sioux had strived in vain to reach and bear within their lines. Ray and Clayton at the moment were strolling placidly forth upon the southward "bench" to receive and welcome the little knot of comrades sent galloping in advance to greet them. There was perhaps just a suspicion of exaggerated nonchalance about their gait and bearing—a regimental weakness, possibly—and no other officer save Lieutenant Field happened to be within earshot when Winsor's voice on the other front was heard in hoarse command:

"Come back there, you fellows! Back or you're goners!"

The sight had proved too much for some of the Sioux. Down again at furious speed came a scattered cloud of young braves, following the lead of the tall, magnificent chief who had been the hero of the earlier attack,—down into the low ground, never swerving or checking pace, straight for the grove, the three or four inquisitive blue-coats in the meantime scurrying for shelter; and the yell that went up at sight of the Indian dash and the quick reopening of the sputtering fire brought Ray, running once again to the northward edge of the timber, wondering what could be amiss. Field was lying on his blanket, just under the bank, as the captain darted by, and grinned his gratification as he heard the brief, assuring words: "Webb's here—all hands with him." An instant later a bullet whizzed through the roots of the old cottonwood above his head, and from far out afield, deadened by the rush of the wind, a dull crackle of shots told that something had recalled the Sioux to the attack, and for three

A DAUGHTER OF THE SIOUX

minutes there was a lively fusillade all along the northward side. Then it slowly died away, and other voices, close at hand,—someone speaking his name,—called the lad's attention. He was weak from loss of blood, and just a little dazed and flighty. He had meant three hours agone that when next he encountered his post commander his manner should plainly show that senior that even a second lieutenant had rights a major was bound to respect. But, only mistily now, he saw bending over him the keen, soldierly features,—the kind, winsome gray eyes, filled with such a world of concern and sympathy,—and heard the deep, earnest tones of the voice he knew so well, calling again his name and mingling cordial praise and anxious inquiry, and all the rancor seemed to float away with the smoke of the last carbine shots. He could only faintly return the pressure of that firm, muscular hand, only feebly smile his thanks and reassurance, and then he, too, seemed floating away somewhere into space, and he could not manage to connect what Webb had been saying with the next words that fastened on his truant senses. It must have been hours later, too, for darkness had settled on the valley. A little fire was burning under the shelter of the bank. A little group of soldiers were chatting in low tone, close at hand. Among them, his arm in a sling, stood a stocky little chap whose face, seen in the flickering light, was familiar to him. So was the eager brogue in which that little chap was speaking. A steward was remonstrating, and only vaguely at first, Field grasped the meaning of his words:—

A DAUGHTER OF THE SIOUX

"The captain said you were not to try to follow, Kennedy, at least not until Dr. Waller saw you. Wait till he gets here. He can't be three miles back now."

"To hell wid ye!" was the vehement answer. "D'ye think I'd be maundherin' here wid the whole command gone on afther thim bloody Sioux. I've made my mark on wan o' thim, an' he's the buck I'm afther."

"He's made his mark on *you,* Kennedy," broke in a soldier voice. "You mad fool, trying to tackle a chief like that—even if he was hit, for he had his whole gang behind him."

"Sure he dared me out, an'—what's this he called me? a d———d whiskey thafe!—me that niver———"

"Oh, shut up, Kennedy," laughed a brother Irishman. "You were full as a goat at 'K' Troop's stables—Where'd ye get the whiskey if———"

"I'll lay you, Lanigan, when I get two hands agin, though I misdoubt wan would do it. It's me horse I want now and lave to go on wid the capt'n. Ready now, sir," he added, with sudden change of tone and manner, for a tall, slender form came striding into the fire light, and Field knew Blake at the instant, and would have called but for the first word from the captain's lips.

"*Your* heart's safe, Kennedy. I wish your head was. Your past master in blasphemy out there won't eat it, at all events."

"Did ye get him, sorr,—afther all?"

A DAUGHTER OF THE SIOUX

"*I* didn't. His English spoiled my aim. 'Twas Winsor shot him. Now, you're to stay here, you and Kilmaine. The doctor may bring despatches, and you follow us with the first to come." An orderly had led forth a saddled horse, and Blake's foot was already in the stirrup. "They say it was Red Fox himself, Kennedy," he added. "Where on earth did you meet him before?"

"Shure, *I* niver knew him, sorr," was the quick reply, as Blake's long, lean leg swung over the big charger's back and the rider settled in saddle.

"But he knew *you* perfectly well. He dared you by name, when we closed on them—you and Mr. Field."

And when an hour later the veteran surgeon came and knelt by the side of the young officer reported seriously wounded, and took his hand and felt his pulse, there was something in the situation that seemed to call for immediate action. "We'll get you back to Frayne to-morrow, Field," said Waller, with kind intent. "Don't—worry now."

"Don't do that, doctor," feebly, surprisingly moaned the fevered lad. "Don't take me back to Frayne!"

A DAUGHTER OF THE SIOUX

CHAPTER XIV

A VANISHED HEROINE

Within forty-eight hours of the coming of Trooper Kennedy with his "rush" despatches to Fort Frayne, the actors in our little drama had become widely separated. Webb and his sturdy squadron, including Ray and such of his troop as still had mounts and no serious wounds, were marching straight on for the Dry Fork of the Powder. They were two hundred fighting men; and, although the Sioux had now three times that many, they had learned too much of the shooting powers of these seasoned troopers, and deemed it wise to avoid close contact. The Indian fights well, man for man, when fairly cornered, but at other times he is no true sportsman. He asks for odds of ten to one, as when he wiped out Custer on the "Greasy Grass," or Fetteman at Fort Phil Kearny,—as when he tackled the Gray Fox,—General Crook—on the Rosebud, and Sibley's little party among the pines of the Big Horn. Ray's plucky followers had shot viciously and emptied far too many saddles for Indian equanimity. It might be well in any event to let Webb's squadron through and wait for further accessions from the agencies at the southeast, or the big, turbulent bands of Uncapapas and Minneconjous at Standing Rock, or the Cheyennes along the Yellowstone.

So back went Lame Wolf and his braves, bearing Stabber with them, flitting northward again toward the glorious country beyond the "Chakadee," and on went Webb, with Blake, Gregg, Ray and their juniors, with Tracy to take care of such as might be

A DAUGHTER OF THE SIOUX

wounded on the way; and, later still, the old post surgeon reached the Elk with guards and hospital attendants, and on the morrow row began his homeward march with the dead and wounded,—a sad and solemn little procession. Only twenty miles he had to go, but it took long hours, so few were the ambulances, so rough the crossings of the ravines; and, not until near nightfall was the last of the wounded,—Lieutenant Field,—borne in the arms of pitying soldiers into the old post hospital, too far gone with fever, exhaustion and some strong mental excitement to know or care that his strange plea had been, perforce, disregarded;—to know or care later that the general himself, the commander they loved and trusted, was bending over him at dawn the following day. Ordering forward all available troops from the line of the railway, "the Chief" had stopped at Laramie only long enough for brief conference with the post commander; then, bidding him come on with all his cavalry, had pushed ahead for Frayne. It couldn't be a long campaign, perhaps, with winter close at hand, but it would be a lively one. Of that the chief felt well assured.

Now, there was something uncanny about this outbreak on the part of the Sioux, and the general was puzzled. Up to September the Indians had been busy with the annual hunt. They were fat, well-fed, prosperous,—had got from the government pretty much everything that they could ask with any show of reason and, so they said, had been promised more. The rows between the limited few of their young men and some bullies among the "rustlers" had been no more frequent nor serious than on previous summers, when matters had been settled without resort

A DAUGHTER OF THE SIOUX

to arms; but this year the very devil seemed to have got into the situation. Something, or probably somebody, said the general, had been stirring the Indians up, exciting—exhorting possibly, and almost the first thing the general did as he climbed stiffly out of his stout Concord wagon, in the paling starlight of the early morning, was to turn to Dade, now commanding the post, and to say he should like, as soon as possible, to see Bill Hay. Meantime he wished to go in and look at the wounded.

It was not yet five o'clock, but Dr. Waller was up and devoting himself to the needs of his patients, and Dade had coffee ready for the general and his single aide-de-camp, but not a sip would the general take until he had seen the stricken troopers. He knew Field by reputation, well and favorably. He had intimately known Field's father in the old days, in the old army, when they served together on the then wild Pacific shores "where rolls the Oregon." The great civil war had divided them, for Field had cast his soldier fortune with his seceding State, but all that was a thing of the past. Here was the son, a loyal soldier of the flag the father had again sworn allegiance to when he took his seat in the House of Representatives. The general thought highly of Field, and was sore troubled at his serious condition. He knew what despatches would be coming from the far South when the telegraph line began the busy clicking of the morning. He was troubled to find the lad in high fever and to hear that he had been out of his head. He was more than troubled at the concern, and something like confusion, in the old doctor's face.

"You don't think him dangerously wounded, do you?" he asked.

A DAUGHTER OF THE SIOUX

"Not dangerously, general," was the reply. "It's—well, he seems to have something on his mind." And more than this the doctor would not say. It was not for him to tell the chief what Webb had confided ere he left the post—that most of the currency for which Field was accountable was so much waste paper. Field lay muttering and tossing in restless misery, unconscious most of the time, and sleeping only when under the influence of a strong narcotic. Dade, with sadness and constraint apparent in his manner, hung back and did not enter the bare hospital room where, with only a steward in attendance, the young soldier lay. The doctor had gone with the general to the bedside, but the captain remained out of earshot at the door.

First call for reveillé was just sounding on the infantry bugles as the trio came forth. "I have sent for Hay already, general," Dade was saying, as they stood on the wooden veranda overlooking the valley of the murmuring river; "but will you not come now and have coffee? He can join us over at my quarters."

Already, however, the orderly was hurrying back. They met him when not half way over to the line of officers' quarters. The few men for duty in the two companies of infantry, left to guard the post, were gathering in little groups in front of their barracks, awaiting the sounding of the assembly. They knew the chief at a glance, and were curiously watching him as he went thoughtfully pacing across the parade by the side of the temporary commander. They saw the orderly coming almost at a run from the direction of the guard-house, saw him halt and salute, evidently making some report, but they could not guess what

A DAUGHTER OF THE SIOUX

made him so suddenly start and run at speed toward the southward bluff, the direction of the trader's corral and stables, while Captain Dade whirled about and signalled Sergeant Crabb, of the cavalry, left behind in charge of the few custodians of the troop barracks. Crabb, too, threw dignity to the winds, and ran at the beck of his superior officer.

"Have you two men who can ride hard a dozen miles or so—and carry out their orders?" was the captain's sharp demand.

"Certainly, sir," answered Crabb, professionally resentful that such question should be asked of men of the ——th Cavalry.

"Send two to report to me at once, mounted. Never mind breakfast."

And by this time, apparently, the chief, the post commander and possibly even the aide-de-camp had forgotten about the waiting coffee. They still stood there where they had halted in the centre of the parade. The doctor, coming from hospital, was signalled to and speedily joined them. The bugle sounded, the men mechanically formed ranks and answered to their names, all the while watching from the corner of their eyes the group of officers, now increased by two infantry subalterns, Lieutenants Bruce and Duncan, who raised their caps to the preoccupied general, such salutation being then a fashion, not a regulation of the service, and stood silently awaiting instructions, for something of consequence was surely at hand. Then the orderly again appeared, returning from his mission, out of breath and speaking with difficulty.

A DAUGHTER OF THE SIOUX

"Craps—I mean the Frenchman, sir, says it was after four, perhaps half past, when they started, Pete drivin'. He didn't see who was in it. 'Twas the covered buckboard he took, sir—the best one."

And then, little by little, it transpired that Hay, the post trader whom the general had need to see, had taken his departure by way of the Rawlins road, and without so much as a whisper of his purpose to any one.

"I knew he had thought of going. He told Major Webb so," said Dade, presently. "But that was before the outbreak assumed proportions. He had given up all idea of it yesterday and so told me."

"Has anything happened to—start him since then?" demanded the bearded general, after a moment's thought.

Dade and the doctor looked into each other's eyes, and the latter turned away. It was not his affair.

"W-ell, something has happened, general," was Dade's slow, constrained reply. "If you will step this way—I'll see you later, gentlemen—" this to his subalterns—"I'll explain as far as I can."

And while Dr. Waller fell back and walked beside the aide-de-camp, gladly leaving to the post commander the burden of a trying explanation, the general, slowly pacing by the captain's side, gave ear to his story.

A DAUGHTER OF THE SIOUX

"Hay cleaned up quite a lot of money," began the veteran, "and had intended starting it to Cheyenne when this Indian trouble broke out. The courier reached us during the night, as you know, and the major ordered Ray to start at dawn and Field to go with him."

"Why, I thought Field was post adjutant!" interposed the general.

"He was, but—well—I beg you to let Major Webb give you his own reasons, general," faltered Dade, sorely embarrassed. "He decided that Field should go——"

"He *asked* to go, I suppose—It runs in the blood," said the general, quickly, with a keen look from his blue-gray eyes.

"I think not, sir; but you will see Webb within a few days and he will tell you all about it. What I know is this, that Field was ordered to go and that he gave the major an order on Hay for two packages containing the money for which he was accountable. Field and Wilkins had had a falling out, and, instead of putting the cash in the quartermaster's safe, Field kept it at Hay's. At guard mounting Hay brought the package to the major, who opened both in presence of the officers of the day. Each package was supposed to contain three or four hundred dollars. Neither contained twenty. Some paper slips inserted between five dollar bills made up the packages. Field was then far to the north and past conferring with. Hay was amazed and distressed—said that someone must have duplicate keys of his safe as well as of his stables."

"Why the stables?" asked the chief, pausing at the gate and studying the troubled face of the honored soldier he so well knew and so fully trusted. He was thinking, too, how this was not the first occasion that the loss of public money had been hidden for the time in just that way—slips inserted between good currency.

"Because it transpires that some of his horses were out that very night without his consent or ken. No one for a moment, to my knowledge, has connected Field with the loss of the money. Hay thought, however, it threw suspicion on *him*, and was mightily upset."

"Then his sudden departure at this time, without a word to anybody looks—odd," said the general, thoughtfully. "But *he* had no need of money. He's one of the wealthiest men in Wyoming. And she—his wife,—needs nothing. He gives her all she can possibly want." By this time they were at the door. A lamp still burned dimly in the hallway, and Dade blew it out, as he ushered the general into the cosily lighted dining-room.

"You'll excuse Mrs. Dade and Esther, I hope, sir. They are not yet up—quite overcome by anxiety and excitement,—there's been a lot about Frayne the last two days.—Take this chair, General. Coffee will be served at once. No, sir, as you say, the Hays have no need of money—he and his wife, that is."

"But you suspect—whom?" asked the general, the blue-gray eyes intent on the troubled face before him, for Dade's very hesitancy told of some untold theory. The doctor and the aide had taken

A DAUGHTER OF THE SIOUX

seats at the other end of the table and dutifully engaged in low-toned conversation.

"That is a hard question for me to answer, General," was the answer. "I have no right to suspect anybody. We had no time to complete the investigation. There are many hangers-on, you know, about Hay's store, and indeed, his house. Then his household, too, has been increased, as perhaps you did not know. Mrs. Hay's niece—a very brilliant young woman—is visiting them, and she and Field rode frequently together."

The general's face was a study. The keen eyes were reading Dade as a skilled physician would interpret the symptoms of a complicated case. "How old—and what is she like, Dade?" he asked.

"The women can answer that better than I, sir. They say she must be twenty-four;—Mrs. Hay says nineteen—She is very dark and very handsome—at times. Most of our young men seem to think so, at least. She certainly rides and dances admirably, and Mr. Field was constantly her partner."

The general began to see light. "Field was constantly with her, was he? Riding just by themselves or with others when they went out?" he asked.

"By themselves, sir. I doubt if any other of our equestriennes would care to ride at her pace. She rather outstrips them all. The major told me they seemed to go—well, every time he saw them, at least,—up to Stabber's village, and that was something he disapproved of, though I dare say she was simply curious to see an Indian village, as an Eastern girl might be."

"Possibly," said the general. "And what did you tell me—she is Mrs. Hay's niece? I don't remember *his* having any niece when they were at Laramie in '66, though I knew something of Mrs. Hay, who was then but a short time married. She spoke Sioux and *patois* French better than English in those days. What is the young lady's name?"

"Miss Flower, sir. Nanette Flower."

The chief dropped his head on his hand and reflected. "It's a good twenty years, and I've been knocking about all over the West since then, but, I'd like to see Mrs. Hay and that young woman, Dade, whether we overhaul Bill or not. I must go on to Beecher at once."

"You will wait for the cavalry from Laramie, will you not, sir?" asked the captain, anxiously.

"I can't. I'll get a bath and breakfast and forty winks later; then see Mrs. Hay and Bill, if he is back. They ought to catch him before he reaches Sage Creek. There are your couriers now," he added, at the sound of spurred heels on the front piazza.

The captain stepped forth into the hallway. A trooper stood at the front door, his hand lifted in salute. Another, in saddle, and holding the reins of his comrade's horse, was at the gate. A rustle of feminine drapery swept downward from the upper floor, and Dade glanced up, half dreading to see Esther's face. But it was his

A DAUGHTER OF THE SIOUX

wife who peered over the balustrade. "I shall be down in ten minutes," she said, in low tone. "Esther is sleeping at last. How did—he—seem this morning?"

"Sleeping, too, but only fitfully. Dr. Waller is here," and then Dade would have ended the talk. He did not wish to speak further of Field or his condition. But she called again, low-toned, yet dominant, as is many a wife in and out of the army.

"Surely you are not letting the general start with only two men!"

"No, he goes by and by." And again Dade would have escaped to the piazza, but once again she held him.

"Then where are you sending these?"

"After Mr. Hay. He—made an early start—not knowing perhaps, the general was coming."

"Start!" she cried, all excitement now. "Start!—Start for where?" and the dressing sacque in aspen-like agitations came in full view at the head of the stairs.

"Rawlins, I suppose. I don't know what it means."

"But *I* do!" exclaimed his better half, in emotion uncontrollable. "*I* do! It means that she has *made* him,—that *she* has gone, too—I mean Nanette Flower!"

A DAUGHTER OF THE SIOUX

CHAPTER XV

A WOMAN'S PLOT

Woman's intuition often far outstrips the slower mental process of the other sex. The mother who has to see a beloved daughter's silent suffering, well knowing another girl to be, however indirectly, the cause of it, sees all manner of other iniquities in that other girl. Kind, charitable and gentle was Mrs. Dade, a wise mother, too, as well as most loving, but she could look with neither kindness nor charity on Miss Flower. She had held her peace; allowed no word of censure or criticism to escape her when the women were discussing that young lady; but all the more vehement was her distrust, because thus pent up and repressed. With the swiftness of feminine thought, for no man had yet suspected, she fathomed the secret of the trader's sudden going; and, carried away by the excitement of the moment and the belief that none but her husband could hear, she had made that startling announcement. And her intuition was unerring. Nanette Flower was indeed gone.

Yet for nearly an hour she stood alone in her conviction. Her husband quickly cautioned silence, and, going forth, gave instructions to the couriers that sent them speeding for the Rawlins road. But at seven o'clock Mrs. Hay herself appeared and asked to see the general, who was taking at the moment his accustomed bracer, tonic and stimulant,—the only kind he was ever known to use—a cold bath. So it was to Mrs. Dade, in all apparent frankness and sincerity, the trader's wife began her tale.

A DAUGHTER OF THE SIOUX

Everyone at Frayne well knew that her anxiety as to the outcome of the battle on the Elk had well nigh equalled that of the wives and sweethearts within the garrison. While her niece, after the first day's excitement, kept to her room, the aunt went flitting from house to house, full of sympathy and suggestion, but obviously more deeply concerned than they had ever seen her. Now, she seemed worried beyond words at thought of her husband's having to go at just this time. It was mainly on Nanette's account, she said. Only last night, with the mail from Laramie, had come a letter posted in San Francisco the week before, telling Miss Flower that her dearest friend and roommate for four years at school, who had been on an extended bridal tour, would pass through Rawlins, eastward bound, on Friday's train, and begging Nanette to meet her and go as far at least as Cheyenne. Her husband, it seems, had been hurriedly recalled to New York, and there was no help for it. Nanette had expected to join her, and go all the way East in late October or early November; had given her promise, in fact, for she was vastly excited by the news, and despite headache and lassitude that had oppressed her for two days past, she declared she must go, and Uncle Will must take her. So, with only a small trunk, hastily packed, of her belongings, and an iron-bound chest of the trader's, the two had started before dawn in Uncle Bill's stout buckboard, behind his famous four mule team, with Pete to drive, and two sturdy ranchmen as outriders, hoping to reach the Medicine Bow by late afternoon, and rest at Brenner's Ranch.

Confidentially, Mrs. Hay told Mrs. Dade that her husband was glad of the excuse to take the route up the Platte instead of the old, rough trail southeastward over the mountains to Rock Creek, for he had a large sum in currency to get to the bank, and there were desperados along the mountain route who well knew he would have to send that money in, and were surely on lookout to waylay him—or it. Ever since pay-day two or three rough characters had been hanging about the store, and Hay suspected they were watching his movements, with the intention of getting word to their comrades in crime the moment he started, and it was almost as much to steal a march on them, as to oblige Nanette, he so willingly left before it was light. The Rawlins road followed the Platte Valley all the way to Brenner's, and, once there, he would feel safe, whereas the Rock Creek trail wound through gulch, ravine and forest most of the distance, affording many a chance for ambuscade. Of course, said Mrs. Hay, if her husband had for a moment supposed the general would wish to see him, he would not have gone, adding, with just a little touch of proper, wifelike spirit, that on the general's previous visits he had never seemed to care whether he saw Mr. Hay or not.

All this did Mrs. Dade accept with courteous yet guarded interest. They were seated in the little army parlor, talking in low tone; for, with unfailing tact, Mrs. Hay had asked for Esther, and expressed her sympathy on hearing of her being unnerved by the excitement through which they had passed. Well she knew that Field's serious condition had not a little to do with poor Esther's prostration, but that was knowledge never to be hinted at. Dade himself she did not wish to meet just now. He was too direct a questioner, and had said and looked things about Nanette that made her dread him. She knew that, however austere and commanding he might be when acting under his own convictions, he was abnormally susceptible to uxorial views, and the way to win the captain's sympathies or avert his censure, was to secure the kindly interest of his wife. Mrs. Hay knew that he had sent couriers off by the Rawlins road—a significant thing in itself—and that couriers had come in from the north with further news from Webb. She knew he had gone to the office, and would probably remain there until summoned for breakfast, and now was her time, for there was something further to be spoken of, and while gentle and civil, Mrs. Dade had not been receptive. It was evident to the trader's wife that her lord and master had made a mistake in leaving when he did. He knew the general was on the way. He knew there was that money business to be cleared up, yet she knew there were reasons why she *wanted* him away,—reasons hardest of all to plausibly explain. There were reasons, indeed, why she was glad Nanette was gone. All Fort Frayne was devoted to Esther Dade and, however unjustly, most of Fort Frayne,—men, women and children,—attributed Field's defection, as they chose to call it, to Nanette—Nanette who had set at naught her aunt's most ardent wishes, in even noticing Field at all. Money, education, everything she could give had been lavished on that girl, and now, instead of casting her net for that well-to-do and distinguished bachelor, the major, thereby assuring for herself the proud position of first lady of Fort Frayne, the wife of the commanding officer, Nanette had been deliberately throwing herself away at a beardless, moneyless second lieutenant, because he danced and rode well. Mrs. Hay did not blame Mrs. Dade at that moment for hating the girl, if

A DAUGHTER OF THE SIOUX

hate she did. She could have shaken her, hard and well, herself, yet was utterly nonplussed to find that Nanette cared next to nothing how badly Field was wounded. What she seemed to care to know was about the casualties among the Sioux, and, now that Stabber's village, the last living trace of it, old men, squaws, children, pappooses, ponies and puppies and other living creatures had, between two days, been whisked away to the hills, there were no more Indians close at hand to whisper information.

She was glad Nanette was gone, because Field, wounded and present, would have advantages over possible suitors absent on campaign—because all the women and a few of the men were now against her, and because from some vague, intangible symptoms, Mrs. Hay had satisfied herself that there was something in the wind Nanette was hiding even from her—her benefactress, her best friend, and it seemed like cold-blooded treachery. Hay had for two days been disturbed, nervous and unhappy, yet would not tell her why. He had been cross-questioning Pete, "Crapaud" and other employees, and searching about the premises in a way that excited curiosity and even resentment, for the explanation he gave was utterly inadequate. To satisfy her if possible, he had confided, as he said, the fact that certain money for which Lieutenant Field was accountable, had been stolen. The cash had been carefully placed in his old-fashioned safe; the missing money, therefore, had been taken while still virtually in his charge. "They might even suspect me," he said, which she knew would not be the case. "They forbade my speaking of it to anybody, but I simply had to tell you." She felt sure there was something he was concealing; something he

A DAUGHTER OF THE SIOUX

would not tell her; something concerning Nanette, therefore, because she so loved Nanette, he shrank from revealing what might wound her. Indeed, it was best that Nanette should go for the time, at least, but Mrs. Hay little dreamed that others would be saying—even this kindly, gentle woman before her—that Nanette should have stayed until certain strange things were thoroughly and satisfactorily explained.

But the moment she began, faltering not a little, to speak of matters at the post, as a means of leading up to Nanette—matters concerning Lieutenant Field and his financial affairs,—to her surprise Mrs. Dade gently uplifted her hand and voice. "I am going to ask you not to tell me, Mrs. Hay," said she. "Captain Dade has given me to understand there was something to be investigated, but preferred that I should not ask about it. Now, the general will be down in fifteen or twenty minutes. I suggest that we walk over the hospital and see how Mr. Field is getting on. We can talk, you know, as we go. Then you will breakfast with us. Indeed, may I not give you a cup of coffee now, Mrs. Hay?"

But Mrs. Hay said no. She had had coffee before coming. She would go and see if there was anything they could do for Field, and would try again to induce Mrs. Dade to listen to certain of her explanations.

But Mrs. Dade was silent and preoccupied. She was thinking of that story of Nanette's going, and wondering whether it could be true. She was wondering if Mrs. Hay knew the couriers had gone to recall Hay, and that if he and Nanette failed to return it might

A DAUGHTER OF THE SIOUX

mean trouble for both. She could accord to Mrs. Hay no confidences of her own, and had been compelled to decline to listen to those with which Mrs. Hay would have favored her. She was thinking of something still more perplexing. The general, as her husband finally told her, had asked first thing to see Hay, and later declared that he wished to talk with Mrs. Hay and see Nanette. Was it possible he knew anything of what she knew— that between Hay's household and Stabber's village there had been communication of some kind—that the first thing found in the Indian pouch brought home by Captain Blake, was a letter addressed in Nanette Flower's hand, and with it three card photographs, two of them of unmistakable Indians in civilized garb, and two letters, addressed, like hers, to Mr. Ralph Moreau,—one care of the Rev. Jasper Strong, Valentine, Nebraska, the other to the general delivery, Omaha?

Yes, that pouch brought in by Captain Blake had contained matter too weighty for one woman, wise as she was, to keep to herself. Mrs. Blake, with her husband's full consent, had summoned Mrs. Ray, soon after his departure on the trail of Webb, and told her of the strange discovery. They promptly decided there was only one thing to do with the letter;—hand or send it, unopened, to Miss Flower. Then, as Blake had had no time to examine further, they decided to search the pouch. There might be more letters in the same superscription.

But there were not. They found tobacco, beeswax, an empty flask that had contained whiskey, vaseline, Pond's Extract, salve, pigments, a few sheets of note paper, envelopes and pencil—odd things to find in the possession of a Sioux—a burning glass, matches, some quinine pills, cigars, odds and ends of little consequence, and those letters addressed to R. Moreau. The first one they had already decided should go to Miss Flower. The others, they thought, should be handed unopened to the commanding officer. They might contain important information, now that the Sioux were at war and that Ralph Moreau had turned out probably to be a real personage. But first they would consult Mrs. Dade. They had done so the very evening of Blake's departure, even as he, long miles away, was telling Kennedy his Irish heart was safe from the designs of one blood-thirsty Sioux; and Mrs. Dade had agreed with them that Nanette's letter should be sent to her forthwith, and that, as Captain Blake had brought it in, the duty of returning the letter devolved upon his wife.

And so, after much thought and consultation, a little note was written, saying nothing about the other contents or about the pouch itself. "Dear Miss Flower:" it read. "The enclosed was found by Captain Blake some time this morning. He had no time to deliver it in person. Yours sincerely. N. B. Blake."

She would enter into no explanation and would say nothing of the consultation. She could not bring herself to sign her name as usually she signed it, Nannie Bryan Blake. She had, as any man or woman would have had, a consuming desire to know what Miss Flower could be writing to a Mr. Moreau, whose correspondence turned up in this remarkable way, in the pouch of a painted Sioux. But she and they deemed it entirely needless to assure Miss Flower no alien eye had peered into the mysterious pages. (It might have resulted in marvellous developments if Miss Flower thought they had.) Note and enclosure were sent first thing next morning by the trusty hand of Master Sanford Ray, himself, and by him delivered in person to Miss Flower, who met him at the trader's gate. She took it, he said; and smiled, and thanked him charmingly before she opened it. She was coming out for her customary walk at the hour of guard mounting, but the next thing he knew she had "scooted" indoors again.

And from that moment Miss Flower had not been seen.

All this was Mrs. Dade revolving in mind as she walked pityingly by the side of the troubled woman, only vaguely listening to her flow of words. They had thought to be admitted to the little room in which the wounded officer lay, but as they tiptoed into the wide, airy hall and looked over the long vista of pink-striped coverlets in the big ward beyond, the doctor himself appeared at the entrance and barred the way.

"Is there nothing we can do?" asked Mrs. Dade, with tears in her voice. "Is he—so much worse?"

"Nothing can be done just now," answered Waller, gravely. "He has had high fever during the night—has been wakeful and flighty again. I—should rather no one entered just now."

And then they noted that even the steward who had been with poor Field was now hovering about the door of the dispensary and that only Dr. Waller remained within the room. "I am

A DAUGHTER OF THE SIOUX

hoping to get him to sleep again presently," said he. "And when he is mending there will be a host of things for you both to do."

But that mending seemed many a day off, and Mrs. Hay, poor woman, had graver cares of her own before the setting sun. Avoiding the possibility of meeting the general just now, and finding Mrs. Dade both silent and constrained at mention of her niece's name, the trader's wife went straightway homeward from the hospital, and did not even see the post commander hurrying from his office, with an open despatch in his hand. But by this time the chief and his faithful aide were out on the veranda, surrounded by anxious wives and daughters, many of whom had been earnestly bothering the doctor at the hospital before going to breakfast. Dade much wished them away, though the news brought in by night riders was both stirring and cheery. The Indians had flitted away from Webb's front, and he counted on reaching and rescuing the Dry Fork party within six hours from the time the courier started. They might expect the good news during the afternoon of Thursday. Scouts and flankers reported finding *travois* and pony tracks leading westward from the scene of Ray's fierce battle, indicating that the Indians had carried their dead and wounded into the fastnesses of the southern slopes of the Big Horn, and that their punishment had been heavy. Among the chiefs killed or seriously wounded was this new, vehement leader whom Captains Blake and Ray thought might be Red Fox, who was so truculent at the Black Hills conference the previous year. Certain of the men, however, who had seen Red Fox at that time expressed doubts. Lieutenant Field, said Webb, had seen him, and could probably say.

A DAUGHTER OF THE SIOUX

Over this despatch the general pondered gravely. "From what I know of Red Fox," said he, "I should think him a leader of the Sitting Bull type,—a shrew, intriguing, mischief-making fellow, a sort of Sioux walking delegate, not a battle leader; but according to Blake and Ray this new man is a fighter."

Then Mrs. Dade came out and bore the general off to breakfast, and during breakfast the chief was much preoccupied. Mrs. Dade and the aide-de-camp chatted on social matters. The general exchanged an occasional word with his host and hostess, and finally surprised neither of them, when breakfast was over and he had consumed the last of his glass of hot water, by saying to his staff officer, "I should like to see Mrs. Hay a few minutes, if possible. We'll walk round there first. Then—let the team be ready at ten o'clock."

But the team, although ready, did not start northward at ten, and the general, though he saw Mrs. Hay, had no speech with her upon the important matters uppermost in his mind during the earlier hours of the day. He found that good lady in a state of wild excitement and alarm. One of the two outriders who had started with her husband and niece at dawn, was mounted on a dun-colored cow pony, with white face and feet. One of the two troopers sent by Dade to overtake and bring them back, was turning a blown and exhausted horse over to the care of Hay's stablemen, as he briefly told his story to the wild-eyed, well nigh distracted woman. Six miles up stream, he said, they had come suddenly upon a dun-colored cow pony, dead in his tracks, with white feet in air and white muzzle bathed in blood; bridle, saddle

A DAUGHTER OF THE SIOUX

and rider gone; signs of struggle in places—but no signs of the party, the team and wagon, anywhere.

"And no cavalry to send out after them!" said Dade, when he reached the spot. Old Crabb was called at once, and mustered four semi-invalided troopers. The infantry supplied half a dozen stout riders and, with a mixed escort, the general, accompanied by Dade and the aide-de-camp, drove swiftly to the scene. Six miles away they found the dead pony. Seven miles away they encountered the second trooper, coming back. He had followed the trail of the four mule team as far as yonder point, said he, and there was met by half a dozen shots from unseen foe, and so rode back out of range. But Dade threw his men forward as skirmishers; found no living soul either at the point or on the banks of the rocky ford beyond; but, in the shallows, close to the shore, lay the body of the second outrider, shot and scalped. In a clump of willows lay another body, that of a pinto pony, hardly cold, while the soft, sandy shores were cut by dozens of hoof tracks—shoeless. The tracks of the mules and wagon lay straight away across the stream bed—up the opposite bank and out on the northward-sweeping bench beyond. Hay's famous four, and well-known wagon, contents and all, therefore, had been spirited away, not toward the haunts of the road agents in the mountains of the Medicine Bow, but to those of the sovereign Sioux in the fastnesses of the storied Big Horn.

A DAUGHTER OF THE SIOUX

CHAPTER XVI

NIGHT PROWLING AT FRAYNE

In the full of the September moon the war-bands of the Sioux had defied agents and peace chiefs, commissioners and soldiers, and started their wild campaign in northern Wyoming. In the full of the October moon the big chief of the whites had swept the last vestige of their warriors from the plains, and followed their bloody trails into the heart of the mountains, all his cavalry and much of his foot force being needed for the work in hand. Not until November, therefore, when the ice bridge spanned the still reaches of the Platte, and the snow lay deep in the brakes and *coulées*, did the foremost of the homeward-bound commands come in view of old Fort Frayne, and meantime very remarkable things had occurred, and it was to a very different, if only temporary, post commander that Sandy Ray reported them as "sighted." Even brave old Dade had been summoned to the front, with all his men, and in their place had come from distant posts in Kansas other troops to occupy the vacant quarters and strive to feel at home in strange surroundings.

A man of austere mold was the new major,—one of the old Covenanter type, who would march to battle shouting hymn tunes, and to Christmas and Thanksgiving chanting doleful lays. He hailed, indeed, from old Puritan stock; had been a pillar in the village church in days before the great war, and emulated Stonewall Jackson in his piety, if he did not in martial prowess. Backed by local, and by no means secular, influences he had risen in the course of the four years' war from a junior lieutenancy to the grade of second in command of his far eastern regiment; had rendered faithful services in command of convalescent camps and the like, but developed none of that vain ambition which prompts the seeking of "the bubble reputation" at the cannon's mouth. All he ever knew of Southern men in ante-bellum days was what he heard from the lips of inspired orators or read from the pens of very earnest anti-slavery editors. Through lack of opportunity he had met no Southerner before the war, and carried his stanch, Calvinistic prejudices to such extent that he seemed to shrink from closer contact even then. The war was holy. The hand of the Lord would surely smite the slave-holding arch rebel, which was perhaps why the Covenanter thought it work of supererogation to raise his own. He finished as he began the war, in the unalterable conviction that the Southern President, his cabinet and all his leading officers should be hung, and their lands confiscated to the state—or its representatives. He had been given a commission in the army when such things were not hard to get—at the reorganization in '66, had been stationed in a Ku Klux district all one winter and in a sanitarium most of the year that followed. He thought the nation on the highroad to hell when it failed to impeach the President of high crimes and misdemeanors, and sent Hancock to harmonize matters in Louisiana. He was sure of it when the son of a Southerner, who had openly flouted him, was sent to West Point. He retained these radical views even unto the twentieth anniversary of the great surrender; and, while devoutly praying for forgiveness of his own sins, could never seem to forgive those whose lot had been cast with the South. He was utterly nonplussed when told that

A DAUGHTER OF THE SIOUX

the young officer, languishing in hospital on his arrival, was the son of a distinguished major-general of the Confederate Army, and he planned for the father a most frigid greeting, until reminded that the former major-general was now a member of Congress and of the committee on military affairs. Then it became his duty to overlook the past.

He had not entered Field's little room, even when inspecting hospital (Flint was forever inspecting something or other)—the doctor's assurance that, though feeble, his patient was doing quite well, was all sufficient. He had thought to greet the former Confederate, a sorely anxious father, with grave and distant civility, as an avowed and doubtless unregenerate enemy of that sacred flag; but, as has been said, that was before it was pointed out to him that this was the Honorable M. C. from the Pelican State, now prominent as a member of the House Committee on Military Affairs. Motherless and sister-less was the wounded boy, yet gentle and almost caressing hands had blessed his pillow and helped to drive fever and delirium to the winds. It was twelve days after they brought him back to Frayne before the father could hope to reach him, coming post haste, too; but by that time the lad was propped on his pillows, weak, sorrowing and sorely troubled, none the less so because there was no one now to whom he could say *why*.

The men whom he knew and trusted were all away on campaign, all save the veteran post surgeon, whom hitherto he had felt he hardly knew at all. The women whom he had best known and trusted were still present at the post. Mrs. Ray and Mrs. Blake

A DAUGHTER OF THE SIOUX

had been his friends, frank, cordial and sincere up to the week of his return from Laramie and his sudden and overwhelming infatuation for Nanette Flower. Then they had seemed to hold aloof, to greet him only with courtesy, and to eye him with unspoken reproach. The woman at Fort Frayne to whom he most looked up was Mrs. Dade, and now Mrs. Dade seemed alienated utterly. She had been to inquire for him frequently, said his attendant, when he was so racked with fever. So had others, and they sent him now jellies and similar delicacies, but came no more in person—just yet at least—but he did not know the doctor so desired. Field knew that his father, after the long, long journey from the distant South, was now close at hand,—would be with him within a few hours, and even with Ray's warm words of praise still ringing in his ears, the young soldier was looking to that father's coming almost with distress. It was through God's mercy and the wisdom of the old surgeon that no word, as yet, had been whispered to him of the discovery made when the money packages were opened—of the tragic fate that had, possibly, befallen Bill Hay and Miss Flower.

That a large sum of money was missing, and that Field was the accountable officer, was already whispered about the garrison. The fact that four officers and Mr. Hay were aware of it in the first place, and the latter had told it to his wife, was fatal to entire secrecy. But, in the horror and excitement that prevailed when the details of the later tragedy were noised about the post, this minor incident had been almost forgotten.

A DAUGHTER OF THE SIOUX

The disappearance of Hay and his brilliant, beautiful niece, however, was not to be forgotten for a moment, day or night, despite the fact that Mrs. Hay, who had been almost crazed with dread and terror when first informed there had been a "hold-up," rallied almost immediately, and took heart and hope when it became apparent that Indians, not white men, were the captors.

"The Sioux would never harm a hair of his head," she proudly declared. "He has been their friend for half a century." Nor had she fears for Nanette. The Sioux would harm nobody her husband sought to protect. When it was pointed out to her that they had harmed the guards,—that one of them was found shot dead and scalped at the shores of the Platte, and the other, poor fellow, had crawled off among the rocks and bled to death within gunshot of the scene,—Mrs. Hay said they must have first shown fight and shot some of the Sioux, for all the Indians knew Mr. Hay's wagon. Then why, asked Fort Frayne, had they molested him—and his?

The general had had to leave for the front without seeing Mrs. Hay. More than ever was it necessary that he should be afield, for this exploit showed that some of the Sioux, at least, had cut loose from the main body and had circled back toward the Platte—Stabber's people in all probability. So, sending Crabb and his little squad across the river to follow a few miles, at least, the trail of the wagon and its captors, and ascertain, if possible, whither it had gone, he hurried back to Frayne; sent messengers by the Laramie road to speed the cavalry, and orders to the colonel to send two troops at once to rescue Hay and his niece; sent wires

A DAUGHTER OF THE SIOUX

calling for a few reinforcements, and was off on the way to Beecher, guarded by a handful of sturdy "doughboys" in ambulances, before ever the body of the second victim was found.

And then, little by little, it transpired that this mysterious war party, venturing to the south bank of the Platte, did not exceed half a dozen braves. Crabb got back in thirty-six hours, with five exhausted men. They had followed the wheel tracks over the open prairie and into the foothills far to the Northwest, emboldened by the evidence of there being but few ponies in the original bandit escort. But, by four in the afternoon, they got among the breaks and ravines and, first thing they knew, among the Indians, for zip came the bullets and down went two horses, and they had to dismount and fight to stand off possible swarms, and, though owning they had seen no Indians, they had proof of having felt them, and were warranted in pushing no further. After dark they began their slow retreat and here they were.

And for seven days that was the last heard, by the garrison, at least, of these most recent captives of the Sioux. Gentle and sympathetic women, however, who called on Mrs. Hay, were prompt to note that though unnerved, unstrung, distressed, she declared again and again her faith that the Indians would never really harm her husband. They might hold him and Nanette as hostages for ransom. They might take for their own purposes his wagon, his mules and that store of money, but his life was safe, yes, and Nanette's too. Of this she was so confident that people began to wonder whether she had not received some assurance to that effect, and when Pete, the stable boy driver, turned up at the end of the first week with a cock-and-bull story about having stolen an Indian pony and shot his way from the midst of the Sioux away up on No Wood Creek, on the west side of the hills, and having ridden by night and hidden by day until he got back to the Platte and Frayne, people felt sure of it. Pete could talk Sioux better than he could jabber English. He declared the Indians were in the hills by thousands, and were going to take Hay and the young lady away off somewhere to be held for safe keeping. He said the two troops that, never even halting at Frayne, had pushed out on the trail, would only get into trouble if they tried to enter the hills from the South, and that they would never get the captives, wherein Pete was right, for away out among the spurs and gorges of the range, fifty miles from Frayne, the pursuers came upon the wreck of the wagon at the foot of an acclivity, up which a force of Sioux had gone in single file. Many warriors it would seem, however, must have joined the party on the way, and from here,—where with the wagon was found Hay's stout box, bereft of its contents,—in four different directions the pony tracks of little parties crossed or climbed the spurs, and which way the captives had been taken, Captain Billings, the commander, could not determine. What the Sioux hoped he might do was divide his force into four detachments and send one on each trail. Then they could fall upon them, one by one, and slay them at their leisure. Billings saw the game, however, and was not to be caught. He knew Bill Hay, his past and his popularity among the red men. He knew that if they meant to kill him at all they would not have taken the trouble to

A DAUGHTER OF THE SIOUX

cart him fifty miles beforehand. He dropped the stern chase then and there, and on the following day skirted the foothills away to the east and, circling round to the breaks of the Powder as he reached the open country, struck and hard hit a scouting band of Sioux, and joined the general three days later, when most he was needed, near the log palisades of old Fort Beecher.

Then there had been more or less of mysterious coming and going among the halfbreed hangers-on about the trader's store, and these were things the new post commander knew not how to interpret, even when informed of them. He saw Mrs. Hay but once or twice. He moved into the quarters of Major Webb, possessing himself, until his own should arrive, of such of the major's belongings as the vigilance of Mistress McGann would suffer. He stationed big guards from his two small companies about the post, and started more hard swearing among his own men, for "getting only two nights in bed," than had been heard at Frayne in long months of less pious post commandership. He strove to make himself agreeable to the ladies, left lamenting for their lords, but as luck would have it, fell foremost into the clutches of the quartermaster's wife, the dominant and unterrified Wilkins.

Just what prompted that energetic and, in many ways, estimable woman, to take the new major into close communion, and tell him not only what she knew, but what she thought, about all manner of matters at the post, can never be justly determined. But within the first few days of his coming, and on the eve of the arrival of General Field, Major Flint was in possession of the story of how devoted young Field had been to Esther Dade, and how cruelly he had jilted her for the brilliant Miss Flower, "her that was gone with the Sioux." The differences between her stout, veteran liege and the smooth-faced stripling had given her text to start with. The story of the money lost had filtered from her lips, and finally that of other peccadilloes, attributable to the young post adjutant, whom, as she said, "The meejor had to rejuice and sind to the front all along of his doin's in gar'son." Dade was gone. There was no man save Wilkins to whom Major Flint felt that he could appeal for confirmation or denial of these stories. Dr. Waller was his senior in the service by ten years at least, and a type of the old-time officer and gentleman of whom such as Flint stood ever in awe. He preferred, therefore, as he thought, to keep the doctor at a distance, to make him feel the immensity of his, the post commander's, station, and so, as Wilkins dare not disavow the sayings of his wife, even had he been so minded, the stories stood.

Flint was thinking of them this very evening when Dr. Waller, happening to meet him on his way from hospital briefly said that General Field should be with them on the morrow. "He leaves Rock Creek to-night, having hired transportation there. I had hoped our lad might be in better spirits by this time."

The major answered vaguely. How could a lad with all these sins upon his soul be in anything but low spirits? Here was a brand to be snatched from the burning, a youth whom prompt, stern measures might redeem and restore, one who should be taught the error of his ways forthwith; only, the coming of the member

A DAUGHTER OF THE SIOUX

of the Military Committee of the House of Representatives might make the process embarrassing. There were other ways, therefore and however, in which this valuable information in the major's possession might be put to use, and of these was the major thinking, more than of the condition of the wounded lad, physical or spiritual, as homeward through the gloaming he wended his way.

Might it not be well to wait until this important and influential personage had reached the post before proceeding further? Might it not be well, confidentially and gradually, as it were, to permit the Honorable M. C. to know that grave irregularities had occurred?—that up to this moment the complete knowledge thereof was locked in the breast of the present post commander?—that the suppression or presentation of the facts depended solely upon that post commander? and then if the member of the House Committee on Military Affairs proved receptive, appreciative, in fact responsive, might not the ends of justice better be subserved by leaving to the parent the duty of personally and privately correcting the son? and, in consideration of the post commander's wisdom and continence, pledging the influence of the Military Committee to certain delectable ends in the major's behalf? Long had Flint had his eye on a certain desirable berth in the distant East—at the national capitol in fact—but never yet had he found statesman or soldier inclined to further his desire. That night the major bade Mr. and Mrs. Wilkins hold their peace as to Field's peccadilloes until further leave was given them to speak. That night the major, calling at Captain Dade's, was concerned to hear that Mrs. Dade was not

A DAUGHTER OF THE SIOUX

at home. "Gone over to the hospital with Mrs. Blake and the doctor," was the explanation, and these gentle-hearted women, it seems, were striving to do something to rouse the lad from the slough of despond which had engulfed him. That night "Pink" Marble, Hay's faithful book-keeper and clerk for many a year, a one-armed veteran of the civil war, calling, as was his invariable custom when the trader was absent, to leave the keys of the safe and desks with Mrs. Hay, was surprised to find her in a flood of tears, for which she declined all explanation; yet the sight of Pete, the half breed, slouching away toward the stables as Marble closed the gate, more than suggested cause, for "Pink" had long disapproved of that young man. That night Crapaud, the other stableman, had scandalized Jerry Sullivan, the bar-keeper, and old McGann, Webb's Hibernian major domo, by interrupting their game of Old Sledge with a demand for a quart of whiskey on top of all that he had obviously and surreptitiously been drinking, and by further indulging in furious threats, in a sputtering mixture of Dakota French and French Dakota, when summarily kicked out. That night, late as twelve o'clock, Mrs. Ray, aroused by the infantile demands of the fourth of the olive branches, and further disturbed by the suspicious growlings and challenge of old Tonto, Blake's veteran mastiff, peeped from the second story window and plainly saw two forms in soldier overcoats at the back fence, and wondered what the sentries found about Blake's quarters to require so much attention. Then she became aware of a third form, rifle-bearing, and slowly pacing the curving line of the bluff—the sentry beyond doubt. Who, then, were these others who had now totally disappeared? She thought to speak of it to Nannie in the morning, and then thought not. There were reasons why nervous alarm of any kind were best averted then from Mrs. Blake. But there came reason speedily why Mrs. Ray could not forget it.

And that night, later still, along toward four o'clock, the persistent clicking of the telegraph instrument at the adjutant's office caught the ear of the sentry, who in time stirred up the operator, and a "rush" message was later thrust into the hand of Major Flint, demolishing a day-old castle in the air.

From Rock Creek, Wyoming,

October 23, 188—. 9:15 P. M.

Commanding   Officer,   Fort   Frayne, *via Fort Laramie.*

Stage capsized Crook Cañon. General Field seriously injured. Have wired Omaha.

(Signed)

Warner,

Commanding Camp.

CHAPTER XVII

A RIFLED DESK

Events moved swiftly in the week that followed. Particulars of the accident to General Field, however, were slow in reaching Fort Frayne; and, to the feverish unrest and mental trouble of the son, was now added a feverish anxiety on the father's account that so complicated the situation as to give Dr. Waller grave cause for alarm. Then it was that, ignoring every possible thought of misbehavior on the part of the young officer toward the gentle girl so dear to them, not only Mrs. Blake and Mrs. Ray, but Mrs. Dade herself, insisted on being made of use,—insisted on being permitted to go to his bedside and there to minister, as only women can, to the suffering and distressed. Waller thought it over and succumbed. The lad was no longer delirious, at least, and if he revealed anything of what was uppermost in his mind it would be a conscious and voluntary revelation. There were some things he had said and that Waller alone had heard, the good old doctor wished were known to certain others of the garrison, and to no one more than Mrs. Dade; and so the prohibition against their visiting the wounded lad was withdrawn, and not only these, but other women, sympathetically attracted, were given the necessary authority.

There was other reason for this. From the commanding officer of the supply camp at Rock Springs had come, finally, a letter that was full of foreboding. General Field, it said, was sorely injured and might not survive. If the department commander had only been at Omaha or Cheyenne, as the anxious father hastened to reach his son, the mishap would never have occurred. The general would gladly have seen to it that suitable transportation from the railway to Frayne was afforded his old-time comrade. But, in his absence, Field shrank from appealing to anyone else, and, through the train conductor, wired ahead to Rock Creek for a stout four-mule team and wagon, with a capable driver. The conductor assured him that such things were to be had for money, and that everything would be in readiness on his arrival. Team, wagon and driver certainly were on hand, but the team looked rickety, so did the wagon, so did the driver, who had obviously been priming for the occasion. It was this rig or nothing, however; and, in spite of a courteous remonstrance from the two officers at the supply camp, who saw and condemned the "outfit," General Field started on time and returned on an improvised trestle three hours later. The "outfit" had been tumbled over a ledge into a rocky creek bottom, and with disastrous results to all concerned except the one who deserved it most—the driver. The ways of Providence are indeed inscrutable.

A surgeon had been sent from Fort Russell, and his report was such that Waller would not let it go in full to his patient. They had carried the old soldier back to camp, and such aid as could be given by the rude hands of untaught men was all he had for nearly twenty-four hours, and his suffering had been great. Internal injuries, it was feared, had been sustained, and at his advanced age that was something almost fatal. No wonder Waller was worried. Then Flint took alarm at other troubles closer at hand. Up to this year he had been mercifully spared all personal contact with our Indian wards, and when he was told by his

A DAUGHTER OF THE SIOUX

sentries that twice in succession night riders had been heard on the westward "bench," and pony tracks in abundance had been found at the upper ford—the site of Stabber's village—and that others still were to be seen in the soft ground not far from Hay's corral, the major was more than startled. At this stage of the proceedings, Sergeant Crabb of the Cavalry was the most experienced Indian fighter left at the post. Crabb was sent for, and unflinchingly gave his views. The Sioux had probably scattered before the squadrons sent after them from the north; had fled into the hills and, in small bands probably, were now raiding down toward the Platte, well knowing there were few soldiers left to defend Fort Frayne, and no cavalry were there to chase them.

"What brings them here? What do they hope to get or gain?" asked Flint.

"I don't know, sir," answered Crabb. "But this I do know, they are after something and expect to get it. If I might make so bold, sir, I think the major ought to keep an eye on them blasted halfbreeds at Hay's."

It set Flint to serious thinking. Pete and Crapaud, paid henchmen of the trader, had been taking advantage of their employer's absence and celebrating after the manner of their kind. One of his officers, new like himself to the neighborhood and to the Indians, had had encounter with the two that rubbed his commissioned fur the wrong way. A sentry, in discharge of his duty, had warned them one evening away from the rear gate of a bachelor den, along officers' row, and had been told to go to

A DAUGHTER OF THE SIOUX

sheol, or words to that effect. They had more business there than he had, said they, and, under the potent sway of "inspiring bold John Barleycorn" had not even abated their position when the officer-of-the-day happened along. They virtually damned and defied him, too.

The officer-of-the-day reported to the commanding officer, and that officer called on Mrs. Hay to tell her he should order the culprits off the reservation if they were not better behaved. Mrs. Hay, so said the servant, was feeling far from well and had to ask to be excused, when who should appear but that ministering angel Mrs. Dade herself, and Mrs. Dade undertook to tell Mrs. Hay of the misconduct of the men, even when assuring Major Flint she feared it was a matter in which Mrs. Hay was powerless. They were afraid of Hay, but not of her. Hearing of Mrs. Hay's illness, Mrs. Dade and other women had come to visit and console her, but there were very few whom she would now consent to see. Even though confident no bodily harm would befall her husband or her niece, Mrs. Hay was evidently sore disturbed about something. Failing to see her, Major Flint sent for the bartender and clerk, and bade them say where these truculent, semi-savage bacchanals got their whiskey, and both men promptly and confidently declared it wasn't at the store. Neither of them would give or sell to either halfbreed a drop, and old Wilkins stood sponsor for the integrity of the affiants, both of whom he had known for years and both of whom intimated that the two specimens had no need to be begging, buying or stealing whiskey, when Bill Hay's private cellar held more than enough to fill the whole Sioux nation. "Moreover," said Pink Marble,

A DAUGHTER OF THE SIOUX

"they've got the run of the stables now the old man's away, and there isn't a night some of those horses ain't out." When Flint said that was something Mrs. Hay ought to know, Pink Marble replied that was something Mrs. Hay did know, unless she refused to believe the evidence of her own senses as well as his, and Pink thought it high time our fellows in the field had recaptured Hay and fetched him home. If it wasn't done mighty soon he, Pink, wouldn't be answerable for what might happen at the post.

All the more anxious did this make Flint. He decided that the exigencies of the case warranted his putting a sentry over Hay's stable, with orders to permit no horse to be taken out except by an order from him, and Crabb took him and showed him, two days later, the tracks of two horses going and coming in the soft earth in front of a narrow side door that led to the corral. Flint had this door padlocked at once and Wilkins took the key, and that night was surprised by a note from Mrs. Hay.

"The stablemen complain that the sentries will not let them take the horses out even for water and exercise, which has never been the case before," and Mrs. Hay begged that the restriction might be removed. Indeed, if Major Flint would remove the sentry, she would assume all responsibility for loss or damage. The men had been with Mr. Hay, she said, for six years and never had been interfered with before, and they were sensitive and hurt and would quit work, they said, if further molested. Then there would be nobody to take their place and the stock would suffer.

A DAUGHTER OF THE SIOUX

In point of fact, Mrs. Hay was pleading for the very men against whom the other employés claimed to have warned her—these two halfbreeds who had defied his sentries,—and Flint's anxieties materially increased. It taxed all his stock of personal piety, and strengthened the belief he was beginning to harbor, that Mrs. Hay had some use for the horses at night—some sojourners in the neighborhood with whom she must communicate, and who could they be but Sioux?

Then Mistress McGann, sound sleeper that she used to be, declared to the temporary post commander, as he was, and temporary lodger as she considered him, that things "was goin' on about the post she'd never heard the likes of before, and that the meejor would never put up with a minute." When Mrs. McGann said "the meejor" she meant not Flint, but his predecessor. There was but one major in her world,—the one she treated like a minor. Being a soldier's wife, however, she knew the deference due to the commanding officer, even though she did not choose to show it, and when bidden to say her say and tell what things "was goin' on" Mistress McGann asseverated, with the asperity of a woman who has had to put her husband to bed two nights running, that the time had never been before that he was so drunk he didn't know his way home, and so got into the back of the bachelor quarters instead of his own. "And to think av his bein' propped up at his own gate by a lousy, frog-eatin' half Frinchman, half salvage!" Yet, when investigated, this proved to be the case, and the further question arose, where did McGann get his whiskey? A faithful, loyal devoted old servitor was McGann, yet Webb, as we have seen, had ever to watch his whiskey carefully lest the Irishman should see it, and seeing taste, and tasting fall. The store had orders from Mrs. McGann, countersigned by Webb, to the effect that her husband was never to have a drop. Flint was a teetotaller himself, and noted without a shadow of disapprobation that the decanters on the sideboard were both empty the very day he took possession, also that the cupboard was securely locked. Mrs. McGann was sure her liege got no liquor there nor at the store, and his confused statement that it was given him by "fellers at the stables," was treated with scorn. McGann then was still under marital surveillance and official displeasure the day after Mrs. McGann's revelations, with unexplained iniquities to answer for when his head cleared and his legs resumed their functions. But by that time other matters were brought to light that laid still further accusation at his door. With the consent of Dr. Waller, Lieutenant Field had been allowed to send an attendant for his desk. There were letters, he said, he greatly wished to see and answer, and Mrs. Ray had been so kind as to offer to act as his amanuensis. The attendant went with the key and came back with a scared face. Somebody, he said, had been there before him.

They did not tell Field this at the time. The doctor went at once with the messenger, and in five minutes had taken in the situation. Field's rooms had been entered and probably robbed. There was only one other occupant of the desolate set that so recently had rung to the music of so many glad young voices. Of the garrison proper at Frayne all the cavalry officers except Wilkins were away at the front; all the infantry officers, five in number, were also up along the Big Horn. The four who had

A DAUGHTER OF THE SIOUX

come with Flint were strangers to the post, but Herron, who had been a classmate of Ross at the Point, moved into his room and took the responsibility of introducing the contract doctor, who came with them, into the quarters at the front of the house on the second floor. These rooms had been left open and unlocked. There was nothing, said the lawful occupant, worth stealing, which was probably true; but Field had bolted, inside, the door of his sleeping room; locked the hall door of his living room and taken the key with him when he rode with Ray. The doctor looked over the rooms a moment; then sent for Wilkins, the post quartermaster, who came in a huff at being disturbed at lunch. Field had been rather particular about his belongings. His uniforms always hung on certain pegs in the plain wooden wardrobe. The drawers of his bureau were generally arranged like the clothes press of cadet days, as though for inspection, but now coats, blouses, dressingsack and smoking jacket hung with pockets turned inside out or flung about the bed and floor. Trousers had been treated with like contempt. The bureau looked like what sailors used to call a "hurrah's nest," and a writing desk, brass-bound and of solid make, that stood on a table by a front window, had been forcibly wrenched open, and its contents were tossed about the floor. A larger desk,—a wooden field desk—stood upon a trestle across the room, and this, too, had been ransacked. Just what was missing only one man could tell. Just how they entered was patent to all—through a glazed window between the bed-room and the now unused dining room beyond. Just who were the housebreakers no man present could say; but Mistress McGann that afternoon

A DAUGHTER OF THE SIOUX

communicated her suspicion to her sore-headed spouse, and did it boldly and with the aid of a broomstick. "It's all along," she said, "av your shtoopin' to dhrink wid them low lived salvages at Hay's. Now, what d'ye know about this?"

But McGann swore piously he knew nothing "barrin' that Pete and Crapaud had some good liquor one night—dear knows when it was—an' I helped 'em dhrink your health,—an' when 'twas gone, and more was wanted, sure Pete said he'd taken a demijohn to the lieutenant's, with Mr. Hay's compliments, the day before he left for the front, and sure he couldn't have drunk all av it, and if the back dure was open Pete would inquire anyhow."

That was all Michael remembered or felt warranted in revealing, for stoutly he declared his and their innocence of having burglariously entered any premises, let alone the lieutenant's. "Sure they'd bite their own noses off fur him," said Mike, which impossible feat attested the full measure of halfbreed devotion. Mistress McGann decided to make further investigation before saying anything to anybody; but, before the dawn of another day, matters took such shape that fear of sorrowful consequences, involving even Michael, set a ban on her impulse to speak. Field, it seems, had been at last induced to sleep some hours that evening, and it was nearly twelve when he awoke and saw his desk on a table near the window. The attendant was nodding in an easy chair; and, just as the young officer determined to rouse him, Mrs. Dade, with the doctor, appeared on tiptoe at the doorway. For a few minutes they kept him interested in letters

A DAUGHTER OF THE SIOUX

and reports concerning his father's condition, the gravity of which, however, was still withheld from him. Then there were reports from Tongue River, brought in by courier, that had to be told him. But after a while he would be no longer denied. He demanded to see his desk and his letters.

At a sign from the doctor, the attendant raised it from the table and bore it to the bed. "I found things in some confusion in your quarters, Field," said Waller, by way of preparation, "and I probably haven't arranged the letters as you would if you had had time. They were lying about loosely—"

But he got no further. Field had started up and was leaning on one elbow. The other arm was outstretched. "What do you mean?" he cried. "The desk hasn't been *opened?*"

Too evidently, however, it had been, and in an instant Field had pulled a brass pin that held in place a little drawer. It popped part way out, and with trembling hands he drew it forth—empty.

Before he could speak Mrs. Dade suddenly held up her hand in signal for silence, her face paling at the instant. There was a rush of slippered feet through the corridor, a hum of excited voices, and both Dr. Waller and the attendant darted for the door.

Outside, in the faint starlight, sound of commotion came from the direction of the guard-house,—of swift footfalls from far across the parade, of the vitreous jar of windows hastily raised. Two or three lights popped suddenly into view along the dark line of officers' quarters, and Waller's voice, with a ring of authority unusual to him, halted a running corporal of the guard.

A DAUGHTER OF THE SIOUX

"What is it?" demanded he.

"I don't know, sir," was the soldier's answer. "There was an awful scream from the end quarters—Captain Ray's, sir." Then on he went again.

And then came the crack, crack of a pistol.

A DAUGHTER OF THE SIOUX

CHAPTER XVIII

BURGLARY AT BLAKE'S

The doctor started at the heels of the corporal, but was distanced long before he reached the scene. The sergeant of the guard was hammering on the front door of Blake's quarters; but, before the summons was answered from within, Mrs. Ray, in long, loose wrapper, came hurrying forth from her own—the adjoining—hallway. Her face was white with dread. "It is I, Nannie. Let us in," she cried, and the door was opened by a terrified servant, as the doctor came panting up the steps. Together he and Mrs. Ray hurried in. "Robbers!" gasped the servant girl—"Gone—the back way!" and collapsed on the stairs. Sergeant and corporal both tore around to the west side and out of the rear gate. Not a sign of fugitives could they see, and, what was worse, not a sign of sentry. Number 5, of the third relief, should at that moment have been pacing the edge of the bluff in rear of the northernmost quarters, and yet might be around toward the flagstaff. "Find Number 5," were the sergeant's orders, and back he hurried to the house, not knowing what to expect. By that time others of the guard had got there and the officer-of-the-day was coming,—the clink of his sword could be heard down the road,—and more windows were uplifted and more voices were begging for information, and then came Mrs. Dade, breathless but calm.

Within doors she found the doctor ministering to a stout female who seemed to have gone off in an improvised swoon—Mrs. Blake's imported cook. Up the stairs, to her own room again, Mrs. Blake was being led by Marion Ray's encircling arm. Three

A DAUGHTER OF THE SIOUX

women were speedily closeted there, for Mrs. Dade was like an elder sister to these two sworn friends, and, not until Mrs. Dade and they were ready, did that lady descend the stairs and communicate the facts to the excited gathering in the parlor, and they in turn to those on the porch in front. By this time Flint himself, with the poet quartermaster, was on hand, and all Fort Frayne seemed to rouse, and Mrs. Gregg had come with Mrs. Wilkins, and these two had relieved the doctor of the care of the cook, now talking volubly; and, partly through her revelations, but mainly through the more coherent statements of Mrs. Dade, were the facts made public. Margaret, the cook, had a room to herself on the ground floor adjoining her kitchen. Belle, the maid, had been given the second floor back, in order to be near to her young mistress. Bitzer, the Blakes' man-of-all-work,—like McGann, a discharged soldier,—slept in the basement at the back of the house, and there was he found, blinking, bewildered and only with difficulty aroused from stupor by a wrathful sergeant. The cook's story, in brief, was that she was awakened by Mrs. Blake's voice at her door and, thinking Belle was sick, she jumped up and found Mrs. Blake in her wrapper, asking was she, Margaret, up stairs a moment before. Then Mrs. Blake, with her candle, went into the dining room, and out jumped a man in his stocking feet from the captain's den across the hall, and knocked over Mrs. Blake and the light, and made for her, the cook; whereat she screamed and slammed her door in his face, and that was really all she knew about it.

But Mrs. Blake knew more. Awakened by some strange consciousness of stealthy movement about the house, she called

A DAUGHTER OF THE SIOUX

Belle by name, thinking possibly the girl might be ill and seeking medicine. There was sound of more movement, but no reply. Mrs. Blake's girlhood had been spent on the frontier. She was a stranger to fear. She arose; struck a light and, seeing no one in her room or the guest chamber and hallway, hastened to the third room, and was surprised to find Belle apparently quietly sleeping. Then she decided to look about the house and, first, went down and roused the cook. As she was coming out of the dining room, a man leaped past her in the hall, hurling her to one side and dashing out the light. Her back was toward him, for he came from Gerald's own premises known as the den. In that den, directly opposite, was one of her revolvers, loaded. She found it, even in the darkness and, hurrying forth again, intending to chase the intruder and alarm the sentry at the rear, encountered either the same or a second man close to the back door, a man who sprang past her like a panther and darted down the steps at the back of the house, followed by two shots from her Smith & Wesson. One of these men wore a soldier's overcoat, for the cape, ripped from the collar seam, was left in her hands. Another soldier's overcoat was later found at the rear fence, but no boots, shoes or tracks thereof, yet both these men, judging from the sound, had been in stocking feet, or possibly rubbers, or perhaps—but that last suspicion she kept to herself, for Mrs. Hay, too, was now among the arrivals in the house, full of sympathy and genuine distress. The alarm, then, had gone beyond the guard-house, and the creators thereof beyond the ken of the guard, for not a sentry had seen or heard anything suspicious until after the shots; then Number 8, Flint's latest

A DAUGHTER OF THE SIOUX

addition, declared that from his post at Hay's corral he had distinctly heard the swift hoofbeats of a brace of ponies darting up the level bench to the westward. Number 5 had turned up safely, and declared that at the moment the scream was heard he was round by the flagstaff, listening to the night chorus of a pack of yelping coyotes, afar out to the northwest, and then he thought he heard scrambling and running down at the foot of the bluff just as the shots were fired. Investigation on his part was what took him out of sight for the moment, and later investigation showed that one marauder, at least, had gone that way, for a capeless greatcoat was found close down by the shore, where some fugitive had tossed it in his flight. This overcoat bore, half erased from the soiled lining, the name of Culligan, Troop "K;" but Culligan had served out his time and taken his discharge a year before. The other overcoat was even older, an infantry coat, with shorter cape, bearing a company number "47," but no name. Both garments savored strongly of the stable.

Then, before quiet was restored, certain search was made about the quarters. It was found the intruders had obtained admission through the basement door at the back, which was never locked, for the sentry on Number 5 had orders to call Bitzer at 5:30 A. M., to start the fires, milk the cow, etc.,—Hogan, Ray's factotum, being roused about the same time. The marauders had gone up the narrow stairway into the kitchen, first lashing one end of a leather halter-strap about the knob of Bitzer's door and the other to the base of the big refrigerator,—a needless precaution, as it took sustained and determined effort, as many a sentry on Number 5 could testify, to rouse Bitzer from even a nap.

It was no trick for the prowlers to softly raise the trap door leading to the kitchen, and, once there, the rest of the house was practically open. Such a thing as burglary or sneak thieving about the officers' quarters had been unheard of at Frayne for many a year. One precaution the visitors had taken, that of unbolting the back door, so that retreat might not be barred in case they were discovered. Then they had gone swiftly and noiselessly about their work.

But what had they taken? The silver was upstairs, intact, under Mrs. Blake's bed; so was the little safe in which was kept her jewelry and their valuable papers. Books, bric-à-brac,—everything down stairs—seemed unmolested. No item was missing from its accustomed place. Mrs. Blake thought perhaps the intruders had not entered her room at all. In Gerald's den were "stacks," as he said, of relics, souvenirs, trophies of chase and war, but no one thing of the intrinsic value of fifty dollars. What could have been the object of their midnight search? was the question all Fort Frayne was asking as people dispersed and went home,—the doctor intimating it was high time that Mrs. Blake was permitted to seek repose. Not until he had practically cleared the house of all but her most intimate friends, Mrs. Dade and Mrs. Ray, would Waller permit himself to ask a question that had been uppermost in his mind ever since he heard her story.

A DAUGHTER OF THE SIOUX

"Mrs. Blake, someone has been ransacking Mr. Field's quarters for letters or papers. Now,—was there anything of that kind left by the captain that—someone may have needed?"

Nannie Blake's head was uplifted instantly from Marion's shoulder. She had been beginning to feel the reaction. For one moment the three women looked intently into each other's faces. Then up they started and trooped away into Gerald's den. The doctor followed. The upper drawer of a big, flat-topped desk stood wide open, and pretty Mrs. Blake opened her eyes and mouth in emulation as she briefly exclaimed—

"It's gone!"

Then Waller went forthwith to the quarters of the commander and caught him still in conference with his quartermaster and the guard, four or five of the latter being grouped without. The major retired to his front room, where, with Wilkins, he received the doctor.

"Major Flint," said Waller, "those overcoats belong to Mr. Hay's stablemen,—Pete and Crapaud. Will you order their immediate arrest?"

"I would, doctor," was the answer, "but they are not at the corral. We know how to account for the hoofbeats in the valley. Those scoundrels have got nearly an hour's start, and we've nobody to send in chase."

Then it presently appeared that the post commander desired to continue conference with his staff officer, for he failed to invite

A DAUGHTER OF THE SIOUX

the post surgeon to be seated. Indeed, he looked up into the doctor's kindling eyes with odd mixture of impatience and embarrassment in his own, and the veteran practitioner felt the slight, flushed instantly, and, with much *hauteur* of manner, took prompt but ceremonious leave.

And when morning came and Fort Frayne awoke to another busy day, as if the excitements of the night gone by had not been enough for it, a new story went buzzing, with the first call for guard mount, about the garrison; and, bigger even than yesterday, the two details, in soldier silence, began to gather in front of the infantry quarters. Major Flint had ordered sentries posted at the trader's home, with directions that Mrs. Hay was not to be allowed outside her gate, and no one, man or woman, permitted to approach her from without except by express permission of the post commander. "General Harney" and "Dan," the two best horses of the trader's stable, despite the presence of the sentry at the front, had been abstracted sometime during the earlier hours of the night, and later traced to the ford at Stabber's old camp, and with Pete and Crapaud, doubtless, were gone.

That day the major wired to Omaha that he should be reinforced at once. One half his little force, he said, was now mounted each day for guard, and the men couldn't stand it. The general, of course, was in the field, but his chief of staff remained at headquarters and was empowered to order troops from post to post within the limits of the department. Flint hoped two more companies could come at once, and he did not care what post

A DAUGHTER OF THE SIOUX

was denuded in his favor. His, he said, was close to the Indian lands,—separated from them, in fact, only by a narrow and fordable river. The Indians were all on the warpath and, aware of his puny numbers, might be tempted at any moment to quit the mountains and concentrate on him. Moreover, he was satisfied there had been frequent communication between their leaders and the household of the post trader at Fort Frayne. He was sure Mrs. Hay had been giving them valuable information, and he expected soon to be able to prove very serious charges against her. Meantime, he had placed her under surveillance. (*That* she had been ever since his coming, although she never realized it.) Fancy the sensation created at Omaha, where the Hays were well known, when this news was received! Flint did not say "under arrest," guarded day and night by a brace of sentries who were sorely disgusted with their duty. He had no doubt his appeals for more troops would be honored, in view of his strenuous representations, but the day passed without assurance to that effect and without a wired word to say his action regarding Mrs. Hay had been approved. It began to worry him. At 3 P. M. Mrs. Hay sent and begged him to call upon her that she might assure and convince him of her innocence. But this the major found means to refuse, promising, however a meeting in the near future, after he had received tidings from the front, which he was awaiting and expecting every moment. He had reluctantly given permission to visit her to Mrs. Dade, Mrs. Ray and two or three other women whose hearts were filled with sympathy and sorrow, and their heads with bewilderment, over the amazing order. Indeed, it was due to Mrs. Dade's advice that she so far triumphed over pride and wrath as to ask to see the major and explain. She had received tidings from her husband and Nanette. She was perfectly willing to admit it,—to tell all about it,—and, now that Pete and Crapaud had turned out to be such unmitigated rascals, to have them caught and castigated, if caught they could be. But all this involved no disloyalty. They had always been friendly with the Sioux and the Sioux with them. Everybody knew it;—no one better than General Crook himself, and if he approved why should a junior disapprove? Indeed, as she asked her friends, what junior who had ever known Mr. Hay and her, or the Indians either, would be apt to disapprove so long as the Indians, when on the warpath, received no aid or comfort from either her husband or herself? "And if they had," said she, further, waxing eloquent over her theme, "could we have *begun* to give them half the aid or comfort—or a thousandth part of the supplies and ammunition—they got day after day through the paid agents of the Interior Department?"

But these were questions army people could not properly discuss,—their mission in life being rather to submit to, than suggest, criticism.

And so another restless day went by and no more news came from either front or rear—from the range to the north or Rock Springs at the south, and Flint was just formulating another fervid appeal to that impassive functionary, the adjutant general at Omaha, when toward evening word came whistling down the line in the person of Master Sanford Ray, that two couriers were in sight "scooting" in from Moccasin Ridge, and Flint and fully

A DAUGHTER OF THE SIOUX

half the soldier strength of Fort Frayne gathered on the northward bluff like the "wan burghers" of ancient Rome, to watch and speed their coming. Who could tell what the day might yet bring forth?

It was well nigh dark before the foremost reached the ford—a scout in worn and tawdry buckskin, wearied and impassive. He gave his despatch to the care of the first officer to accost him and took the way to the store, briefly saying in reply to questions, that he was "too dry to speak the truth." So they flocked, at respectful distance, about the major as he read the hurried lines. The general bade the post commander wire the entire message to Washington, and to take all precautions for the protection of the few settlers about him. The columns under Colonel Henry and Major Webb had united near the head waters of the Clear Fork of the Powder; had had a rattling running fight with Lame Wolf's people; had driven them into the mountains and were following hot on the trail, but that Stabber's band and certain disaffected Sioux had cut loose from the main body and gone south. Whistling Elk, a young chief of much ambition had quarrelled with certain of the Red Cloud element, and joined Stabber, with his entire band. "Look out for them and watch for signals any day or night from Eagle Butte."

Flint read with sinking heart. Indian fighting was something far too scientific for his martial education and too much for his skeleton command. In the gathering dusk his face looked white and drawn, and old Wilkins, breasting his way up the slope, puffed hard, as he begged for news. There was still another

A DAUGHTER OF THE SIOUX

despatch, however, which was evidently adding to the major's perturbation, for it concerned him personally and for the moment Wilkins went unheard.

The general desires that you send the couriers back within twenty-four hours of their arrival, after you have had time to scout the line of the Platte say twenty miles each way, giving full report of every Indian seen or heard of. He enjoins vigilance and hopes to keep the Sioux so busy that they can send no more in your direction. Should they do so, however, he will pursue at once. He trusts that you are doing everything possible to comfort and reassure Mrs. Hay, and that you can send good news of Lieutenant Field.

And this when he had just refused to remove the sentries or to visit Mrs. Hay:—this when he had just been told by Dr. Waller that Lieutenant Field was distinctly worse.

"He is simply fretting his heart out here," were the doctor's words to him but a short time before, "and, while unable to mount a horse, he is quite strong enough now to take the trip by ambulance, slowly, that is, to Rock Springs. I fear his father is failing. I fear Field will fail if not allowed to go. I recommend a seven days' leave, with permission to apply to Omaha for thirty—he'll probably need it."

"I can't permit government teams and ambulances to be used for any such purpose," said the major, stoutly. "It is distinctly against orders."

"Then, sir, he can go in my spring wagon and we'll hire mules from Mrs. Hay," was the doctor's prompt reply. "He can do no good here, major. He may do much good there."

But Flint was full of information and official zeal. The matter of Field's going had been broached before, and, when told of it, the Wilkins pair had been prompt with their protests. "Of course he'd be wantin' to get away," said Wilkins, "wid all that money to account for, let alone these other things." The Irishman was hot against the young West Pointer who had derided him. He doubtless believed his own words. He never dreamed how sorely the lad now longed to see his father,—how deep was his anxiety on that father's account,—how filled with apprehension on his own, for that rifled desk had brought him reason for most painful thought. Wilkins and Field had been antagonistic from the start. Neither could see good in the other and, egged on by his worthy spouse's exhortations, the quartermaster had seized the opportunity to fill the post commander's too receptive mind with all his own suspicions—and this at a crucial time.

"I can't listen to it, Dr. Waller," said the major, sternly. "Here's a matter of near a thousand dollars that young man has got to answer for the moment he is well enough to stir. And if he can't account for it—you well know what my duty will demand."

A DAUGHTER OF THE SIOUX

CHAPTER XIX

A SLAP FOR THE MAJOR

The columns of Colonel Henry and Major Webb, as said "the Chief," had united, and here were two men who could be counted on to push the pursuit "for all they were worth." Hitherto, acting in the open country and free from encumbrance, the Indians had been hard to reach. Now they were being driven into their fastnesses among the mountains toward the distant shelter whither their few wounded had been conveyed, and where the old men, the women and children were in hiding. Now it meant that, unless the troops could be confronted and thrown back, another transfer of tepees and *travois*, ponies and dogs, wounded and aged would have to be made. Lame Wolf had thought his people safe behind the walls of the Big Horn and the shifting screen of warriors along the foothills, but the blue skirmish lines pushed steadily on into the fringing pines, driving the feathered braves from ridge to ridge, and Lame Wolf had sense enough to see that here were leaders that "meant business" and would not be held. Henry had ten veteran troops at his back when he united with Webb, who led his own and the Beecher squadron, making eighteen companies, or troops, of Horse, with their pack mules, all out at the front, while the wagon train and ambulances were thoroughly guarded by a big battalion of sturdy infantry, nearly all of them good marksmen, against whose spiteful Springfields the warriors made only one essay in force, and that was more than enough. The blue coats emptied many an Indian saddle and strewed the prairie with ponies, and sent Whistling Elk and his people to the right about in sore dismay, and then it dawned on Lame Wolf that he must now either mislead the cavalry leader,—throw him off the track, as it were,—or move the villages, wounded, prisoners and all across the Big Horn river, where hereditary foemen, Shoshone and Absaraka, would surely welcome them red-handed.

It was at this stage of the game he had his final split with Stabber. Stabber was shrewd, and saw unerringly that with other columns out—from Custer on the Little Horn and Washakie on the Wind River,—with reinforcements coming from north and south, the surrounding of the Sioux in arms would be but a matter of time. He had done much to get Lame Wolf into the scrape and now was urging hateful measures as, unless they were prepared for further and heavier losses, the one way out, and that way was—surrender.

Now, this is almost the last thing the Indian will do. Not from fear of consequences at the hands of his captors, for he well knows that, physically, he is infinitely better off when being coddled by Uncle Sam than when fighting in the field. It is simply the loss of *prestige* among his fellow red men that he hates and dreads. Therefore, nothing short of starvation or probable annihilation prompts him, as a rule, to yield himself a prisoner. Stabber urged it rather than risk further battle and further loss, but Stabber had long been jealous of the younger chief, envied him his much larger following and his record as a fighter, and Stabber, presumably, would be only too glad to see him fallen

A DAUGHTER OF THE SIOUX

from his high estate. They could then enjoy the hospitality of a generous nation (a people of born fools, said the unreasoning and unregenerate red man) all winter, and, when next they felt sufficiently slighted to warrant another issue on the warpath, they could take the field on equal terms. Lame Wolf, therefore, swore he'd fight to the bitter end. Stabber swore he'd gather all his villagers, now herding with those of Wolf; and, having segregated his sheep from the more numerous goats, would personally lead them whither the white man could not follow. At all events he made this quarrel the pretext for his withdrawal with full five score fighting men, and Lame Wolf cursed him roundly as the wretch deserved and, all short-handed now, with hardly five hundred braves to back him, bent his energies to checking Henry's column in the heart of the wild hill country.

And this was the situation when the general's first despatches were sent in to Frayne,—this the last news to reach the garrison from the distant front for five long days, and then one morning, when the snow was sifting softly down, there came tidings that thrilled the little community, heart and soul—tidings that were heard with mingled tears and prayers and rejoicings, and that led to many a visit of congratulation to Mrs. Hay, who, poor woman, dare not say at the moment that she had known it all as much as twenty-four hours earlier, despite the fact that Pete and Crapaud were banished from the roll of her auxiliaries.

Even as the new couriers came speeding through the veil of falling flakes, riding jubilantly over the wide-rolling prairie with their news of victory and battle, the post commander at Fort

Frayne was puzzling over a missive that had come to him, he knew not how, mysterious as the anarchists' warnings said to find their way to the very bedside of the guarded Romanoffs. Sentry Number 4 had picked it up on his post an hour before the dawn—a letter addressed in bold hand to Major Stanley Flint, commanding Fort Frayne, and, presuming the major himself had dropped it, he turned it over to the corporal of his relief, and so it found its way toward reveillé into the hands of old McGann, wheezing about his work of building fires, and Michael laid it on the major's table and thought no more about it until two hours later, when the major roused and read, and then a row began that ended only with the other worries of his incumbency at Frayne.

Secretly Flint was still doing his best to discover the bearer when came the bold riders from the north with their thrilling news. Secretly, he had been over at the guard-house interviewing as best he could, by the aid of an unwilling clerk who spoke a little Sioux, a young Indian girl whom Crabb's convalescent squad, four in number, had most unexpectedly run down when sent scouting five miles up the Platte, and brought, screaming, scratching and protesting back to Frayne. Her pony had been killed in the dash to escape, and the two Indians with her seemed to be young lads not yet well schooled as warriors, for they rode away pellmell over the prairie, leaving the girl to the mercy of the soldiers. Flint believed her to be connected in some way with the coming of the disturbing note, which was why he compelled her detention at the guard-house. Under Webb's *régime* she would have been questioned by Hay, or some one of his household. Under Flint, no one of Hay's family or retainers could be allowed

A DAUGHTER OF THE SIOUX

to see her. He regarded it as most significant that her shrillest screams and fiercest resistance should have been reserved until just as her guardians were bearing her past the trader's house. She had the little light prison room to herself all that wintry morning, and there, disdainful of bunk or chair, enveloped in her blanket, she squatted disconsolate, greeting all questioners with defiant and fearless shruggings and inarticulate protest. Not a syllable of explanation, not a shred of news could their best endeavors wring from her. Yet her glittering eyes were surely in search of some one, for she looked up eagerly every time the door was opened, and Flint was just beginning to think he would have to send for Mrs. Hay when the couriers came with their stirring news and he had to drop other affairs in order to forward this important matter to headquarters.

Once again, it seems, Trooper Kennedy had been entrusted with distinguished duty, for it was he who came trotting foremost up the road, waving his despatch on high. A comrade from Blake's troop, following through the ford, had turned to the left and led his horse up the steep to the quarters nearest the flagstaff. This time there was no big-hearted post commander to bid the Irishman refresh himself *ad libitum*. Flint was alone at his office at the moment, and knew not this strange trooper, and looked askance at his heterodox garb and war-worn guise. Such laxity, said he to himself, was not permitted where *he* had hitherto served, which was never on Indian campaign. Kennedy, having delivered his despatches, stood mutely expectant of question and struggling with an Irishman's enthusiastic eagerness to tell the details of heady fight. But Flint had but one method of getting at

A DAUGHTER OF THE SIOUX

facts—the official reports—and Kennedy stood unnoticed until, impatient at last, he queried:—

"Beg pardon, sir, but may we put up our horses?"

"Who's we?" asked the major, bluntly. "And where are the others?"

"Trigg, sir—Captain Blake's troop. He went to the captain's quarters with a package."

"He should have reported himself first to the post commander," said the major, who deemed it advisable to make prompt impression on these savage hunters of savage game.

"Thim wasn't his ordhers, surr," said Kennedy, with zealous, but misguided loyalty to his comrades and his regiment.

"No one has a right, sir, to give orders that are contrary in spirit to the regulations and customs of the service," answered the commander, with proper austerity. "Mr. Wilkins," he continued, as the burly quartermaster came bustling in, "have the other trooper sent to report at once to me and let this man wait outside till I am ready to see him."

And so it happened that a dozen members of the garrison gathered, from the lips of a participant, stirring particulars of a spirited chase and fight that set soldiers to cheering and women and children to extravagant scenes of rejoicing before the official head of the garrison was fairly ready to give out the news. Kennedy had taken satisfaction for the commander's slights by

A DAUGHTER OF THE SIOUX

telling the tidings broadcast to the crowd that quickly gathered, and, in three minutes, the word was flying from lip to lip that the troops had run down Lame Wolf's main village after an all day, all night rush to head them off, and that with very small loss they had been able to capture many of the families and to scatter the warriors among the hills. In brief, while Henry, with the main body, had followed the trail of the fighting band, Webb had been detached and, with two squadrons, had ridden hard after a Shoshone guide who led them by a short cut through the range and enabled them to pounce on the village where were most of Lame Wolf's noncombatants, guarded only by a small party of warriors, and, while Captains Billings and Ray with their troops remained in charge of these captives, Webb, with Blake and the others had pushed on in pursuit of certain braves who had scampered into the thick of the hills, carrying a few of the wounded and prisoners with them. Among those captured, or recaptured, were Mr. Hay and Crapaud. Among those who had been spirited away was Nanette Flower. This seemed strange and unaccountable.

And yet Blake had found time to write to his winsome wife,—to send her an important missive and most important bit of news. It was with these she came running in to Mrs. Ray before the latter had time to half read the long letter received from her soldier husband, and we take the facts in the order of their revelation.

"Think of it, Maidie!" she cried. "Think of it! Gerald's first words, almost, are 'Take good care of that pouch and contents,' and now pouch and contents are gone! Whoever dreamed that they would be of such consequence? He says the newspaper will explain."

And presently the two bonny heads were bent over the big sheets of a dingy, grimy copy of a Philadelphia daily, and there, on an inner page, heavily marked, appeared a strange item, and this Quaker City journal had been picked up in an Ogalalla camp. The item read as follows:

AN UNTAMED SIOUX

The authorities of the Carlisle School and the police of Harrisburg are hunting high and low for a young Indian known to the records of the Academy as Ralph Moreau, but borne on the payrolls of Buffalo Bill's Wild West aggregation as Eagle Wing—a youth who is credited with having given the renowned scout-showman more trouble than all his braves, bronchos and "busters" thereof combined. Being of superb physique and a daring horseman, Moreau had been forgiven many a peccadillo, and had followed the fortunes of the show two consecutive summers until Cody finally had to get rid of him as an intolerable nuisance.

It seems that when a lad of eighteen, "Eagle Wing" had been sent to Carlisle, where he ran the gamut of scrapes of every conceivable kind. He spoke English picked up about the agencies; had influential friends and, in some clandestine way, received occasional supplies of money that enabled him to take French leave when he felt like it. He was sent back from Carlisle to Dakota as irreclaimable, and after a year or two on his native heath, reappeared among the haunts of civilization as one of Buffalo Bill's warriors. Bill discharged him at Cincinnati and, at the instance of the Indian Bureau, he was again placed at Carlisle, only to repeat on a larger scale his earlier exploits and secure a second transfer to the Plains, where his opportunities for devilment were limited. Then Cody was induced to take him on again by profuse promises of good behavior, which were kept until Pennsylvania soil was reached two weeks ago, when he broke loose again; was seen in store clothes around West Philadelphia for a few days, plentifully supplied with money, and next he turned up in the streets of Carlisle, where he assaulted an attaché of the school, whose life was barely saved by the prompt efforts of other Indian students. Moreau escaped to Harrisburg, which he proceeded to paint his favorite color that very night, and wound up the entertainment by galloping away on the horse of a prominent official, who had essayed to escort him back to Carlisle. It is believed that he is now in hiding somewhere about the suburbs, and that an innate propensity for devilment will speedily betray him to the clutches of the law.

A few moments after reading this oddly interesting story the two friends were in consultation with Mrs. Dade, who, in turn, called in Dr. Waller, just returning from the hospital and a not too satisfactory visit to Mr. Field. There had been a slight change for the better in the condition of General Field that had enabled Dr. Lorain of Fort Russell and a local physician to arrange for his speedy transfer to Cheyenne. This had in a measure relieved the anxiety of Waller's patient, but never yet had the veteran practitioner permitted him to know that he was practically a

A DAUGHTER OF THE SIOUX

prisoner as well as a patient. Waller feared the result on so high-strung a temperament, and had made young Field believe that, when strong and well enough to attempt the journey, he should be sent to Rock Springs. Indeed, Dr. Waller had no intention of submitting to Major Flint's decision as final. He had written personally to the medical director of the department, acquainting him with the facts, and, meanwhile, had withdrawn himself as far as possible, officially and socially, from the limited circle in which moved his perturbed commanding officer.

He was at a distant point of the garrison, therefore, and listening to the excited and vehement comments of the younger of the three women upon this strange newspaper story, and its possible connection with matters at Frayne, at the moment when a dramatic scene was being enacted over beyond the guard-house.

Kennedy was still the center of a little group of eager listeners when Pink Marble, factotum of the trader's store, came hurrying forth from the adjutant's office, speedily followed by Major Flint. "You may tell Mrs. Hay that while I cannot permit her to visit the prisoner," he called after the clerk, "I will send the girl over—under suitable guard."

To this Mr. Marble merely shrugged his shoulders and went on. He fancied Flint no more than did the relics of the original garrison. A little later Flint personally gave an order to the sergeant of the guard and then came commotion.

First there were stifled sounds of scuffle from the interior of the guard-house; then shrill, wrathful screams; then a woman's voice

A DAUGHTER OF THE SIOUX

unlifted in wild upbraidings in an unknown tongue, at sound of which Trooper Kennedy dropped his rein and his jaw, stood staring one minute; then, with the exclamation: "Mother of God, but I know that woman!" burst his way through the crowd and ran toward the old log blockhouse at the gate,—the temporary post of the guard. Just as he turned the corner of the building, almost stumbling against the post commander, there came bursting forth from the dark interior a young woman of the Sioux, daring, furious, raging, and, breaking loose from the grasp of the two luckless soldiers who had her by the arms, away she darted down the road, still screaming like some infuriated child, and rushed straight for the open gateway of the Hays. Of course the guard hastened in pursuit, the major shouting "Stop her! Catch her!" and the men striving to appear to obey, yet shirking the feat of seizing the fleeing woman. Fancy, then, the amaze of the swiftly following spectators when the trader's front door was thrown wide open and Mrs. Hay herself sprang forth. Another instant and the two women had met at the gate. Another instant still, and, with one motherly arm twining about the quivering, panting, pleading girl and straining her to the motherly heart, Mrs. Hay's right hand and arm flew up in the superb gesture known the wide frontier over as the Indian signal "Halt!" And halt they did, every mother's son save Kennedy, who sprang to the side of the girl and faced the men in blue. And then another woman's voice, rich, deep, ringing, powerful, fell on the ears of the amazed, swift-gathering throng, with the marvellous order: "Stand where you are! You shan't touch a hair of her head! She's a chief's daughter. She's my own kin and I'll answer for her to the

A DAUGHTER OF THE SIOUX

general himself. As for you," she added, turning now and glaring straight at the astounded Flint, all the pent-up sense of wrath, indignity, shame and wrong overmastering any thought of prudence or of "the divinity that doth hedge" the commanding officer, "As for you," she cried, "I pity you when our own get back again! God help you, Stanley Flint, the moment my husband sets eyes on you. D'you know the message that came to him this day?" And now the words rang louder and clearer, as she addressed the throng. "*I* do, and so do officers and gentlemen who'd be shamed to have to shake hands with such as he. He's got my husband's note about him now, and what my husband wrote was this—'I charge myself with every dollar you charge to Field, and with the further obligation of thrashing you on sight'—and, mark you, he'll do it!"

A DAUGHTER OF THE SIOUX

CHAPTER XX

THE SIOUX SURROUNDED

In the hush of the wintry night, under a leaden sky, with snowflakes falling thick and fast and mantling the hills in fleecy white, Webb's column had halted among the sturdy pines, the men exchanging muttered, low-toned query and comment, the horses standing with bowed heads, occasionally pawing the soft coverlet and sniffing curiously at this filmy barrier to the bunch grass they sought in vain. They had feasted together, these comrade troopers and chargers, ere the sun went down,—the men on abundant rations of agency bacon, flour and brown sugar, found with black tailed deer and mountain sheep in abundance in the captured village, and eked out by supplies from the pack train,—the horses on big "blankets" of oats set before them by sympathetic friends and masters. Then, when the skies were fairly dark, Webb had ordered little fires lighted all along the bank of the stream, leaving the men of Ray's and Billings' troops to keep them blazing through the long night watches to create the impression among the lurking Sioux that the whole force was still there, guarding the big village it had captured in the early afternoon, and then, in silence, the troopers had saddled and jogged away into the heart of the hills, close on the heels of their guides.

There had been little time to look over the captures. The main interest of both officers and men, of course, centred in Mr. Hay, who was found in one of the tepees, prostrate from illness and half frantic from fever and strong mental excitement. He had

Page 227

A DAUGHTER OF THE SIOUX

later tidings from Frayne, it seems, than had his rescuers. He could assure them of the health and safety of their wives and little ones, but would not tell them what was amiss in his own household. One significant question he asked: Did any of them know this new Major Flint? No? Well, God help Flint, if ever he, Hay, got hold of him.

"He's delirious," whispered Webb, and rode away in that conviction, leaving him to Ray and Billings.

Three miles out, on the tortuous trail of the pursued, the column halted and dismounted among the pines. Then there was brief conference, and the word "Mount" was whispered along the Beecher squadron, while Blake's men stood fast. With a parting clasp of the hand Webb and "Legs" had returned to the head of their respective commands, "Legs" and his fellows to follow steadily the Indian trail through the twisting ravines of the foothills; Webb to make an all-night forced march, in wide *détour* and determined effort, to head off the escaping warriors before they could reach the rocky fastnesses back of Bear Cliff. Webb's chief scout "Bat," chosen by General Crook himself, had been a captive among the Sioux through long years of his boyhood, and knew the Big Horn range as Webb did the banks of the Wabash. "They can stand off a thousand soldiers," said the guide, "if once they get into the rocks. They'd have gone there first off only there was no water. Now there's plenty snow."

So Blake's instructions were to follow them without pushing, to let them feel they were being pursued, yet by no means to hasten them, and, if the general's favorite scout proved to be all he promised as guide and pathfinder, Webb might reasonably hope by dint of hard night riding, to be first at the tryst at break of day. Then they would have the retreating Sioux, hampered by their few wounded and certain prisoners whom they prized, hemmed between rocky heights on every side, and sturdy horsemen front and rear.

It was eight by the watch at the parting of the ways. It was 8:30 when Blake retook the trail, with Sergeants Schreiber and Winsor, the latter borrowed from Ray, far in the van. Even had the ground been hard and stony these keen-eyed soldier scouts could have followed the signs almost as unerringly as the Indians, for each had had long years of experience all over the West; but, despite the steadily falling snow, the traces of hoofs and, for a time, of *travois* poles could be readily seen and followed in the dim gray light of the blanketed skies. Somewhere aloft, above the film of cloud, the silvery moon was shining, and that was illumination more than enough for men of their years on the trail.

For over an hour Blake followed the windings of a ravine that grew closer and steeper as it burrowed into the hills. Old game trails are as good as turnpikes in the eyes of the plainsman. It was when the ravine began to split into branches that the problem might have puzzled them, had not the white fleece lain two inches deep on the level when "Lo" made his dash to escape. Now the rough edges of the original impression were merely rounded over by the new fallen snow. The hollows and ruts and depressions led on from one deep cleft into another, and by

A DAUGHTER OF THE SIOUX

midnight Blake felt sure the quarry could be but a few miles ahead and Bear Cliff barely five hours' march away. So, noiselessly, the signal "Halt!" went rearward down the long, dark, sinuous column of twos, and every man slipped out of saddle— some of them stamping, so numb were their feet. With every mile the air had grown keener and colder. They were glad when the next word whispered was, "Lead on" instead of "Mount."

By this time they were far up among the pine-fringed heights, with the broad valley of the Big Horn lying outspread to the west, invisible as the stars above, and neither by ringing shot nor winged arrow had the leaders known the faintest check. It seemed as though the Indians, in their desperate effort to carry off the most important or valued of their charges, were bending all their energies to expediting the retreat. Time enough to turn on the pursuers when once the rocks had closed about them,— when the wounded were safe in the fastnesses, and the pursuers far from supports. But, at the foot of a steep ascent, the two leading scouts,—rival sergeants of rival troops but devoted friends for nearly twenty years,—were seen by the next in column, a single corporal following them at thirty yards' distance, to halt and begin poking at some dark object by the wayside. Then they pushed on again. A dead pony, under a quarter inch coverlet of snow, was what met the eyes of the silently trudging command as it followed. The high-peaked wooden saddle tree was still "cinched" to the stiffening carcass. Either the Indians were pushed for time or overstocked with saddlery. Presently there came a low whistle from the military "middleman" between the scouts and a little advance guard. "Run ahead," growled the

A DAUGHTER OF THE SIOUX

sergeant commanding to his boy trumpeter. "Give me your reins." And, leaving his horse, the youngster stumbled along up the winding trail; got his message and waited. "Give this to the captain," was the word sent back by Schreiber, and "this" was a mitten of Indian tanned buckskin, soft and warm if unsightly, a mitten too small for a warrior's hand, if ever warrior deigned to wear one,—a mitten the captain examined curiously, as he ploughed ahead of his main body, and then returned to his subaltern with a grin on his face:

"Beauty draws us with a single hair," said he, "and can't shake us even when she gives us the mitten. Ross," he added, after a moment's thought, "remember this. With this gang there are two or three sub-chiefs that we should get, alive or dead, but the chief end of man, so far as 'K' Troop's concerned, is to capture that girl, unharmed."

And just at dawn, so gray and wan and pallid it could hardly be told from the pale moonlight of the earlier hours, the dark, snake-like column was halted again, nine miles further in among the wooded heights. With Bear Cliff still out of range and sight, something had stopped the scouts, and Blake was needed at the front. He found Schreiber crouching at the foot of a tree, gazing warily forward along a southward-sloping face of the mountain that was sparsely covered with tall, straight pines, and that faded into mist a few hundred yards away. The trail,—the main trail, that is,—seemed to go straight away eastward, and, for a short distance, downward through a hollow or depression; while, up the mountain side to the left, the north, following the spur or shoulder, there were signs as of hoof tracks, half sheeted by the new-fallen snow, and through this fresh, fleecy mantlet ploughed the trooper boots in rude, insistent pursuit. The sergeants' horses were held by a third soldier a few yards back behind the spur, for Winsor was "side scouting" up the heights.

The snowfall had ceased for a time. The light was growing broader every moment, and presently a soft whistle sounded somewhere up the steep, and Schreiber answered. "He wants us, sir," was all he said, and in five minutes they had found him, sprawled on his stomach on a projecting ledge, and pointing southeastward, where, boldly outlined against the gray of the morning sky, a black and beetling precipice towered from the mist-wreathed pines at its base. Bear Cliff beyond a doubt!

"How far, sergeant?" asked the captain, never too reliant on his powers of judging distance.

"Five miles, sir, at least; yet some three or four Indians have turned off here and gone—somewhere up there." And, rolling half over, Winsor pointed again toward a wooded bluff, perhaps three hundred feet higher and half a mile away. "That's probably the best lookout this side of the cliff itself!" he continued, in explanation, as he saw the puzzled look on the captain's face. "From there, likely, they can see the trail over the divide—the one Little Bat is leading the major and, if they've made any time at all, the squadron should be at Bear Cliff now."

They were crawling to him by this time, Blake and Schreiber, among the stunted cedars that grew thickly along the rocky ledge.

A DAUGHTER OF THE SIOUX

Winsor, flat again on his stomach, sprawled like a squirrel close to the brink. Every moment as the skies grew brighter the panorama before them became more extensive, a glorious sweep of highland scenery, of boldly tossing ridges east and south and west—the slopes all mantled, the trees all tipped, with nature's ermine, and studded now with myriad gems, taking fire at the first touch of the day god's messenger, as the mighty king himself burst his halo of circling cloud and came peering over the low curtain far at the eastward horizon. Chill and darkness and shrouding vapor vanished all in a breath as he rose, dominant over countless leagues of wild, unbroken, yet magnificent mountain landscape.

"Worth every hour of watch and mile of climb!" muttered Blake. "But it's Indians, not scenery, we're after. What are we here for, Winsor?" and narrowly he eyed Ray's famous right bower.

"If the major got there first, sir,—and I believe he did,—they have to send the prisoners and wounded back this way."

"Then we've got 'em!" broke in Schreiber, low-toned, but exultant. "Look sir," he added, as he pointed along the range. "They are signalling now."

From the wooded height ten hundred yards away, curious little puffs of smoke, one following another, were sailing straight for the zenith, and Blake, screwing his field glasses to the focus, swept with them the mountain side toward the five-mile distant cliff, and presently the muscles about his mouth began to twitch—sure sign with Blake of gathering excitement.

A DAUGHTER OF THE SIOUX

"You're right, sergeant," he presently spoke, repressing the desire to shout, and striving, lest Winsor should be moved to invidious comparisons, to seem as *nonchalant* as Billy Ray himself. "They're coming back already." Then down the mountain side he dove to plan and prepare appropriate welcome, leaving Winsor and the glasses to keep double powered watch on the situation.

Six-fifty of a glorious, keen November morning, and sixty troopers of the old regiment were distributed along a spur that crossed, almost at right angles, the line of the Indian trail. Sixty fur-capped, rough-coated fellows, with their short brown carbines in hand, crouching behind rocks and fallen trees, keeping close to cover and warned to utter silence. Behind them, two hundred yards away, their horses were huddled under charge of their disgusted guards, envious of their fellows at the front, and cursing hard their luck in counting off as number four. Schreiber had just come sliding, stumbling, down from Winsor's perch to say they could hear faint sound of sharp volleying far out to the eastward, where the warriors, evidently, were trying to "stand off" Webb's skirmish line until the *travois* with the wounded and the escort of the possible prisoners should succeed in getting back out of harm's way and taking surer and higher trail into the thick of the wilderness back of Bear Cliff. "Some of 'em must come in sight here in a minute, sir," panted the veteran sergeant. "We could see them plainly up there—a mule litter and four *travois*, and there must be a dozen in saddle."

A dozen there were, for along the line of crouching men went sudden thrill of excitement. Shoulders began to heave; nervous

A DAUGHTER OF THE SIOUX

thumbs bore down on heavy carbine hammers, and there was sound of irrepressible stir and murmur. Out among the pines, five hundred yards away, two mounted Indians popped suddenly into view, two others speedily following, their well-nigh exhausted ponies feebly shaking their shaggy, protesting heads, as their riders plied the stinging quirt or jabbed with cruel lance; only in painful jog trot could they zig zag through the trees. Then came two warriors, leading the pony of a crippled comrade. "Don't fire—Don't harm them! Fall back from the trail there and let them in. They'll halt the moment they see our tracks! Get 'em alive, if possible!" were Blake's rapid orders, for his eyes were eagerly fixed on other objects beyond these dejected leaders— upon stumbling mules, lashed fore and aft between long, spliced saplings and bearing thus a rude litter—Hay's pet wheelers turned to hospital use. An Indian boy, mounted, led the foremost mule; another watched the second; while, on each side of the occupant of this Sioux palanquin, jogged a blanketed rider on jaded pony. Here was a personage of consequence—luckier much than these others following, dragged along on *travois* whose trailing poles came jolting over stone or hummock along the rugged path. It was on these that Blake's glittering eyes were fastened. "Pounce on the leaders, you that are nearest!" he ordered, in low, telling tones, the men at his left; then turned to Schreiber, crouching close beside him, the fringe of his buckskin hunting shirt quivering over his bounding heart. "There's the prize I want," he muttered low. "Whatever you do, let no shot reach that litter. Charge with me the moment the leaders yell. You men to the right," he added, slightly raising his

A DAUGHTER OF THE SIOUX

voice, "be ready to jump with me. Don't shoot anybody that doesn't show fight. Nab everything in sight."

"Charge with me the moment the leaders yell."

A DAUGHTER OF THE SIOUX

"Whoo-oop!" All in a second the mountain woke, the welkin rang, to a yell of warning from the lips of the leading Sioux. All in a second they whirled their ponies about and darted back. All in that second Blake and his nearmost sprang to their feet and flung themselves forward straight for the startled convoy. In vain the few warriors bravely rallied about their foremost wounded; the unwieldy litter could not turn about; the frantic mules, crazed by the instant pandemonium of shouts and shots,—the onward rush of charging men,—the awful screams of a brace of squaws, broke from their leading reins; crashed with their litter against the trees, hurling the luckless occupant to earth. Back drove the unhit warriors before the dash of the cheering line. Down went first one pony, then a second, in his bloody tracks. One after another, litter, *travois*, wounded and prisoner, was clutched and seized by stalwart hands, and Blake, panting not a little, found himself bending staring over the prostrate form flung from the splintered wreck of the litter, a form writhing in pain that forced no sound whatever from between grimly clinching teeth, yet that baffled effort, almost superb, to rise and battle still—a form magnificent in its proportions, yet helpless through wounds and weakness. Not the form Blake thought to see, of shrinking, delicate, dainty woman, but that of the furious warrior who thrice had dared him on the open field—the red brave well known to him by sight and deed within the moon now waning, but, only within the day gone by, revealed to him as the renegade Ralph Moreau,—Eagle Wing of the Ogalalla Sioux.

Where then was Nanette?

A DAUGHTER OF THE SIOUX

"Look out for this man, corporal!" he called, to a shouting young trooper. "See that no harm comes to him." Then quickly he ran on to the huddle of *travois*. Something assured him she could not be far away. The first drag litter held another young warrior, sullen and speechless like the foremost. The next bore a desperately wounded brave whose bloodless lips were compressed in agony and dumb as those of the dead. About these cowered, shivering and whimpering, two or three terror-stricken squaws, one of them with a round-eyed pappoose staring at her back. A pony lay struggling in the snow close by. Half a dozen rough soldier hands were dragging a stricken rider from underneath. Half a dozen more were striving to control the wild plungings of another mettlesome little beast, whose rider, sitting firmly astride, lashed first at his quivering flank and then at the fur gauntleted hands,—even at the laughing, bearded faces—sure sign of another squaw, and a game one. Far out to the front the crackle of carbine and rifle told that Webb was driving the scattered braves before him,—that the comrade squadron was coming their way,—that Bear Cliff had been sought by the Sioux in vain,—that Indian wiles and strategy, Indian pluck and staying power, all had more than met their match. Whatever the fate of Lame Wolf's fighting force, now pressed by Henry's column, far in the southward hills, here in sight of the broad Big Horn valley, the white chief had struck a vital blow. Village, villagers, wounded and prisoners were all the spoil of the hated soldiery. Here at the scene of Blake's minor affair there appeared still in saddle just one undaunted, unconquered amazon whose black eyes flashed through the woolen hood that hid the rest of her

A DAUGHTER OF THE SIOUX

face, whose lips had uttered as yet no sound, but from whom two soldiers recoiled at the cry of a third. "Look at the hand of her, fellers! It's whiter than mine!"

"That's all right, Lanigan," answered the jovial voice of the leader they loved and laughed with. "Hold that pony steady. Now, by your-ladyship's leave," and two long, sinewy arms went circling about the shrinking rider's waist, and a struggling form was lifted straightway out of saddle and deposited, not too gracefully, on its moccasined feet. "We will remove this one impediment to your speech," continued Blake, whereat the muffling worsted was swiftly unwound, "and then we will listen to our meed of thanks. Ah, no wonder you did not need a side-saddle that night at Frayne. You ride admirably *à califourchon*. My compliments, Mademoiselle La Fleur; or should I say—Madame Moreau."

For all answer Blake received one quick, stinging slap in the face from that mittenless little right hand.

CHAPTER XXI

THANKSGIVING AT FRAYNE

Thanksgiving Day at Frayne! Much of the garrison was still afield, bringing back to their lines and, let us hope, to their senses, the remnant of Stabber's band, chased far into the Sweetwater Hills before they would stop, while Henry's column kept Lame Wolf in such active movement the misnamed chieftain richly won his later sobriquet "The Skipper." The general had come whirling back from Beecher in his Concord wagon, to meet Mr. Hay as they bore that invalid homeward from the Big Horn. Between the fever-weakened trader and the famous frontier soldier there had been brief conference—all that the doctors felt they could allow—and then the former had been put to bed under the care of his devoted wife, while the latter, without so much as sight of a pillow, had set forth again out Sweetwater way to wind up the campaign. This time he went in saddle, sending his own team over the range of the Medicine Bow to carry a convalescent subaltern to the side of a stricken father; the sender ignorant, possibly, of the post commander's prohibition; ignoring it, if, as probable, it was known to him. The good old doctor himself had bundled the grateful lad and sent a special hospital attendant with him. Mrs. Dade and her devoted allies up the row had filled with goodies a wonderful luncheon basket, while Mrs. Hay had sent stores of wine for the use of both invalids, and had come down herself to see the start, for, without a word indicative of reproof, the general had bidden Flint remove the blockade, simply saying he would assume all responsibility, both for Mrs. Hay and the young Indian girl, given refuge under the trader's roof until the coming of her own people still out with Stabber's band. Flint could not fathom it. He could only obey.

And now, with the general gone and Beverly Field away, with Hay home and secluded, by order, from all questioning or other extraneous worry; with the wounded soldiers safely trundled into hospital, garrison interest seemed to centre for the time mainly in that little Ogalalla maid—Flint's sole Sioux captive—who was housed, said the much interrogated domestic, in Mrs. Hay's own room instead of Miss Flower's, while the lady of the house, when she slept at all, occupied a sofa near her husband's bedside.

Then came the tidings that Blake, with the prisoners from No Wood Creek and Bear Cliff was close at hand, and everybody looked with eager eyes for the coming across the snowy prairie of that homeward bound convoy—that big village of the Sioux, with its distinguished captives, wounded and unwounded; one of the former, the young sub-chief Eagle Wing, alias Moreau;—one of the latter a self-constituted martyr, since she was under no official restraint,—Nanette Flower, hovering ever about the litter bearing that sullen and still defiant brave, whose side she refused to leave.

Not until they reached Fort Frayne; not until the surgeon, after careful examination, declared there was no need of taking Moreau into hospital,—no reason why he should not be confined in the prison room of the guard-house,—were they able to induce the silent, almost desperate girl to return to her aunt.

A DAUGHTER OF THE SIOUX

Not until Nanette realized that her warrior was to be housed within wooden walls whence she would be excluded, could Mrs. Hay, devoted to the last, persuade the girl to reoccupy her old room and to resume the dress of civilization. Barring that worsted hood, she was habited like a chieftain's daughter, in gaily beaded and embroidered garments, when recaptured by Blake's command. Once within the trader's door, she had shut herself in her old room, the second floor front, refusing to see anybody from outside the house, unless she could be permitted to receive visits from the captive Sioux, and this the major, flintily, forebade. It was nightfall when the litter-bearers reached the post, Hay's rejoicing mules braying unmelodious ecstasy at sight of their old stable. It was dark when the wounded chief was borne into the guard-house, uttering not a sound, and Nanette was led within the trader's door, yet someone had managed to see her face, for the story went all over the wondering post that very night,—women flitting with it from door to door,—that every vestige of her beauty was gone;—she looked at least a dozen years older. Blake, when questioned, after the first rapture of the home-coming had subsided, would neither affirm nor deny. "She would neither speak to me nor harken," said he, whimsically. "The only thing she showed was teeth and—temper."

Then presently they sent a lot of the Sioux—Stabber's villagers and Lame Wolf's combined,—by easy stages down the Platte to Laramie, and then around by Rawhide and the Niobrara to the old Red Cloud agency, there to be fed and coddled and cared for, wounded warriors and all, except a certain few, including this accomplished orator and chieftain, convalescing under guard at

A DAUGHTER OF THE SIOUX

Frayne. About his case there hung details and complications far too many and intricate to be settled short of a commission. Already had the tidings of this most important capture reached the distant East. Already both Indian Bureau and Peace Societies had begun to wire the general in the field and "work" the President and the Press at home. Forgotten was the fact that he had been an intolerable nuisance to Buffalo Bill and others who had undertaken to educate and civilize him. The Wild West Show was now amazing European capitals and, therefore, beyond consulting distance. Forgotten were escapades at Harrisburg, Carlisle and Philadelphia. Suppressed were circumstances connecting him with graver charges than those of repeated roistering and aggravated assault. Ignored, or as yet unheard, were the details of his reappearance on the frontier in time to stir up most of the war spirit developed that September, and to take a leading part in the fierce campaign that followed. He was a pupil of the nation, said the good people of the Indian Friends Societies—a youth of exceptional intelligence and promise, a son of the Sioux whose influence would be of priceless value could he be induced to complete his education and accept the views and projects of his eastern admirers. It would never do to let his case be settled by soldiers, settlers and cowboys, said philanthropy. They would hang him, starve him, break his spirit at the very least. (They were treating him particularly well just now, as he had sense enough to see.) There must be a deputation,—a committee to go out at once to the West, with proper credentials, per diem, mileage and clerks, to see to it that these unfortunate children of the mountain and prairie were accorded fair

A DAUGHTER OF THE SIOUX

treatment and restored to their rights, especially this brilliant young man Moreau. The general was beyond reach and reasoning with, but there was Flint, eminent for his piety, and untrammelled in command; Flint, with aspirations of his own, the very man to welcome such influence as theirs, and, correspondingly, to give ear to their propositions. Two days after the safe lodgment of Eagle Wing behind the bars, the telegrams were coming by dozens, and one week after that deserved incarceration Fort Frayne heard with mild bewilderment the major's order for Moreau's transfer to the hospital. By that time letters, too, were beginning to come, and, two nights after this removal to the little room but lately occupied by Lieutenant Field—this very Thanksgiving night, in fact,—the single sentry at the door stood attention to the commanding officer, who in person ushered in a womanly form enveloped in hooded cloak, and with bowed head Nanette Flower passed within the guarded portal, which then closed behind her and left her alone with her wounded brave.

Blake and Billings had been sent on to Red Cloud, guarding the presumably repentant Ogalallas. Webb, Ray, Gregg and Ross were still afield, in chase of Stabber. Dade, with four companies of infantry, was in the Big Horn guarding Henry's wagon train. There was no one now at Frayne in position to ask the new commander questions, for Dr. Waller had avoided him in every possible way, but Waller had nobly done the work of his noble profession. Moreau, or Eagle Wing, was mending so very fast there was no reason whatever why the doctor should object to his receiving visitors. It was Flint alone who would be held

A DAUGHTER OF THE SIOUX

responsible if anything went wrong. Yet Fort Frayne, to a woman, took fire at the major's action. Two days previous he might have commanded the support of Mrs. Wilkins, but Nanette herself had spoiled all chance of that. It seems the lady had been to call at Mrs. Hay's the previous day—that Mrs. Hay had begged to be excused,—that Mrs. Wilkins had then persisted, possibly as a result of recent conference with Flint, and had bidden the servant say she'd wait until Miss Flower could come down, and so sailed on into the parlor, intent on seeing all she could of both the house and its inmates. But not a soul appeared. Mrs. Hay was watching over her sleeping husband, whose slow recovery Flint was noting with unimpatient eye. Voices low, yet eager, could be heard aloft in Nanette's room. The servant, when she came down, had returned without a word to the inner regions about the kitchen, and Mrs. Wilkins's wait became a long one. At last the domestic came rustling through the lower floor again, and Mrs. Wilkins hailed. Both were Irish, but one was the wife of an officer and long a power, if not indeed a terror, in the regiment. The other feared the quartermaster's wife as little as Mrs. Wilkins feared the colonel's, and, when ordered to stand and say why she brought no answer from Miss Flower, declined to stand, but decidedly said she brought none because there was none.

"Did ye tell her I'd wait?" said Mrs. Wilkins.

"I did," said Miss McGrath, "an' she said 'Let her,' an' so I did." Then in came Mrs. Hay imploring hush, and, with rage in her Hibernian heart, the consort of the quartermaster came away.

A DAUGHTER OF THE SIOUX

There was not one woman in all Fort Frayne, therefore, to approve the major's action in permitting this wild girl to visit the wilder Indian patient. Mrs. Hay knew nothing of it because Nanette well understood that there would be lodged objection that she dare not disregard—her uncle's will. One other girl there was, that night at Frayne, who marked her going and sought to follow and was recalled, restrained at the very threshold by the sound of a beloved voice softly, in the Sioux tongue, calling her name. One other girl there was who knew not of her going, who shrank from thought of meeting her at any time,—in any place,—and yet was destined to an encounter fateful in its results in every way.

Just as tattoo was sounding on the infantry bugle, Esther Dade sat reading fairy stories at the children's bedside in the quarters of Sergeant Foster, of her father's company. There had been Thanksgiving dinner with Mrs. Ray, an Amazonian feast since all their lords were still away on service, and Sandy Ray and Billy, Jr., were perhaps too young to count. Dinner was all over by eight o'clock, and, despite some merry games, the youngsters' eyes were showing symptoms of the sandman's coming, when that privileged character, Hogan, Ray's long-tried trooper now turned *major domo*, appeared at the doorway of the little army parlor. He had been bearer of a lot of goodies to the children among the quarters of the married soldiers, and now, would Mrs. Dade please speak with Mrs. Foster, who had come over with him, and Mrs. Dade departed for the kitchen forthwith. Presently she returned. "I'm going back awhile with Mrs. Foster," said she. "She's sitting up to-night with poor Mrs. Wing, who—

A DAUGHTER OF THE SIOUX

" But there was no need of explanation. They all knew. They had laid so recently their wreaths of evergreen on the grave of the gallant soldier who fell, fighting at the Elk, and now another helpless little soul had come to bear the buried name, and all that were left for mother and babe was woman's boundless charity. It was Thanksgiving night, and while the wail of the bereaved and stricken went up from more than one of these humble tenements below the eastward bluff, there were scores of glad and grateful hearts that lifted praise and thanksgiving to the throne on high, even though they knew not at the moment but that they, too, might, even then, be robbed of all that stood between them and desolation. Once it happened in the story of our hard-fighting, hard-used little army that a bevy of fair young wives, nearly half a score in number, in all the bravery of their summer toilets, sat in the shadow of the flag, all smiles and gladness and applause, joining in the garrison festivities on the Nation's natal day, never dreaming of the awful news that should fell them ere the coming of another sun; that one and all they had been widowed more than a week; that the men they loved, whose names they bore, lay hacked and mutilated beyond recognition within sight of those very hills where now the men from Frayne were facing the same old foe. In the midst of army life we are, indeed, in death, and the thanksgiving of loving ones about the fireside for mercies thus far shown, is mingled ever with the dread of what the morrow may unfold.

"Let me go, too, mamma," was Esther's prompt appeal, as she heard her mother's words. "I can put the children to bed while you and Mrs. Foster are over there."

A DAUGHTER OF THE SIOUX

And so with Hogan, lantern bearing, mother and daughter had followed the sergeant's wife across the broad, snow-covered parade; had passed without comment, though each was thinking of the new inmate, the brightly-lighted hospital building on the edge of the plateau, and descended the winding pathway to the humble quarters of the married soldiers, nestling in the sheltered flats between the garrison proper and the bold bluffs that again close bordered the rushing stream. And here at Sergeant Foster's doorway Esther parted from the elders, and was welcomed by shrieks of joy from three sturdy little cherubs—the sergeant's olive branches, and here, as the last notes of tattoo went echoing away under the vast and spangled sky, one by one her charges closed their drooping lids and dropped to sleep and left their gentle friend and reader to her own reflections.

There was a soldier dance that night in one of the vacant messrooms. Flint's two companies were making the best of their isolation, and found, as is not utterly uncommon, quite a few maids and matrons among the households of the absent soldiery quite willing to be consoled and comforted. There were bright lights, therefore, further along the edge of the steep, beyond those of the hospital, and the squeak of fiddle and drone of 'cello, mingled with the plaintive piping of the flute, were heard at intervals through the silence of the wintry night. No tramp of sentry broke the hush about the little rift between the heights— the major holding that none was necessary where there were so many dogs. Most of the soldiers' families had gone to the dance; all of the younger children were asleep; even the dogs were still, and so, when at ten o'clock Esther tiptoed from the children's

A DAUGHTER OF THE SIOUX

bedside and stood under the starlight, the murmur of the Platte was the only sound that reached her ears until, away over at the southwest gate the night guards began the long-drawn heralding of the hour. "Ten o'clock and all's well" it went from post to post along the west and northward front, but when Number Six, at the quartermaster's storehouse near the southeast corner, should have taken up the cry where it was dropped by Number Five, afar over near the flagstaff, there was unaccountable silence. Six did not utter a sound.

Looking up from the level of "Sudstown," as it had earlier been named, Esther could see the black bulk of the storehouse close to the edge of the plateau. Between its westward gable end and the porch of the hospital lay some fifty yards of open space, and through this gap now gleamed a spangled section of the western heavens. Along the bluff, just under the crest, ran a pathway that circled the southeastward corner and led away to the trader's store, south of the post. Tradition had it that the track was worn by night raiders, bearing contraband fluids from store to barracks in the days before such traffic was killed by that common sense promoter of temperance, soberness and chastity—the post exchange. Along that bluff line, from the storehouse toward the hospital, invisible, doubtless, from either building or from the bluff itself, but thrown in sharp relief against that rectangular inlet of starry sky, two black figures, crouching and bearing some long, flat object between them, swift and noiseless were speeding toward the hospital. The next instant they were lost in the black background of that building. Then, as suddenly and a moment later, one of them reappeared, just for a moment, against the

A DAUGHTER OF THE SIOUX

brightly lighted window,—the southernmost window on the easterward side—the window of the room that had been Beverly Field's—the window of the room now given over to Eagle Wing, the Sioux,—the captive for whose safe keeping a special sentry within the building, and this strangely silent Number Six without, were jointly responsible. Then that silhouetted figure was blotted from her sight in general darkness, for the lights within as suddenly went out.

And at that very moment a sound smote upon her ear, unaccountable at that hour and that side of the garrison— hoofbeats swiftly coming down into the hollow from the eastward bluff,—hoofbeats and low, excited voices. Foster's little house was southernmost of the settlement. The ground was open between it and the heights, and despite the low, cautious tones, Esther heard the foremost rider's muttered, angering words. "Dam fool! Crazy! Heap crazy! Too much hurry. Ought t' let him call off first!" Then an answer in guttural Sioux.

And then in an instant it dawned upon the girl that here was new crime, new bloodshed, perhaps, and a plot to free a villianous captive. Her first thought was to scream for aid, but what aid could she summon? Not a man was within hail except these, the merciless haters of her race and name. To scream would be to invite their ready knives to her heart—to the heart of any woman who might rush to her succor. The cry died in her throat, and, trembling with dread and excitement, she clung to the door post and crouched and listened, for stifled mutterings could be heard, a curse or two in vigorous English, a stamping of impatient

A DAUGHTER OF THE SIOUX

ponies, a warning in a woman's tone. Then, thank God! Up at the storehouse corner a light came dancing into view. In honest soldier tones boomed out the query "What's the matter, Six?" and then, followed by a scurry of hoofs, a mad lashing of quirts, a scramble and rush of frightened steeds, and a cursing of furious tongues, her own brave young voice rang out on the night. "This way, sergeant! Help—Quick!"

Black forms of mounts and riders sped desperately away, and then with all the wiry, sinewy strength of her lithe and slender form, Esther hurled herself upon another slender figure, speeding after these, afoot. Desperately she clung to it in spite of savage blows and strainings. And so they found her, as forth they came,—a rush of shrieking, startled, candle-bearing women,—of bewildered and unconsciously blasphemous men of the guard— her arms locked firmly about a girl in semi-savage garb. The villain of the drama had been whisked away, leaving the woman who sought to save him to the mercy of the foe.

CHAPTER XXII

BEHIND THE BARS

In the whirl and excitement following the startling outcry from the flats, all Fort Frayne was speedily involved. The guard came rushing through the night, Corporal Shannon stumbling over a prostrate form,—the sentry on Number Six, gagged and bound. The steward shouted from the hospital porch that Eagle Wing, the prisoner patient, had escaped through the rear window, despite its height above the sloping ground. A little ladder, borrowed from the quartermaster's corral, was found a moment later. An Indian pony, saddled Sioux fashion, was caught running, riderless, toward the trader's back gate, his horsehair bridle torn half way from his shaggy head. Sergeant Crabb, waiting for no orders from the major, no sooner heard that Moreau was gone, than he rushed his stable guard to the saddleroom, and in fifteen minutes had, not only his own squad, but half a dozen "casual" troopers circling the post in search of the trail, and in less than half an hour was hot in chase of two fleeing horsemen, dimly seen ahead through the starlight, across the snowy wastes. That snowfall was the Sioux's undoing. Without it the trail would have been invisible at night. With it, the pursued were well-nigh hopeless from the start. Precious time had been lost in circling far out south of the post before making for the ford, whither Crabb's instinct sent him at once, to the end that he and two of his fellows ploughed through the foaming waters, barely five hundred yards behind the chase, and, as they rode vehemently onward through the starlight, straining every nerve, they heard nothing of the happenings about the Fosters' doorway, where by this time post commander, post surgeon, post quartermaster and acting post adjutant, post ordnance, quartermaster and commissary sergeants, many of the post guard and most of the post laundresses had gathered—some silent, anxious and bewildered, some excitedly babbling; while, within the sergeant's domicile, Esther Dade, very pale and somewhat out of breath, was trying with quiet self possession to answer the myriad questions poured at her, while Dr. Waller was ministering to the dazed and moaning sentry, and, in an adjoining tenement, a little group had gathered about an unconscious form. Someone had sent for Mrs. Hay, who was silently, tearfully chafing the limp and almost lifeless hands of a girl in Indian garb. The cloak and skirts of civilization had been found beneath the window of the deserted room, and were exhibited as a means of bringing to his senses a much bewildered major, whose first words on entering the hut gave rise to wonderment in the eyes of most of his hearers, and to an impulsive reply from the lips of Mrs. Hay.

"I warned the general that girl would play us some Indian trick, but he ordered her release," said Flint, and with wrathful emphasis came the answer.

"The general warned you *this* girl would play you a trick, and, thanks to no one but you, she's done it!"

Then rising and stepping aside, the long-suffering woman revealed the pallid, senseless face,—not of the little Indian maid, her shrinking charge and guest,—but of the niece she loved and had lived and lied for many and trying years—Nanette La Fleur, a long-lost sister's only child.

So Blake knew what he was talking about that keen November morning among the pines at Bear Cliff. He had unearthed an almost forgotten legend of old Fort Laramie.

But the amaze and discomfiture of the temporary post commander turned this night of thanksgiving, so far as he was concerned, into something purgatorial. The sight of his sentry, bound, gagged and bleeding,—the discovery of the ladder and of the escape of the prisoner, for whom he was accountable, had filled him with dismay, yet for the moment failed to stagger his indomitable self esteem. There had been a plot, of course, and the instant impulse of his soul was to fix the blame on others and to free himself. An Indian trick, of course, and who but the little Indian maid within the trader's gates could be the instrument! Through her, of course, the conspirators about the post had been enabled to act. She was the general's *protegée*, not his, and the general must shoulder the blame. Even when Flint saw Nanette, self convicted through her very garb and her presence at the scene of the final struggle,—even when assured it was she and not the little Ogalalla girl who had been caught in the act,—that the latter, in fact, had never left the trader's house, his disproportioned mind refused to grasp the situation. Nanette, he declared, with pallid face, "must have been made a victim." "Nothing could have been farther from her thoughts than complicity in the escape of Eagle Wing." "She had every reason to desire his restoration to health, strength and to the fostering

A DAUGHTER OF THE SIOUX

care of the good and charitable body of Christian people interested in his behalf." "All this would be endangered by his attempt to rejoin the warriors on the warpath." The major ordered the instant arrest of the sentry stationed at the door of the hospital room—shut out by the major's own act from all possibility of seeing what was going on within. He ordered under arrest the corporal of the relief on post for presumable complicity, and, mindful of a famous case of Ethiopian skill then new in the public mind, demanded of Dr. Waller that he say in so many words that the gag and wrist thongs on the prostrate sentry had not been self applied. Waller impassively pointed to the huge lump at the base of the sufferer's skull, "Gag and bonds he might have so placed, after much assiduous practice," said he, "but no man living could hit himself such a blow at the back of the head."

"Who could have done it, then?" asked Flint. It was inconceivable to Waller's mind that any one of the soldiery could have been tempted to such perfidy for an Indian's sake. There was not at the moment an Indian scout or soldier at the post, or an Indian warrior, not a prisoner, unaccounted for. There had been halfbreeds hanging about the store prior to the final escapade of Pete and Crapaud, but these had realized their unpopularity after the battle on the Elk, and had departed for other climes. Crapaud was still under guard. Pete was still at large, perchance, with Stabber's braves. There was not another man about the trader's place whom Flint or others could suspect. Yet the sergeant of the guard, searching cautiously with his lantern about the post of Number Six, had come upon some

A DAUGHTER OF THE SIOUX

suggestive signs. The snow was trampled and bloody about the place where the soldier fell, and there were here and there the tracks of moccasined feet,—those of a young woman or child going at speed toward the hospital, running, probably, and followed close by a moccasined man. Then those of the man, alone, went sprinting down the bluff southeastward over the flats some distance south of the Foster's doorway and up the opposite bluff, to a point where four ponies, shoeless, had been huddled for as much, perhaps, as half an hour. Then all four had come scampering down close together into the space below the hospital, not fifty yards from where the sentry fell, and the moccasined feet of a man and woman had scurried down the bluff from the hospital window, to meet them west of Foster's shanty. Then there had been confusion,—trouble of some kind: One pony, pursued a short distance, had broken away; the others had gone pounding out southeastward up the slope and out over the uplands, then down again, in wide sweep, through the valley of the little rivulet and along the low bench southwest of the fort, crossing the Rock Springs road and striking, further on, diagonally, the Rawlins trail, where Crabb and his fellows had found it and followed.

But all this took hours of time, and meanwhile, only half revived, Nanette had been gently, pityingly borne away to a sorrowing woman's home, for at last it was found, through the thick and lustrous hair, that she, too, had been struck a harsh and cruel blow; that one reason, probably, why she had been able to oppose no stouter resistance to so slender a girl as Esther Dade was that she was already half dazed through the stroke of some

A DAUGHTER OF THE SIOUX

blunt, heavy weapon, wielded probably by him she was risking all to save.

Meantime the major had been pursuing his investigations. Schmidt, the soldier sentry in front of Moreau's door, a simple-hearted Teuton of irreproachable character, tearfully protested against his incarceration. He had obeyed his orders to the letter. The major himself had brought the lady to the hospital and showed her in. The door that had been open, permitting the sentry constant sight of his prisoner, had been closed by the commanding officer himself. Therefore, it was not for him, a private soldier, to presume to reopen it. The major said to the lady he would return for her soon after ten, and the lady smilingly (Schmidt did not say how smilingly,—how bewitchingly smilingly, but the major needed no reminder) thanked him, and said, by that time she would be ready. In a few minutes she came out, saying, (doubtless with the same bewitching smile) she would have to run over home for something, and she was gone nearly half an hour, and all that time the door was open, the prisoner on the bed in his blankets, the lamp brightly burning. It was near tattoo when she returned, with some things under her cloak, and she was breathing quick and seemed hurried and shut the door after thanking him, and he saw no more of her for fifteen minutes, when the door opened and out she came, the same cloak around her, yet she looked different, somehow, and must have tiptoed, for he didn't hear her heels as he had before. She didn't seem quite so tall, either, and that was all, for he never knew anything more about it till the steward came running to tell of the escape.

A DAUGHTER OF THE SIOUX

So Schmidt could throw but little light upon the situation, save to Flint himself, who did not then see fit to say to anyone that at no time was it covenanted that Miss Flower should be allowed to go and come unattended. In doing so she had deluded someone beside the sentry.

It was late in the night when Number Six regained his senses and could tell *his* tale, which was even more damaging. Quite early in the evening, so he said,—as early as nine o'clock,—he was under the hospital corner, listening to the music further up along the bluff. A lady came from the south of the building as though she were going down to Sudstown. Mrs. Foster had gone down not long before, and Hogan, with a lantern, and two officers' ladies. But this one came all alone and spoke to him pleasant-like and said she was so sorry he couldn't be at the dance. She'd been seeing the sick and wounded in hospital, she said, and was going to bring some wine and jellies. If he didn't mind, she'd take the path around the quartermaster's storehouse outside, as she was going to Mr. Hay's, and didn't care to go through by the guard-house. So Six let her go, as he "had no orders agin it" (even though it dawned upon him that this must be the young lady that had been carried off by the Sioux). That made him think a bit, he said, and when she came back with a basket nicely covered with a white napkin, she made him take a big chicken sandwich. "Sure I didn't know how to refuse the lady, until she poured me out a big tumbler of wine—wine, she said, she was taking in to Sergeant Briggs and Corporal Turner that was shot at the Elk, and she couldn't bear to see me all alone out there in the cold." But Six said he dasn't take the wine. He got six months "blind"

Page 259

A DAUGHTER OF THE SIOUX

once for a similar solecism, and, mindful of the major's warning (this was diplomatic) Six swore he had sworn off, and had to refuse the repeated requests of the lady. He suspicioned her, he said, because she was so persistent. Then she laughed and said good-night and went on to the hospital. What became of the wine she had poured out? (This from the grim and hitherto silent doctor, seated by the bedside.) She must have tossed it out or drunk it herself, perhaps, Six didn't know. Certainly no trace of it could be found in the snow. Then nothing happened for as much as twenty minutes or so, and he was over toward the south end of his post, but facing toward the hospital when she came again down the steps, and this time handed him some cake and told him he was a good soldier not to drink even wine, and asked him what were the lights away across the Platte, and he couldn't see any, and was following her pointing finger and staring, and then all of a sudden he saw a million lights, dancing, and stars and bombs and that was all he knew till they began talking to him here in hospital. Something had hit him from behind, but he couldn't tell what.

Flint's nerve was failing him, for here was confirmation of the general's theory, but there was worse to come and more of it.

Miss McGrath, domestic at the trader's, had told a tale that had reached the ears of Mistress McGann, and 'twas the latter that bade the major summon the girl and demand of her what it was she had seen and heard concerning "Crappo" and the lady occupant of the second floor front at the trader's home. Then it was that the major heard what others had earlier conjectured—

A DAUGHTER OF THE SIOUX

that there had been clandestine meetings, whispered conferences and the like, within the first week of the lovely niece's coming to Fort Frayne. That notes had been fetched and carried by "Crappo" as well as Pete; that Miss Flower was either a somnambulist or a good imitation of one, as on two occasions the maid had "peeked" and seen her down-stairs at the back door in the dead hours of the night, or the very early morning. That was when she first came. Then, since the recapture, Miss McGrath felt confident that though never again detected down stairs, Miss Flower had been out at night, as Miss McGrath believed her to have been the night, when was it? "when little Kennedy had his scrap wid the Sioux the boys do be all talkin' about"—the night, in fact, that Stabber's band slipped away from the Platte, Ray's troop following at dawn. Questioned as to how it was possible for Miss Flower to get out without coming down stairs, Miss McGrath said she wasn't good at monkeyshines herself, but "wimmen that could ride sthraddle-wise" were capable of climbs more difficult than that which the vine trellis afforded from the porch floor to the porch roof. Miss McGrath hadn't been spying, of course, because her room was at the back of the house, beyond the kitchen, but how did the little heel tracks get on the veranda roof?—the road dust on the matting under the window? the vine twigs in that "quare" made skirt never worn by day? That Miss Flower could and did ride "asthraddle" and ride admirably when found with the Sioux at Bear Cliff, everybody at Frayne well knew by this time. That she had so ridden at Fort Frayne was known to no officer or lady of the garrison then present, but believed by Miss McGrath because

A DAUGHTER OF THE SIOUX

of certain inexpressibles of the same material with the "quare" made skirt; both found, dusty and somewhat bedraggled, the morning Captain Blake was having his chase after the Indians, and Miss Flower was so "wild excited like." All this and more did Miss McGrath reveal before being permitted to return to the sanctity of her chamber, and Flint felt the ground sinking beneath his feet. It might even be alleged of him now that he had connived at the escape of this most dangerous and desperate character, this Indian leader, of whom example, prompt and sharp, would certainly have been made, unless the general and the ends of justice were defeated. But what stung the major most of all was that he had been fairly victimized, hoodwinked, cajoled, wheedled, flattered into this wretched predicament, all through the wiles and graces of a woman. No one knew it, whatever might be suspected, but Nanette had bewitched him quite as much as missives from the East had persuaded and misled.

And so it was with hardened and resentful heart that the major sought her on the morrow. The general and the commands afield would soon be coming home. Such Indians as they had not "rounded up" and captured were scattered far and wide. The campaign was over. Now for the disposition of the prisoners. It was to tell Mrs. Hayand Nanette, especially Nanette, why the sentries were re-established about their home and that, though he would not place the trader's niece within a garrison cell, he should hold her prisoner beneath the trader's roof to await the action of superior authority on the grievous charges lodged at her door. She was able to be up, said Miss McGrath,—not only up but down—down in the breakfast room, looking blither and more like herself than she had been since she was brought home.

"Say that Major Flint desires to see her and Mrs. Hay," said Flint, with majesty of mien, as, followed by two of his officers, he was shown into the trader's parlor.

And presently they came—Mrs. Hay pale and sorrowing; Miss Flower, pale, perhaps, but triumphantly defiant. The one sat and covered her face with her hands as she listened to the major's few words, cold, stern and accusing. The other looked squarely at him, with fearless, glittering eyes:—

"You may order what you like so far as I'm concerned," was the utterly reckless answer of the girl. "I don't care what you do now that I know he is safe—free—and that you will never lay hands on him again."

"That's where you are in error, Miss Flower," was the major's calm, cold-blooded, yet rejoiceful reply. It was for this, indeed, that he had come. "Ralph Moreau was run down by my men soon after midnight, and he's now behind the bars."

A DAUGHTER OF THE SIOUX

CHAPTER XXIII

A SOLDIER ENTANGLED

December and bitter cold. The river frozen stiff. The prairie sheeted in unbroken snow. Great log fires roaring in every open fireplace. Great throngs of soldiery about the red hot barrack stoves, for all the columns were again in winter columns, and Flint's two companies had "got the route" for home. They were to march on the morrow, escorting as far as Laramie the intractables of Stabber's band, some few of the Indians to go in irons, among them Ralph Moreau, or Eagle Wing, now a notorious character.

The general was there at Frayne, with old "Black Bill," erstwhile chief inspector of the department, once a subaltern in days long gone by when Laramie was "Ultima Thule" of the plains forts. The general had heard Flint's halting explanation of his laxity in Moreau's case, saying almost as little in reply as his old friend Grant when "interviewed" by those of whom he disapproved. "Black Bill" it was who waxed explosive when once he opened on the major, and showed that amazed New Englander something of the contents of Moreau's Indian kit, including the now famous hunting pouch, all found with Stabber's village. A precious scoundrel, as it turned out, was this same Moreau, with more sins to answer for than many a convicted jail bird, and with not one follower left to do him reverence except, perhaps, that lonely girl, self secluded at the Hays. Hay himself, though weak, was beginning to sit up. Dade, Blake and Ray were all once more housed in garrison. Truscott and Billings, with their hardy troopers, had taken temporary station at the post, until the general had decided upon the disposition of the array of surrendered Indians, nearly three hundred in number, now confined under strong guard in the quartermaster's corral at the flats, with six "head devils," including Eagle Wing, in the garrison prison.

All the officers, with two exceptions, were again for duty at Frayne. Webb, laid by the heels at Beecher, his feet severely frozen, and Beverly Field, who, recalled from a brief and solemn visit to a far southern home, had reached the post at nightfall of the 10th. There had hardly been allowed him time to uplift a single prayer, to receive a word of consolation from the lips of friends and kindred who loved the honored father, borne to his last resting place. "Come as soon as possible," read the message wired him by Ray, and, though the campaign was over, it was evident that something was amiss, and, with all his sorrow fresh upon him, the lad, sore in body and soul, had hastened to obey.

And it was Ray who received and welcomed him and took him straightway to his own cosy quarters, that Mrs. Ray, and then the Blakes, might add their sympathetic and cordial greeting,—ere it came to telling why it was that these, his friends despite that trouble that could not be talked of, were now so earnest in their sympathy,—before telling him that his good name had become involved, that there were allegations concerning him which the chief had ordered "pigeon-holed" until he should come to face them. A pity it is that Bill Hay could not have been there, too, but his fever had left him far too weak to leave his room. Only

A DAUGHTER OF THE SIOUX

Ray and Blake were present and it was an interview not soon, if ever, to be forgotten.

"I'm no hand at breaking things gently, Field," said Ray, when finally the three were closeted together in the captain's den. "It used to worry Webb that you were seen so often riding with Miss—Miss Flower up to Stabber's village, and, in the light of what has since happened, you will admit that he had reasons. Hear me through," he continued, as Field, sitting bolt upright in the easy chair, essayed to speak. "Neither Captain Blake nor I believe one word to your dishonor in the matter, but it looks as though you had been made a tool of, and you are by no means the first man. It was to see this fellow, Moreau—Eagle Wing— whom you recognized at the Elk,—she was there so frequently— was it not?"

Into Field's pale face there had come a look of infinite distress. For a moment he hesitated, and little beads began to start out on his forehead.

"Captain Ray," he finally said, "they tell me—I heard it from the driver on the way up from Rock Springs—that Miss Flower is virtually a prisoner, that she had been in league with the Sioux, and yet, until I can see her—can secure my release from a promise, I have to answer you as I answered you before—I cannot say."

Blake started impatiently and heaved up from his lounging chair, his long legs taking him in three strides to the frost-covered window at the front. Ray sadly shook his dark, curly head.

A DAUGHTER OF THE SIOUX

"You *are* to see her, Field. The general—bless him for a trump!—wouldn't listen to a word against you in your absence; but that girl has involved everybody—you, her aunt, who has been devotion itself to her, her uncle, who was almost her slave. She deliberately betrayed him into the hands of the Sioux. In fact this red robber and villain, Moreau, is the only creature she hasn't tried to 'work,' and he abandoned her after she had lied, sneaked and stolen for him."

"Captain Ray!" The cry came from pallid lips, and the young soldier started to his feet, appalled at such accusation.

"Every word of it is true," said Ray. "She joined him after his wounds. She shared his escape from the village at our approach. She was with him when Blake nabbed them at Bear Cliff. She was going with him from here. What manner of girl was that, Field, for you to be mixed up with?"

"He is her half brother!" protested Field, with kindling eyes. "She told me—everything—told me of their childhood together, and—"

"Told you a pack of infernal lies!" burst in Blake, no longer able to contain himself. "Made you a cat's paw; led you even to taking her by night to see him when she learned the band were to jump for the mountains—used you, by God, as he used *her*, and, like the Indian she is, she'd turn and stab you now, if you stood in her way or his. Why, Field, that brute's her lover, and she's his—"

A DAUGHTER OF THE SIOUX

"It's a lie! You shall not say it, sir!" cried Field, beside himself with wrath and amaze, as he stood quivering from head to foot, still weak from wounds, fever and distress of mind. But Ray sprang to his side. "Hush, Blake! Hush, Field! Don't speak. What is it, Hogan?" And sharply he turned him to the door, never dreaming what had caused the interruption.

"The general, sir, to see the captain!"

And there, in the hallway, throwing off his heavy overcoat and "arctics," there, with that ever faithful aide in close attendance, was the chief they loved; dropped in, all unsuspecting, just to say good-bye. "I knocked twice," began Hogan, but Ray brushed him aside, for, catching sight of the captain's face, the general was already at the door. Another moment and he had discovered Field, and with both hands extended, all kindliness and sympathy, he stepped at once across the room to greet him.

"I was so very sorry to hear the news," said he. "I knew your father well in the old days. How's your wound? What brought you back so soon?"

And then there was one instant of awkward silence and then— Ray spoke.

"That was my doing, general. I believed it best that he should be here to meet you and—every allegation at his expense. Mr. Field, I feel sure, does not begin to know them yet, especially as to the money."

"It was all recovered," said the general. "It was found almost intact—so was much of that that they took from Hay. Even if it hadn't been, Hay assumed all responsibility for the loss."

With new bewilderment in his face, the young officer, still white and trembling, was gazing, half stupefied, from one to the other.

"What money?" he demanded. "I never heard—"

"Wait," said the general, with significant glance at Ray, who was about to speak. "I am to see them—Mrs. Hay and her niece—at nine o'clock. It is near that now. Webb cannot be with us, but I shall want you, Blake. Say nothing until then. Sit down, Mr. Field, and tell me about that leg. Can you walk from here to Hay's, I wonder?"

Then the ladies, Mrs. Ray and her charming next door neighbor, appeared, and the general adjourned the conference forthwith, and went with them to the parlor.

"Say nothing more," Ray found time to whisper. "You'll understand it all in twenty minutes."

And at nine o'clock the little party was on its way through the sharp and wintry night, the general and Captain Blake, side by side, ahead, the aide-de-camp and Mr. Field close following. Dr. Waller, who had been sent for, met them near the office. The sentries at the guard-house were being changed as the five tramped by along the snapping and protesting board walk, and a sturdy little chap, in fur cap and gauntlets, and huge buffalo overcoat, caught sight of them and, facing outward, slapped his

A DAUGHTER OF THE SIOUX

carbine down to the carry—the night signal of soldier recognition of superior rank as practised at the time.

"Tables are turned with a vengeance," said the general, with his quiet smile. "That's little Kennedy, isn't it? I seem to see him everywhere when we're campaigning. Moreau was going to eat his heart out next time they met, I believe."

"So he said," grinned Blake, "before Winsor's bullet fetched him. Pity it hadn't killed instead of crippling him."

"He's a bad lot," sighed the general. "Wing won't fly away from Kennedy, I fancy."

"Not if there's a shot left in his belt," said Blake. "And Ray is officer-of-the-day. There'll be no napping on guard this night."

At the barred aperture that served for window on the southward front, a dark face peered forth in malignant hate as the speakers strode by. But it shrank back, when the sentry once more tossed his carbine to the shoulder, and briskly trudged beneath the bars. Six Indians shared that prison room, four of their number destined to exile in the distant East,—to years, perhaps, within the casemates of a seaboard fort—the last place on earth for a son of the warlike Sioux.

"They know their fate, I understand," said Blake, as the general moved on again.

"Oh, yes. Their agent and others have been here with Indian Bureau orders, permitting them to see and talk with the

A DAUGHTER OF THE SIOUX

prisoners. Their shackles are to be riveted on to-night. Nearly time now, isn't it?"

"At tattoo, sir. The whole guard forms then, and the four are to be moved into the main room for the purpose. I am glad this is the last of it."

"Yes, we'll start them with Flint at dawn in the morning. He'll be more than glad to get away, too. He hasn't been over lucky here, either."

A strange domestic—(the McGrath having been given warning and removed to Sudsville) showed them into the trader's roomy parlor, the largest and most pretentious at the post. Hay had lavished money on his home and loved it and the woman who had so adorned it. She came in almost instantly to greet them, looking piteously into the kindly, bearded face of the general, and civilly, yet absently, welcoming the others. She did not seem to realize that Field, who stood in silence by the side of Captain Blake, had been away. She had no thought, apparently, for anyone but the chief himself,—he who held the destinies of her dear ones in the hollow of his hand. His first question was for Fawn Eyes, the little Ogalalla maiden whose history he seemed to know. "She is well and trying to be content with me," was the reply. "She has been helping poor Nanette. She does not seem to understand or realize what is coming to him. Have they—ironed him—yet?"

"Hush! She's coming"—She was there.

A DAUGHTER OF THE SIOUX

"I believe not," said the general. "But it has to be done to-night. They start so early in the morning."

"And you won't let her see him, general. No good can come from it. She declares she will go to him in the morning, if you prohibit it to-night," and the richly jewelled hands of the unhappy woman were clasped almost in supplication.

"By morning he will be beyond her reach. The escort starts at six."

"And—these gentlemen here—" She looked nervously, appealingly about her. "Must they—all know?"

"These and the inspector general. He will be here in a moment. But, indeed, Mrs. Hay, it *is* all known, practically," said the general, with sympathy and sorrow in his tone.

"Not all—not all, general! Even I don't know all—She herself has said so. Hush! She's coming."

She was there! They had listened for swish of skirts or fall of slender feet upon the stairway, but there had not been a sound. They saw the reason as she halted at the entrance, lifting with one little hand the costly Navajo blanket that hung as a portière. In harmony with the glossy folds of richly dyed wool, she was habited in Indian garb from head to foot. In two black, lustrous braids, twisted with feather and quill and ribbon, her wealth of hair hung over her shoulders down the front of her slender form. A robe of dark blue stuff, rich with broidery of colored bead and bright-hued plumage, hung, close clinging, and her feet were

A DAUGHTER OF THE SIOUX

shod in soft moccasins, also deftly worked with bead and quill. But it was her face that chained the gaze of all, and that drew from the pallid lips of Lieutenant Field a gasp of mingled consternation and amaze. Without a vestige of color; with black circles under her glittering eyes; with lines of suffering around the rigid mouth and with that strange pinched look about the nostrils that tells of anguish, bodily and mental, Nanette stood at the doorway, looking straight at the chief. She had no eyes for lesser lights. All her thought, apparently, was for him,—for him whose power it was, in spite of vehement opposition, to deal as he saw fit with the prisoner in his hands. Appeal on part of Friends Societies, Peace and Indian Associations had failed. The President had referred the matter in its entirety to the general commanding in the field, and the general had decided. One moment she studied his face, then came slowly forward. No hand extended. No sign of salutation,—greeting,—much less of homage. Ignoring all others present, she addressed herself solely to him.

"Is it true you have ordered him in irons and to Fort Rochambeau?" she demanded.

"It is."

"Simply because he took part with his people when your soldiers made war on them?" she asked, her pale lips quivering.

"You well know how much else there was," answered the general, simply. "And I have told you he deserves no pity—of yours."

A DAUGHTER OF THE SIOUX

"Oh, you say he came back here a spy!" she broke forth, impetuously. "It is not so! He never came near the post,—nearer than Stabber's village, and there he had a right to be. You say 'twas he who led them to the warpath,—that he planned the robbery here and took the money. He never knew they were going, till they were gone. He never stole a penny. That money was loaned him honestly—and for a purpose—and with the hope and expectation of rich profit thereby."

"By you, do you mean?" asked the general, calmly, as before.

"By me? No! What money had I? He asked it and it was given him—by Lieutenant Field."

A gasp that was almost a cry following instantly on this insolent assertion—a sound of stir and start among the officers at whom she had not as yet so much as glanced, now caused the girl to turn one swift, contemptuous look their way, and in that momentary flash her eyes encountered those of the man she had thus accused. Field stood like one turned suddenly to stone, gazing at her with wild, incredulous eyes. One instant she seemed to sway, as though the sight had staggered her, but the rally was as instantaneous. Before the general could interpose a word, she plunged on again:—

"He, at least, had a heart and conscience. He knew how wrongfully Moreau had been accused,—that money was actually needed to establish his claim. It would all have been repaid if your soldiers had not forced this wicked war, and—" and now in her vehemence her eyes were flashing, her hand uplifted, when,

A DAUGHTER OF THE SIOUX

all on a sudden, the portière was raised the second time, and there at the doorway stood the former inspector general, "Black Bill." At sight of him the mad flow of words met sudden stop. Down, slowly down, came the clinched, uplifted hand. Her eyes, glaring as were Field's a moment agone, were fixed in awful fascination on the grizzled face. Then actually she recoiled as the veteran officer stepped quietly forward into the room.

"And what?" said he, with placid interest. "I haven't heard you rave in many a moon, Nanette. You are your mother over again—without your mother's excuse for fury."

But a wondrous silence had fallen on the group. The girl had turned rigid. For an instant not a move was made, and, in the hush of all but throbbing hearts, the sound of the trumpets pealing forth the last notes of tattoo came softly through the outer night.

Then sudden, close at hand, yet muffled by double door and windows, came other sounds—sounds of rush and scurry,— excited voices,—cries of halt! halt!—the ring of a carbine,—a yell of warning—another shot, and Blake and the aide-de-camp sprang through the hallway to the storm door without. Mrs. Hay, shuddering with dread, ran to the door of her husband's chamber beyond the dining room. She was gone but a moment. When she returned the little Ogalalla maid, trembling and wild-eyed, had come running down from aloft. The general had followed into the lighted hallway,—they were all crowding there by this time,—and the voice of Captain Ray, with just a tremor

A DAUGHTER OF THE SIOUX

of excitement about it, was heard at the storm door on the porch, in explanation to the chief.

"Moreau, sir! Broke guard and stabbed Kennedy. The second shot dropped him. He wants Fawn Eyes, his sister."

A scream of agony rang through the hall, shrill and piercing. Then the wild cry followed:

"You shall not hold me! Let me go to him, I say—I am his wife!"

CHAPTER XXIV

THE DEATH SONG OF THE SIOUX

That was a gruesome night at Frayne. Just at tattoo the door leading to the little cell room had been thrown open, and the sergeant of the guard bade the prisoners come forth,—all warriors of the Ogalalla band and foremost of their number was Eagle Wing, the battle leader. Recaptured by Crabb and his men after a desperate flight and fight for liberty, he had apparently been planning ever since a second essay even more desperate. In sullen silence he had passed his days, showing no sign of recognition of any face among his guards until the morning Kennedy appeared—all malice forgotten now that his would-be slayer was a helpless prisoner, and therefore did the Irishman greet him jovially. "That man would knife you if he had half a chance," said the sergeant. "Watch out for him!"

"You bet I'll watch out," said Kennedy, never dreaming that, despite all search and vigilance, Moreau had managed to obtain and hide a knife.

In silence they had shuffled forth into the corridor. The heavy portal swung behind them, confining the other two. Another door opened into the guardroom proper, where stood the big, red hot stove and where waited two blacksmiths with the irons. Once in the guard room every window was barred, and members of the guard, three deep, blocked in eager curiosity the doorway leading to the outer air. In the corridor on one side stood three infantry soldiers, with fixed bayonets. On the other, facing them,

A DAUGHTER OF THE SIOUX

three others of the guard. Between them shuffled the Sioux, "Wing" leading. One glance at the waiting blacksmiths was enough. With the spring of a tiger, he hurled himself, head foremost and bending low, straight at the open doorway, and split his way through the astonished guards like center rush at foot ball, scattering them right and left; then darted round the corner of the guard-house, agile as a cat.

And there was Kennedy confronting him! One furious lunge he made with gleaming knife, then shot like an arrow, straight for the southward bluff. It was bad judgment. He trusted to speed, to dim starlight, to bad aim, perhaps; but the little Irishman dropped on one knee and the first bullet tore through the muscles of a stalwart arm; the second, better aimed, pierced the vitals. Then they were on him, men by the dozen, in another instant, as he staggered and fell there, impotent and writhing.

They bore him to the cell again,—the hospital was too far,—and Waller and his aides came speedily to do all that surgery could accomplish, but he cursed them back. He raved at Ray, who entered, leading poor, sobbing little Fawn Eyes, and demanded to be left alone with her. Waller went out to minister to Kennedy, bleeding fast, and the others looked to Ray for orders when the door was once more opened and Blake entered with Nanette.

"By the general's order," said he, in brief explanation, and in an instant she was on her knees beside the dying Sioux. There and thus they left them. Waller said there was nothing to be done. The junior surgeon, Tracy,—he whom she had so fascinated

A DAUGHTER OF THE SIOUX

only those few weeks before,—bent and whispered: "Call me if you need. I shall remain within hearing." But there came no call. At taps the door was once more softly opened and Tracy peered within. Fawn Eyes, rocking to and fro, was sobbing in an abandonment of grief. Nanette, face downward, lay prone upon a stilled and lifeless heart.

Flint and his escort duly went their way, and spread their story as they camped at Laramie and "the Chug." The general tarried another week at Frayne. There was still very much to keep him there; so, not until he and "Black Bill" came down did we at other stations learn the facts. The general, as usual, had little to say. The colonel talked for both.

A woful time, it seems, they had had with poor Nanette when at last it became necessary to take her away from her dead brave. She raged and raved at even her pleading aunt. Defiant of them all, from the general down, and reckless of law or fact, she vowed it was all a conspiracy to murder Moreau in cold blood. They gave him the knife, she declared, although it later developed that she had tossed it through the open window. They had given him the chance to escape—the sight of Kennedy, "who had striven to kill him twice before," and then of the blacksmiths, with their degrading shackles—all just to tempt him to make a dash for freedom;—just as they had lured and murdered Crazy Horse— Crazy Horse, his brave kinsman—not ten years before,—then had placed a dead shot on the path to life and liberty—a man who killed him in cold blood, as deliberately planned. These were her accusations, and that story took strong hold in certain circles

A DAUGHTER OF THE SIOUX

in the far East, where "love of truth" inspired its widespread publication, but not its contradiction when the facts became known. The same conditions obtain to-day in dealing with affairs across the sea.

Nanette said many other things before her final breakdown; and Hay and his sorrowing wife found their load of care far heaviest, for the strain of Indian blood, now known to all, had steeled the soul of the girl against the people at Fort Frayne, men and women both—against none so vehemently as those who would have shown her sympathy—none so malignantly as those who had suffered for her sake.

This was especially true of Field. In the mad hope of "getting justice," as she termed it, for the dead, she had demanded speech of the general, and, in presence of "Black Bill" and the surgeon, he had given her a hearing. It proved fatal to her cause, for in her fury at what she termed "the triumph of his foes," she lost all sense of right or reason, and declared that it was Field who had warned Stabber's band and sent them fleeing to unite with Lame Wolf,—Field who took the trader's horses and rode by night with Kennedy to warn them it was Webb's intention to surround the village at dawn and make prisoners of the men. It was Field, she said, who furnished the money Moreau needed to establish his claim to a gold mine in the Black Hills, the ownership of which would make them rich and repay Field a dozen times over. It was Field who sought to protect her kindred among the Sioux in hopes, she said it boldly, of winning her. But the general had heard enough. The door was opened and Ray and Blake were

A DAUGHTER OF THE SIOUX

ushered in. The former briefly told of the finding of her note in Field's room the night the adjutant was so mysteriously missing. The note itself was held forth by the inspector general and she was asked if she cared to have it opened and read aloud. Her answer was that Field was a coward, a dastard to betray a woman who had trusted him.

"Oh, he didn't," said Blake, drily. "'Twas just the other way. He couldn't be induced to open his head, so his friends took a hand. You got word of the outbreak through your Indian followers. You wrote to Field and sent the note by Pete, bidding him join you at that godless hour, telling him that you would provide the horses and that you must ride to Stabber's camp to see Moreau for the last time, as he was going at once to the Black Hills. You made Field believe he was your half brother, instead of what he was. You brought Moreau back to the post and took something, I can't say what, down to him from Mr. Hay's,—he waiting for you on the flats below the trader's corral. You should have worn your moccasins, as well as a divided skirt, that night instead of French-heeled *bottines*. The rest—others can tell."

The others were Kennedy and the recaptured, half recalcitrant Pete; the latter turned state's evidence. Kennedy told how he had wandered down into the flats after "the few dhrinks" that made him think scornful of Sioux; of his encounter with Eagle Wing, his rescue by Field and a girl who spoke Sioux like a native. He thought it was little Fawn Eyes when he heard her speak, and until he heard this lady; then he understood. He had been pledged to secrecy by the lieutenant, and never meant to tell a

A DAUGHTER OF THE SIOUX

soul, but when he heard the lie the lady told about the lieutenant, it ended any promise.

Then Pete, an abject, whining wretch, was ushered in, and his story, when dragged out by the roots, was worst of all. Poor Mrs. Hay! She had to hear it, for they sent for her; somebody had to restrain Nanette. Pete said he had known Nanette long time, ever since baby. So had Crapaud. Yes, and they had known Eagle Wing, Moreau, always—knew his father and mother. Knew Nanette's father and mother. But Black Bill interposed. No need to go into these particulars, as substantiating Mrs. Hay and himself, said he. "The lady knows perfectly well that I know all about her girlhood," so Pete returned to modern history. Eagle Wing, it seems, came riding often in from Stabber's camp to see Nanette by night, and "he was in heap trouble, always heap trouble, always want money," and one night she told Pete he must come with her, must never tell of it. She had money, she said, her own, in the trader's safe, but the door was too heavy, she couldn't open it, even though she had the key. She had opened the store by the back door, then came to him to help her with the rest. He pulled the safe door open, he said, and then she hunted and found two big letters, and took them to the house, and next night she opened the store again, and he pulled open the safe, and she put back the letters and sent him to Mr. Field's back door with note, and then over to saddle Harney and Dan, and "bring 'em out back way from stable." Then later she told him Captain Blake had Eagle Wing's buckskin pouch and letters, and they must get them or somebody would hang Eagle Wing, and she kept them going, "all time going," meeting messengers from

A DAUGHTER OF THE SIOUX

the Sioux camps, or carrying letters. She fixed everything for the Sioux to come and capture Hay and the wagon;—fixed everything, even to nearly murdering the sentry on Number Six. Pete and Spotted Horse, a young brave of Stabber's band, had compassed that attempted rescue. She would have had them kill the sentry, if need be, and the reason they didn't get Wing away was that she couldn't wait until the sentries had called off. They might even then have succeeded, only her pony broke away, and she clung to Eagle Wing's until he—he had to hit her to make her let go.

The wild girl, in a fury declared it false from end to end. The poor woman, weeping by her side, bowed her head and declared it doubtless true.

Her story,—Mrs. Hay's,—was saddest of all. Her own father died when she was very, very young. He was a French Canadian trader and traveller who had left them fairly well to do. Next to her Indian mother, Mrs. Hay had loved no soul on earth as she had her pretty baby sister. The girls grew up together. The younger, petted and spoiled, fell in love with a handsome, reckless young French half breed, Jean La Fleur; against all warnings, became his wife, and was soon bullied, beaten and deserted. She lived but a little while, leaving to her more prosperous and level-headed sister, now wedded to Mr. Hay, their baby daughter, also named Nanette, and by her the worthy couple had done their very best. Perhaps it would have been wiser had they sent the child away from all association with the Sioux, but she had lived eight years on the Laramie in daily contact with them, sharing the Indian sports and games, loving their free life, and rebelling furiously when finally taken East. "She" was the real reason why her aunt spent so many months of each succeeding year away from her husband and the frontier. One of the girl's playmates was a magnificent young savage, a son of Crow Killer, the famous chief. The father was killed the day of Crazy Horse's fierce assault on the starving force of General Crook at Slim Buttes in '76, and good, kind missionary people speedily saw promise in the lad, put him at school and strove to educate him. The rest they knew. Sometimes at eastern schools, sometimes with Buffalo Bill, but generally out of money and into mischief, Eagle Wing went from one year to another, and Nanette, foolishly permitted to meet him again in the East, had become infatuated. All that art and education, wealth, travel and luxury combined could do, was done to wean her from her passionate adoration of this superb young savage. There is no fiercer, more intense, devotion than that the Sioux girl gives the warrior who wins her love. She becomes his abject slave. She will labor, lie, steal, sin, suffer, die, *gladly* die for him, if only she believes herself loved in turn, and this did Nanette more than believe, and believing, slaved and studied between his irregular appearances that she might wheedle more money from her aunt to lavish on her brave. When discovered meeting him in secret and by night, she was locked in her third story room and thought secure, until the day revealed her gone by way of the lightning rod. They had to resort to more stringent measures, but time and again she met him, undetected until too late, and when at last her education was declared complete, she had amazed her aunt by

A DAUGHTER OF THE SIOUX

expressing willingness to go to Frayne, when the good woman thought the objectionable kinsman abroad with Buffalo Bill. Until too late, Mrs. Hay knew nothing of his having been discharged and of his preceding them to the West. Then Nanette begged her for more money, because he was in dreadful trouble;—had stabbed a police officer at Omaha, whose people, so Moreau said, agreed not to prosecute him if one thousand dollars could be paid at once. Hay's patience had been exhausted. He had firmly refused to contribute another cent to settle Moreau's scrapes, even though he was a distant kinsman of his wife, and they both were fond of his little sister Fawn Eyes. It had never occurred to Mrs. Hay that Nan could steal from or plot against her benefactors, but that was before she dreamed that Nanette had become the Indian's wife. After that, anything might happen. "If she could do *that* for love of Moreau," said she, "there was nothing she could not do."

And it would seem there was little short of deliberate murder she had not done for her Sioux lover, who had rewarded her utter self-sacrifice by a savage blow with a revolver butt. "Poor Nanette!" sobbed Mrs. Hay, and "Poor Nanette!" said all Fort Frayne, their distrust of her buried and forgotten as she lay, refusing herself to everyone; starving herself in dull, desperate misery in her lonely room. Even grim old "Black Bill," whom she had recognized at once,—Bill, who had been the first to confirm Blake's suspicions as to her identity,—had pity and compassion for her. "It's the way of the blood," said Blake. "She is

A DAUGHTER OF THE SIOUX

"'Bred out of that bloody strain
That haunted us in our familiar paths.'"

"She could do no different," said the general, "having fixed her love on him. It's the strain of the Sioux. *We* call her conduct criminal:—they call it sublime."

And one night, while decision in Nanette's case was still pending, and, still self-secluded, she hid within the trader's home, refusing speech with anyone but little Fawn Eyes, a sleighing party set out from Frayne for a spin by moonlight along the frozen Platte. Wagon bodies had been set on runners, and piled with hay. The young people from officers' row, with the proper allowance of matrons and elders, were stowed therein, and tucked in robes and furs, Esther Dade among them, gentle and responsive as ever, yet still very silent. Field, in his deep mourning, went nowhere. He seemed humiliated beyond words by his connection with this most painful affair. Even the general failed to cheer and reassure him. He blamed himself for everything and shrank even from his friends. They saw the dim glow of the student lamp in his quarters, as they jingled cheerily away. They were coming homeward, toward ten o'clock. The moon was shining brilliantly along the bold heights of the southern bank, and, insensibly, chat and laughter gradually ceased as they came again in sight of the twinkling lights of Frayne, and glanced aloft at a new-made scaffolding, standing black against the sky at the crest of Fetterman Bluff. "Eagle Wing roosts high," said a thoughtless youngster. "The general let them have their way to the last. What's that?" he added, with sudden stop.

A DAUGHTER OF THE SIOUX

The sleigh had as suddenly been reined in. The driver, an Irish trooper, crossed himself, for, on the hush of the breathless winter night, there rose and fell—shrill, quavering, now high, now low, in mournful minor, a weird, desolate, despairing chant, the voice of a heart-broken woman, and one and all they knew at once it was Nanette, after the manner of her mother's people, alone on the lofty height, alone in the wintry wilderness, sobbing out her grief song to the sleeping winds, mourning to the last her lost, her passionately loved brave.

Then, all on a sudden, it ceased. A black form started from under the scaffolding to the edge of the bluff. Then again, weird, wild, uncanny, a barbaric, almost savage strain burst from the lips of the girl. "Mother of Heavin!" cried the driver. "Can no one shtop that awful keen. It's her death song she's singin'!"

Two young officers sprang from the sleigh, but at the instant another cry arose. Another form, this one of horse and rider, appeared at the crest, silhouetted with the girl's against the stars. They saw the rider leap from saddle, almost within arms' length of the singer; saw her quickly turn, as though, for the first time, aware of an intruder. Then the wailing song went out in sudden scream of mingled wrath, hatred and despair, and, like the Sioux that she was at heart, the girl made one mad rush to reach the point of bluff where was a sheer descent of over eighty feet. A shriek of dread went up from the crowded sleigh; a cry of rejoicing, as the intruder sprang and clasped her, preventing her reaching the precipice. But almost instantly followed a moan of anguish, for slipping at the crest, together, firmly linked, they

A DAUGHTER OF THE SIOUX

came rolling, sliding, shooting down the steep incline of the frozen bluff, and brought up with stunning force among the ice blocks, logs and driftwood at the base.

They bore them swiftly homeward,—Field senseless and sorely shaken,—Nanette's fierce spirit slowly drifting away from the bruised and broken tenement held there, so pityingly, in the arms of Esther Dade. Before the Christmas fires were lighted in the snowbound, frontier fort, they had laid all that was mortal of the brave, deluded girl in the little cemetery of Fort Frayne, her solemn story closed, on earth, forever.

A DAUGHTER OF THE SIOUX

L'ENVOI

Nearly two years later, with the old regiment still serving along the storied Platte, they were talking of her one moonlit evening at the flagstaff. The band, by this time a fixture at Frayne, had been playing delightfully, and some of the girls and young gallants had been waltzing on the Rays' veranda. A few new faces were there. Two faces, well known, were missing,—those of Esther Dade and Beverly Field. The latter had never been the same man since the tragic events that followed so closely on the heels of the Lame Wolf campaign. Wounds had slowly healed. Injuries, physical, were well nigh forgotten; but, mentally, he had been long a sufferer. For months after the death of Nanette, even when sufficiently restored to be on duty, he held shrinkingly aloof from post society. Even Webb, Blake and Ray were powerless to pull him out of his despond. He seemed to feel,—indeed he said so, that his brief entanglement with that strange, fascinating girl had clouded his soldier name for all time. To these stanch friends and advisers he frankly told the whole story, and they, in turn, had told it to the general, to the colonel commanding the regiment and to those whose opinions they most valued; but Field could speak of it to none others. Frankly he admitted that from the moment he met the girl he fell under the influence of a powerful fascination. Within twenty-four hours of his return from the Laramie trip they were riding together, and during that ride she asked to be taken to Stabber's village, and there had talked long with that magnificent young Sioux. Later, Field surprised her in tears, and then she told him a pitiful tale. Eagle Wing had been educated, she said, by her aunt and uncle,—was indeed their nephew and her own cousin. He had been wild and had given them much trouble, and her aunt was in bitter distress over his waywardness. It was to plead with him that she, Nanette, had gone. "Moreau" had been taught mining and mineralogy, it seems, and declared that he had "located" a most promising mine in the Black Hills. He could buy off every claim if he had a thousand dollars, and the mine might be worth millions. Hay pooh-poohed the story. Mrs. Hay could not persuade him. Then "Moreau" became threatening. He would join the hostiles, he swore, if his aunt would not help him. Indeed, and here Field's young face burned with shame, Nanette told him that she understood that he, Field, was an only son who might inherit wealth in days to come, and could draw upon his father now for any reasonable sum; and, within the week of his meeting her, he was on the point of offering everything she needed, but that he disbelieved the Indian's story. Then, one night, there came a note begging him to meet her at once. She had a dreadful message, she said, from "Moreau." The fellow had frequently been prowling about the trader's during the dark hours, and now she was afraid of him, yet must see him, and see him at once, even if she had to ride to Stabber's camp. Field's eyes were blinded and he went. Hay's horses were ready beyond the corral, and she rode astride on one of Hay's own saddles. They found "Moreau" awaiting them at the ford, and there was a scene Field could not understand, for they spoke in the Sioux language. That night it was that, all in tears at the Indian's obduracy, she owned that he was her own brother, not merely a cousin, and together they had all gone back toward Frayne. "Moreau" was to wait on the flats

A DAUGHTER OF THE SIOUX

until she could return to the house. She had been striving to get him to make certain promises, she said, contingent on her giving him something from her own means. Field said he remonstrated with her to the utmost, but she told him no woman with Sioux blood in her veins ever deserted a brother—or lover. And so she had returned with a packet, presumably of money, and there they found the Indian clinched with Kennedy. Kennedy was rescued in the nick of time, and pledged to silence. The Indian rode away triumphant. Nanette climbed back to her window, exhausted, apparently, by her exertions, and Field started for his quarters, only to find the entire garrison astir. The rest they knew.

Asked how she came to know of the money in the trader's safe, he said no secret had been made of it by either Hay or him. She had asked him laughingly about his quarrel with Wilkins, and seemed deeply interested in all the details of subaltern life. Either Hay or he, fortunately, could have made good the missing sum, even had most of it not been found amongst Stabber's plunder. Field had never seen her again until the night the general took him to confront her at the Hays', and, all too late, had realized how completely she had lured and used him. In pride, honor, self-respect, he had been sorely wounded, and, even when assured that the general attached no blame to him, and that his name was no longer involved, he would have resigned his commission and quit the service had it not been for these soldiers three, Webb, Blake and Ray. They made him see that, all the more because his father's death had left him independent—sole master of quite a valuable property—he must stick to the sword and live down the possible stain.

A DAUGHTER OF THE SIOUX

And stay he did, refusing even a chance to go abroad the following spring, and devoting himself assiduously to his duties, although he shrank from society. They made him sometimes spend a quiet evening at Ray's or Blake's, where twice Miss Dade was found. But that young lady was quick to see that her hostess had been scheming, as loving women will. And then, when he went hoping to see her, yet half afraid, she came no more. They could not coax her. The early spring had taken him forth on long campaign. The ensuing fall had taken her to the far distant East, for gallant old Dade was breaking down. The doctors sent him on prolonged sick leave. Then was Fort Frayne indeed a desolate post to Beverly Field, and when midwinter came, and with it the news that Dade had but little while to live, he took counsel with Ray, and a month's leave, not much of which was spent in the South. The old regiment was represented at the sad and solemn little ceremony when the devoted husband, father and fellow soldier was laid at rest.

Nor was Field a happier man when he rejoined from leave, and they all thought they knew why. Letters came, black-bordered, with Esther's superscription, sometimes, but only for Mrs. Blake or Mrs. Ray. There was never one for Field. And so a second summer came and went and a second September was ushered in, and in the flood of the full moonlight there was again music and dancing at Fort Frayne, but not for Field, not for Esther Dade. They were all talking of Nanette, Daughter of the Dakotas, and Esther, Daughter of the Regiment, as they called her in her father's Corps, and the mail came late from Laramie, and letters were handed round as tattoo sounded, and Mrs. Blake, eagerly

A DAUGHTER OF THE SIOUX

scanning a black-bordered page, was seen suddenly to run in doors, her eyes brimming over with tears.

Later that night Hogan tapped at Field's front door and asked would the lieutenant step over to Mrs. Ray's a minute, and he went.

"Read that," said Mrs. Ray, pointing to a paragraph on the third page of the black-bordered missive that had been too much for Mrs. Blake. And he read:

"Through it all Esther has been my sweetest comfort, but now I must lose her, too. Our means are so straitened that she has *made* me see the necessity. Hard as it is, I must yield to her for the help that it may bring. She has been studying a year and is to join the staff of trained nurses at St. Luke's the first of October."

For a moment there was silence in the little army parlor. Field's hands were trembling, his face was filled with trouble. She knew he would speak his heart to her at last, and speak he did:—

"All these months that she has been studying I've been begging and pleading, Mrs. Ray. *You* know what I went for last winter,— all to no purpose. I'm going again now, if I have to stay a patient at St. Luke's to coax her out of it."

But not until Christmas came the welcome "wire:"

Patient discharged. Nurse finally accepts new engagement.

A DAUGHTER OF THE SIOUX

The End

A DAUGHTER OF THE SIOUX

www.ingramcontent.com/pod-product-compliance
Lightning Source LLC
Chambersburg PA
CBHW072354290526
45794CB00001B/63